Fugitive Pedagogy

Fugitive Pedagogy

CARTER G. WOODSON AND THE ART OF BLACK TEACHING

Jarvis R. Givens

HARVARD UNIVERSITY PRESS
Cambridge, Massachusetts, and London, England

Publication of this book has been supported through the generous provisions of the
Maurice and Lula Bradley Smith Memorial Fund

FIRST HARVARD UNIVERSITY PRESS PAPERBACK EDITION, 2022
FIRST PRINTING

Library of Congress Cataloging-in-Publication Data

Names: Givens, Jarvis R., author.
Title: Fugitive pedagogy : Carter G. Woodson and the art of black teaching /
    Jarvis R. Givens.
Description: Cambridge, Massachusetts : Harvard University Press, 2021. |
    Includes index.
Identifiers: LCCN 2020042439 | ISBN 9780674983687 (cloth) |
    ISBN 9780674278752 (pbk.)
Subjects: LCSH: Woodson, Carter Godwin, 1875-1950. | African
    Americans—Education—History—20th century. | Critical
    pedagogy—United States—History—20th century. | African
    American teachers—History—20th century.
Classification: LCC LC2741 .G48 2021 | DDC 973/.0496073007202—dc23
LC record available at https://lccn.loc.gov/2020042439

Contents

Preface: A New Grammar for Black Education

For the horrors of the American Negro's life there has been almost no language.

—JAMES BALDWIN, *The Fire Next Time* (1963)

Our language, when it comes to black education, is impoverished. Knowing how education has been a site of deep hurt and suffering on the one hand and yet a sacred site of black spiritual strivings on the other, we might look to more precise grammar to name and wrestle with this embattled reality. I desired a way to write about education as black people experienced it, in the interstices of this liminal reality—wedged between their collective striving and the antiblack domination they sought to escape—a way of writing that would account for the intentional ways black people navigated these deeply violent contexts and dreamed up new worlds and new ways of being. The problem of language is one that plagues black education studies and one that is widespread in the academy more generally, because for so long black life has been *a problem* for thought. Only language that goes beyond the descriptive can aid the observer who desires to sift through such a lived paradox and the futures it structured. But not just any language will do.

James Baldwin pointed us to a source: "The privacy of [the American Negro's] experience, which is only beginning to be recognized in language, and which is denied or ignored in official and popular speech—hence the Negro idiom—lends credibility to any system that pretends to clarify it."[1] A dynamic language is needed to appreciate the complexities of black life. Black idiom, for its interpretive capacity and ability to archive vexing yet important textured aspects of life within the Veil, offers such nuance—historical knowledge, sets of relations, and ways of knowing carried in black speech acts—a black way of saying, these "verbal race rituals and customs" do theoretical work.[2]

As such, this book relies on the fugitive slave archetype, and on *fugitive pedagogy*—a term that is neither (to borrow from folklorists) fully "emic" (from within) nor "etic" (from without) but a hybrid of the two. The fugitive slave emerged as a folk hero and cultural symbol in curriculums developed by black teachers. The fugitive slave appeared in school naming practices and within commemorative ceremonies in school activities and rituals. Black Americans established a heroic tradition around the stories and names associated with this pedagogy of escape in their schools and classrooms. As a folk hero in black curricular imaginations, the fugitive slave carried important insights about the interior life of teachers and students. This was the "fugitive spirit" of black education, to borrow from the poet and literary critic Nathaniel Mackey. Fugitive spirit was fact, metaphor, and formal disposition in black literary practices and (I extend this to include) black education more broadly.[3] Fugitivity has taken on heightened analytical significance in recent decades for the study of black politics and culture, and it can be understood as a contemporary idiom anchored by old knowledge from the black past.[4]

As I put closure on my research in the African American Studies Department at the University of California, Berkeley, I realized that to truly appreciate Carter G. Woodson or his iconic 1933 book, *The Mis-education of the Negro*, required a serious engagement with the veiled world of black education and black teachers only partially visible to the white public of their time and the historical record left behind. The black teachers and students called on in this book became portals into a heritage of *fugitive pedagogy*. I hope to tell their story in a way that moves beyond mere description and narratives of heroic struggle, and instead tease out central conflicts pertaining to questions of black ontology and the deeper meaning of education in black people's struggle for human goodness and flourishing: for a new world to be and new ways to be in the world. As Toni Morrison showed through her fictional character Sixo: a language is only worth speaking or writing or singing if you can see a future in it.[5] I look to black teachers of the past, whose fugitive acts can teach us so much about the future. They represent a tradition that has been plundered from today's black educators, who are its rightful inheritors. I see the cast of characters in this book as standard bearers. A tradition passed through these teachers and their students. Their heritage is one worthy of both praise and deep study.

Fugitive Pedagogy

How some of these slaves learned in spite of opposition makes a beautiful story. Knowing the value of **learning as a means of escape** and having longing for it, too, because it was forbidden, many slaves continued their education under adverse circumstances.

—CARTER G. WOODSON, *The Negro in Our History* (1922)

Introduction: Blackness and the Art of Teaching

But some of us would try to steal
A little from the book.
And put the words together,
And learn by hook or crook.

"Learning to Read" (1872)
—FRANCES ELLEN WATKINS HARPER, teacher and abolitionist

Tessie McGee read to her class in a steady measured tone, quietly engaging in a calculated act of subversion. She was black, twenty-eight years old, and taught history in 1933–1934 at the only black secondary school in Webster Parish, Louisiana.[1] The state's all-white Department of Education and local school board gave clear instructions: teachers were to keep a preapproved outline openly displayed on their desks, which they were to follow closely to acquaint their students with the targeted learning objectives.[2] Black educators and families in Webster Parish had little formal control over curriculum, even though the school was paid for with funds raised by "double taxing" themselves—cultivating neighborhood patches of cotton that they handed over to local school officials. Despite being tax-paying citizens, blacks found state allocations of resources to be far less for their children's education as compared with white children's.[3] On many occasions, McGee made what she deemed to be necessary revisions to the mandatory curriculum. Based on her own judgment, and perhaps at the recommendation of fellow black teachers, she often read passages from Carter G. Woodson's "book on the Negro," which rested comfortably in her lap. She kept the book out of sight, understanding the likely repercussions were she to be caught. Like most black educators, Miss McGee was a public employee and vulnerable to the disciplinary practices of Jim Crow authorities. But she was undeterred. "She read to us from that book," one of McGee's students recounted. "When the principal

Webster Parish Training School, Minden, Louisiana. Fisk University, John Hope and
Aurelia E. Franklin Library, Julius Rosenwald Photo Collection.

would come in, she would . . . simply lift her eyes to the outline that resided
on the desk and teach us from the outline. When the principal disappeared,
her eyes went back to the book in her lap."[4]

The scenario from Miss McGee's classroom illuminates what this book
calls *fugitive pedagogy*. My use of the term *fugitive* draws inspiration from
the literary scholars Steven Best's and Saidiya Hartman's discussion of "fugitive justice." Although focused on slavery, redress, and the historicity of
what is lost and irrecoverable in the future, Best and Hartman introduce the
idea of "two competing narratives of the fugitive's identity."[5] Fugitive con-
notes the dual image of one who escapes enslavement or jailed confinement,
which justifies one's capture and even death at the hands of law enforcement.
Yet as Best and Hartman explain, the violence of enslavement, "legal" capture, and brutality engenders, as well, the countervailing narrative of and by
the fugitive as victim of antiblack domination. Adapting such a conceptualization to American education reveals parallel, equally competing historical
images. On the one hand, the dominant story of the nation's past had long
vilified, devalued, and disrespected black people, thereby justifying racial discrimination in the forms of enslavement and later segregation, disfranchise-

ment, lynching, and imprisonment. On the other hand, this very exclusion, violence, and confinement in a land that professed the ideals of liberty and justice for all prompted a counterhistorical narrative and way of knowing—indeed one represented in the extensive factual evidence contained in Carter G. Woodson's books, which documented the wrongs done to black Americans but also their achievements and contributions to the modern world. And as the case of Tessie McGee makes clear, much of this type of black education occurred in a covert manner.

Black education was a fugitive project from its inception—outlawed and defined as a criminal act regarding the slave population in the southern states and, at times, too, an object of suspicion and violent resistance in the North. Similar to black America's political struggles in general, the quest for freedom through education extended from their grassroots efforts in the time of slavery. While very distinct contexts, there was never a complete break from slavery to freedom. For over a century, scholars have consistently relied on descriptors that signify how secrecy and subversion formed part and parcel of black education. In the 1920s Carter G. Woodson observed that enslaved black people pursued "learning as a means of escape." Present-day historians, such as Thomas Webber, note that the enslaved established ways of doing and being in the quarter communities that served educational purposes and that this system of knowledge and values was held internally, away from the watchful eye of masters and overseers.[6] Heather Williams has masterfully reconstructed enslaved people's pursuit of literacy "in the secret places." She then revealed that even as black people were legally permitted to become educated in the postbellum South, the violent suppression of their efforts persisted, and they continued to resist in the best ways they knew how.[7]

More pointedly to the subject of this book, the historian James Anderson has argued that by the end of the Civil War there were "cumulative experiences and cumulative traditions and values that transmitted over a long period of time" about literacy and education. This educational worldview "enter[ed] into freedom and emancipation with the slave population."[8] Attentive to this observation, *Fugitive Pedagogy* charts the constitutive elements and political relationships that formed the core of the black educational heritage in slavery and how they carried over as the political foundation for what came after. The subversive educational acts by black Americans during the Civil War period through Jim Crow were tied to a longer history of fugitive educational practices that began in the time of slavery.[9]

After the Civil War and especially in the decades following the end of Reconstruction, black education in the South was violently suppressed or starved of adequate state funding and left to perish. Between 1864 and 1876 well over six hundred black southern schools were burned. At the turn of the twentieth century, W. E. B. Du Bois described whites' fierce opposition to black education as having "showed itself in ashes, insult, and blood."[10] Students and their teachers met with white aggression, and consequently black education was only partially revealed to the public eye. The *plot*—by which I mean the embedded political aims of its pedagogy—continued to be concealed and held close.[11] An amassed set of values and traditions, I am arguing, stood at the core of the covert demeanors and tool kit of practices necessary to advance the plot of black education. Glenda Gilmore has written about black women builders of schools as "double agents" during Jim Crow.[12] Vanessa Siddle Walker has exposed the private partnerships between black educators and the NAACP. These teachers were "hidden provocateurs," she argues, forced to keep their political ties underground because of their economic vulnerability as employees of the state and given their physical vulnerability as black people living under de jure segregation.[13] Across this genealogy of scholarship emerges a persistent thread. When it came to the pursuit of freedom through education, black people consistently deployed fugitive tactics. Enslaved people learned in secret places. During Jim Crow, black educators wore a mask of compliance in order to appease the white power structure, while simultaneously working to subvert it.

While my conceptualization of fugitive pedagogy ushers in a new paradigmatic framing of black education in a general sense, its meaning will be largely couched in the particular, emblematic narrative of Carter G. Woodson (1875–1950)—the author of Miss McGee's concealed textbook. Woodson was the son *and student* of former slaves, a veteran schoolteacher of nearly thirty years, and he became the second black American to receive a PhD from Harvard in 1912, after W. E. B. Du Bois. However, while he is the central character of this book, I am no less interested in the educational world that surrounded Woodson as I am in the educator himself. *Fugitive Pedagogy* calls attention to a tradition that passed through Carter G. Woodson, not one that began with him or for which he was solely responsible. The book's baseline narrative tells of Woodson, a man born in the first generation after Emancipation, who published numerous scholarly monographs and articles and founded the Association for the Study of Negro Life and History (ASNLH) in 1915 and Negro History Week in 1926 (what has become today Black History Month). Celebrated as "the father of Black History," Woodson represented much more than this, however. As *Fugitive Pedagogy* brings to light, he was first and foremost a schoolteacher—having taught English, French, and History and having served as a public school principal in West Virginia and Washington, DC. His life's work was influenced and made possible by the pedagogical work of black schoolteachers.

Nor is this book an attempt to retell Woodson's life story in exhaustive biographical detail. Instead it offers a schematic treatment of his development from student to teacher to educational leader and theorist. Embedded in this particular narrative is a more general story of black education, one that stretches from the time of slavery through Jim Crow. This second, more expansive narrative is a conceptual story of antiblack exclusion and confinement on the one hand and blacks' engagement in fugitive educational politics on the other. The dialectic formed between the two narratives is key to understanding the fugitive character of *black educational heritage*. In this sense, the book uses a seminal historical figure to read a broader social and intellectual history through that person's journey.

In *Fugitive Pedagogy* I analyze the educational world surrounding Woodson as illustrative of a larger phenomenon that elevates the stories of his colaborers for the purpose of rendering a work of history, cultural theory, and pedagogical insight. Indeed, teachers like Tessie McGee were representative of the tens of thousands of Woodson's colaborers across the country. Her actions were closer to the rule than to the exception. Using Woodson to anchor the story, however, allows for a more cohesive narrative and analysis that is both thick and expansive, while comprising fragmented story elements from teachers and students to whom he was connected.[14] In the Webster Parish Training School, Tessie McGee's dissident method of instruction constitutes a textbook example of fugitive pedagogy. The physical and intellectual acts by black teachers and students explicitly critiqued and negated white supremacy and antiblack protocols of domination, but they often did so in discreet or partially concealed fashion. Embedded in McGee's actions is the heritage of black education: a lived tension between antiblack persecution in "the American School"—which refers to the schooling apparatus of the United States that manifested in diverse institutional forms, laws, and social policies—and the intellectual and embodied acts of subversion black people deployed to navigate those constraints.[15] The content of Woodson's textbook, the organizations he founded and was a part of, as well as McGee's subversive pedagogical acts through the employment of Woodson's words and ideas, all embody a fugitive project. Woodson's textbook rejected the degrading representations of black life in official school curricula, which always had physical implications as well.[16] McGee escaped this official curriculum by way of the "hidden transcript" literally resting on her lap. The public display of the "official" outline was a masked performance of complicity—an embodied text that accompanied the subversive content in Woodson's history book. McGee's physical act of switching texts taught a lesson to her students who witnessed it. She demonstrated how defiance could at times be disguised by public performances of deference to the coercive regime of school authorities.

Equally important, teachers like McGee gained access to these alternative scripts of knowledge through "insurgent intellectual networks" to which they were connected—institutions like Woodson's ASNLH and black teacher associations.[17] The latter associations betray an expansive veiled yet networked black educational world, one where black Americans said one thing and did another, meaning that the true political intentions undergirding black educational strivings were rarely on full display, given rampant antiblack violence. African Americans responded often in quiet, calculated acts of resistance against oppressive school settings that reflected a world order built on black subjection. As a collective endeavor, fugitive pedagogy comprised networks of teachers as well as their students. For example, the principal entering McGee's classroom was a black man named J. L. Jones. Records suggest that he was an advocate for including black culture and history in the curriculum.[18] He was a leading member in the Louisiana Colored Teachers' Association, which explicitly endorsed Carter G. Woodson and his work. It is not implausible, then, to consider that Jones and McGee may have very likely conspired together, the principal testing the teacher to ensure she could protect herself and the school if a white official entered the room. Their interactions performed for students a strategy of technical compliance without actually complying. Wearing the mask, as Paul Laurence Dunbar called it, was part and parcel of black teachers' professional disposition.[19]

In black segregated schools, the intrusion of white surveillance had a hand in shaping school ecology. It was not atypical for white people to drop by un-announced during the school day, either to show off "their negro school" to visitors or for some other routine inspection. While disruptive to the school day, these visits were primarily meant to demonstrate power, which was essential to reproducing domination.[20] This is to say, the person walking into McGee's classroom could just as easily have been a white school official. Black educators walked a tightrope in their efforts to challenge the school system and social reality in which they found themselves. These circumstances meant that critical aspects of their work had to be done covertly. If they were to fall or be caught, there was no safety net to catch them.[21] Just a few years prior, a black principal was threatened and fired in Oklahoma, and his teachers reprimanded, after a Klan-run white school board learned that Woodson's textbook, *The Negro in Our History,* had—as they put it—"crept into *our* Negro schools."[22] Examples of this kind of violent oversight are plentiful. They move forward and backward in time as far as black teachers are concerned.

Oliver Pope had been teaching in his hometown of Templeton, Virginia, in 1908 when the white superintendent (also a former Confederate soldier) made an unexpected visit to his schoolroom. The visit just so happened to coincide with a class discussion on the Negro vote during Reconstruction. The superintendent challenged Pope in front of his students and soon afterward terminated his teaching contract. A worse fate came to Harry and Harriette Moore. They were married, and both were schoolteachers as well as civil rights activists in Florida. The Moores were fired in 1946 because of their activism surrounding equal pay for black teachers. Their home was bombed on Christmas in 1951, killing them both, after their organizing to challenge the wrongful conviction of four young black men, one of whom was killed in police custody.[23]

The vulnerability of black teachers as a professional group had long been a sharp reality, and it continued to be the case after the Supreme Court ruled in favor of school desegregation in the mid-twentieth century. Black educators were aware of this, as were many of their students who witnessed moments when their teachers were forced to conceal their pedagogical objectives in the presence of intrusive white power. Subjection to surveillance and violence, motivated by no causal logic whatsoever, was a fact of blackness.[24] Black American educators developed strategies to contest this reality, which ranged from broad institutional realms down to the interpersonal and psychic levels.

Fugitive Pedagogy talks pointedly, in a more interpretive sense, about black education at the level of experience. Black people's political clarity meant they understood their teaching and learning to be perpetually taking place under persecution, even as they created learning experiences of joy and empowerment. As one student recalled of his Kentucky school, it was as though he and his classmates were being initiated into "a kind of freemasonry" of the race, as in a secret society replete with unspoken yet understood meanings about the work black education was to do, things that people came to know as a taken-for-granted kind of truth—an affective epistemology—knowledge shared between teachers, principals, and often times the students themselves, because of their shared vulnerability.[25] This kind of living history sat in classrooms like McGee's. She was not alone in teaching from Woodson's books. Sales records indicate a wide circulation among black teachers.[26] But the full impact of fugitive pedagogy far transcends the quantification of individual subversive acts such as hers. The broader effect of such practices on black American teaching, along with the roots of such practices in a long tradition, is the primary topic of this book.

This book has much to say about persecution and the art of teaching in the black American experience.[27] It begins by drawing a narrative line that connects the dots between those enslaved persons who stole away to learn and the teachers and students whose actions occurred in what Saidiya Hartman calls "the afterlife of slavery," or what Woodson referred to as "the sequel to slavery."[28] This tradition is marked by both racist condemnation and blacks' repeated acts of escape and rebellion.[29] It also takes seriously work that reveals the aggressive structural neglect and intentional devaluing of black educational strivings in this country's history, a story of continued backlash that demanded unceasing vigilance on the part of black people.[30]

Scholars have documented the long history of black people striving to learn in the face of physical violence as well as intensely racist intellectual and ideological currents. This tradition is well documented in the narratives written by the formerly enslaved, which have been a major source for scholarship on black education and literary traditions before the Civil War.[31] The tradition is also prevalent in the historical writings on black education during Jim Crow.[32]

Recent scholarship has done well to complicate and revise earlier representations that depicted black teachers as mere accommodationists, helpless victims, or hindrances to black people's struggle for freedom.[33] As more is revealed about the lives of these educators, it becomes clear that scholars must evaluate them on their own terms. Black teachers were a distinct group of political actors. They were even set apart from other black American professionals and leaders. Due to Jim Crow wages, many black educators "supplemented incomes by stints as laborers and domestics." One South Carolina educator expressed this reality in plain language at a 1922 teachers convention: "He teaches 'tis true, but he also farms, preaches, laws, barbers, insures, clerks, typewrites, keeps books, sews, cooks, nurses, launders, dresses hair, and God only knows what else, in order to eke out an existence."[34] Despite common perceptions, black teachers were rarely comfortably middle-class, even as they benefitted from an elevated social status in black American communities.

Furthermore, while black educators did not always participate in traditional forms of public protest, the work done in their classrooms had direct implications for the black freedom struggle, a movement that was sparked and carried out by their students and that black teachers often strategically supported in the shadows, if not in the open. One scholar has made this case clear when writing about black teachers in Birmingham as "schoolhouse activists." Through a sociohistorical analysis, we see such educators implementing pedagogical practices within school walls that instilled political ideals and values that their students put into action, outside the classroom.[35] Black teachers engaged in these practices well before World War II. Moreover, they incubated a socioemotional context for learning that inspired freedom dreams in later generations. We need only look to the autobiographies of Civil Rights and Black Power leaders, activists, and intellectuals to observe this fact.[36]

This book moves beyond the purely narrative and descriptive to analyze how the transgressive nature of education was embedded at the very core of black thought and activism. In doing this, new conceptual tools are generated: a new grammar of and for black education.[37] The theory of fugitive pedagogy accounts for the physical and intellectual acts of subversion engaged in by black people over the course of their educational strivings. Such acts as McGee's physically concealing the textbook, the students witnessing her do this and afterward return to Woodson's text, all stand in relationship to one another as a proxy for a world of black subversive practices of teaching and learning.

Fugitivity: The Metanarrative of Black Education

Fugitive Pedagogy asks: What has been the nature of black people's relationship to the American School? And how have they worked to enact their own visions of teaching and learning within this structural context? In pursuing these questions, I take seriously the reality that black life has been shaped by the history of racial chattel slavery and the futures it structured.

Responding to the queries above, I deploy fugitivity as an analytic to parse through key aspects of black social and political life as it pertains to education. The terminology builds from the historicity of the fugitive slave—enslaved blacks that engaged in both physical and psychic forms of flight.[38] This subversion manifested in various forms—whether this be running away for a day, hiding in the trunk of a tree, alternative spiritual practices, climbing into holes in the ground at night to have school, or the establishment of maroon societies in the dismal swamps of Virginia. More pointedly to enslaved people's fugitive pursuits of education, I argue that their insistence on black educability—that African-descended people were reasoning rational subjects—disrupted "the chattel principle," the very laws and logics condemning them to a subgenre of the human species, a people who could be legitimately owned as property, even in the womb.[39] Fugitivity enunciates subversive practices of black social life in the African Diaspora, over and against the persistent violence of white supremacy and its technologies of surveillance and domination that were bound up in and animated by the chattel principle. It is the constant seeking of an outside to white supremacy that might elusively be understood as black freedom. The language honors the plot that is an insistence on black living, even amid the perpetual threat of black social death, the latter being a dominant ideology that black people always refused, even as it had real consequences given that those who benefitted from their domination were empowered and backed by the broader political structure and the law.[40]

Fugitivity—and fugitive pedagogy in particular—is the metanarrative of black educational history. It is a social and rhetorical frame by which we might interpret black Americans' pursuit to enact humanizing and affirming practices of teaching and learning. To this latter point, I am referring to the reality that the literate slave was akin to a fugitive slave, particularly when we take into account antiliteracy laws, which criminalized reading and writing by black Americans, making it a punishable offense. The first proscription of this kind emerged as early as the Slave Code of 1740, enacted in response to the Stono Slave Rebellion, which—it is key to note—preceded the American Revolution. This legislative response stemmed from the belief that the rebel slaves communicated their plans for insurrection using the written word.[41] The South Carolina legislature decided that "the having of slaves taught to write, or suffering them to be employed in writing, may be *attended with great inconveniences*." The law would be extended to include free blacks in 1800. And Georgia, in 1770, made both reading and writing illegal for the enslaved.[42] Antiliteracy laws and ideology approached universal standing in the South during the decades immediately preceding the Civil War—but, to be clear, it was a carryover from the colonial period. Irrespective of their frequency or when and how they were enforced, antiliteracy proscriptions represent a set of structural antagonisms, as laws and law-like social customs, to which fugitive pedagogy was a response.

Black education was suppressed across regional boundaries, even in places that never technically banned black education. Suspicion about black education was strongest in the South, where it posed the most immediate threat. Prior to the Civil War, the overwhelming majority of black people lived in southern states, and in the eyes of the law, their education was deemed criminal activity. But legal proscriptions of black education grew out of antiblack attitudes shared across the South and North. A few southern cities (Baltimore and New Orleans, for instance) and several northern cities (Boston, Cincinnati, New York, Philadelphia) had schools for free blacks prior to Emancipation, but even in these cities, suspicion and surveillance of black education prevailed. In northern cities, the greatest opposition arose when whites feared that schools might attract unwanted black migrants, instigate black political activism, and especially when black Americans sought entrance to white schools. In Canterbury, Connecticut, a white Quaker teacher named Prudence Crandall allowed a black girl to enter her private school in the early

1830s. When her white students withdrew, she opened the school to black girls, attracting students from free black families as far away as Philadelphia, Providence, New York, and Boston. In response, the townspeople harassed the black girls on the streets, piled manure on the school property, and set it on fire. Yale professors and students protested in front of the homes of New Haven residents who supported an idea posed by black leaders to establish a black college there in 1831. They claimed, "The founding of colleges for educating colored youth is an unwarranted and *dangerous undertaking*." Antiliteracy laws in southern states made explicit a shared antipathy for black education, linked to a general disdain for black people, that featured prominently in the American national culture.[43] Black achievement and criminality were closely linked transgressions in an antiblack world.

The criminality of black learning was a psychosocial reality. According to Frederick Douglass's master: a slave having learned to read and write was a slave "running away with himself": stealing oneself, not just stealing away to the North or stealing away to Jesus but stealing away to one's own imagination, seeking respite in independent thought. The theft of one's mind was directly relational to, perhaps even a precondition for, the theft of one's body. For these reasons, enslaved people who could read and write were branded as "objects of suspicion," marked as black-fugitive-learning-flesh.[44]

So while "a literate slave was supposed to be a contradiction in terms," black people's educational strivings were acted out in the space of this contradiction.[45] Thinking in these structural terms, I would go as far as to suggest that literate slaves and their symbolic (as well as literal) descendants—black teachers—represented an ongoing strike by black people against the conditions of slave work, whereby black folks were captive laborers to be super-exploited within a national political-economic system predicated on chattel slavery and its afterlives. The literate slave represents a protracted refusal by black people against the arbitrary logics of racial capitalism imposed on their lives.[46] They insisted that they were *more than a hand without a head*, to paraphrase Frederick Douglass.[47] Black teachers were the progenies of literate slaves, whose educational strivings were an embodiment of fugitive spirit. The literacy and independent thought of the latter were coterminous with flight, and black teachers post-Emancipation emerged as a professional class who embodied the very ideas of black aspiration and progress, making them symbols of inspiration and, simultaneously, prime targets of white aggression.[48]

The language of fugitivity absorbs and reconfigures long-standing scholarly observations that education and freedom have been inextricably bound in black American life.[49] As stated earlier, black people appropriated schooling to work in service of their freedom dreams, having recognized the functions of education in the context of the American social order. This articulation, however, that black people saw education as a bridge to freedom only reveals but so much of the story. Upon closer examination, we witness that black education was certainly about freedom—but more precisely, part of a more expansive plot against the current configuration of the modern world and, particularly, the perversely color-coded arrangement of the human species. Fugitive pedagogy names the educational acts of escape constituting the precondition of black freedom implied by the very notion of "education *as* freedom." Fugitive pedagogy, then, might be thought of as what it means to put this philosophical ideal into practice. This is not a contradiction to the familiar extrapolation—that black people saw education as freedom—but instead a restating of the narrative to elevate critical parts of the story, namely, to underscore how this philosophical ideal widely held by black people was lived out and enacted.

Black education was a schooling project set against the entire order of things. This is something we must be clear about. In its resounding assertion that black people were rational subjects—that they were not simply hands without a head (captive laborers with no capacity for reason)—black education has been a persistent disruption to the known world instituted through racial chattel slavery. This is the assertion embedded in the abolitionist David Walker's claim that "for colored people to acquire learning in this country, makes tyrants quake and tremble on their sandy foundation." It anchors Frederick Douglass's incisive observation that "knowledge unfits a child to be a slave." The insistence on black educability troubled notions like those imparted by Thomas Jefferson—the precursor to the American Common School Movement—when he asserted that the Negro was incapable of producing poetry, or original and reflective thought. Writing of Phillis Wheatley, Jefferson maintained that poetry written by "the blacks" was simply "beneath the dignity of criticism." This was not just about a distaste for Wheatley's lyrical style or some lack of technique. It was an insistence that black people were beneath the threshold of humanistic potentiality. Jefferson's claim rested on the belief that mastery of the arts and sciences and the production of literature were a visible sign of reason, the apex of human civilization—achievements beyond the realm of possibility for black people. The plot of black education insisted otherwise. In this sense, fugitive pedagogy was the pursuit of an otherwise arrangement of the world and what it meant to be human.[50]

Fugitivity as a Historically Situated Analytic

While fugitivity is anchored by the historical figure of the fugitive slave, it also indexes a broader repertoire of secret acts and subterfuge in black life and culture. Zora Neale Hurston, the Black Renaissance anthropologist, writer, and cultural critic, wrote about this fugitive interiority as the crux of black culture—what she referred to as a "feather-bed resistance": "The white man is always trying to know into somebody else's business. All right, I'll set something outside the door of my mind for him to play with and handle. He can read my writing but he sho' can't read my mind. I'll put this play toy in his hand, and he will seize it and go away. Then I'll say my say and sing my song."[51] As Hurston extrapolates, black people constructed an interior world within their veiled existence, in the shadow of the antiblack color line, even as they had to engage in various practices of acquiescing to the mainstream social order. And there were those before Hurston who put it in simpler terms: "Got one mind for me and another for the master to see." This duality, while a result of domination, was repurposed as a pragmatic disposition.[52]

This book deploys fugitivity as more than an elaborate metaphor. It literally and figuratively emerges from the historical records of black education, extending directly from the discourse of black American teachers and educational communities. They named schools after fugitive slaves, and these historical figures repeatedly appear in curriculum content developed by black teachers. The infinitely returning figure of the fugitive slave can be tracked through the curricular imaginations of these educators as represented by textbooks they wrote for schoolchildren, whereas fugitive slaves were studiously absent in the official curriculum prescribed by white authorities (see Chapter 4). The striking reality of this last point is what initially prompted the use of fugitivity in this book. The subversive language also mimics the allegorical terms taken up by educators to describe their own practices at times, their insistence on "showing two faces" or working around white school authorities (see Chapter 5).[53] Fugitive pedagogy cuts across the archive in multiple ways. The language of fugitivity is first informed by this thematic in the historical record. It is then taken up at the symbolic level as a tool for interpretation, to analyze how black Americans navigated antiblack exclusion and confinement in the American School, how it became embodied as a professional disposition and set of practices.

I ground this project in the language of fugitivity as opposed to "resistance" or "agency," because the concept, in its historical reference, holds in place both the realities of constraint *and* black Americans' constant straining against said confinement. It is careful not to overstate either. Fugitivity is never one or the other. As Fred Moten aptly notes, and I paraphrase: escape is an activity; it's not an achievement.[54] The possible threat of recapture always lingered—similar to an abrupt firing, as was the fate of many black educators, when physical harm was not used as a strategy of coercion.[55] Escape was always unresolved and uncertain, both for the fugitive slave and the fugitive pedagogue. The precarity and vulnerability of black people within the American School curtailed any permanent resolve that might be achieved by their infinite acts of educational resistance. As such, *Fugitive Pedagogy* is neither a history of triumph nor one of defeat. It is instead one of protracted struggle, one in which progress unfolds in perturbed fashion, one where we see black people wrestling with the object of education as a humanistic endeavor, one to be weaponized against their domination.

Critical parts of black education had always taken place underground—sometimes *under a desk*, as in the case of Tessie McGee's use of Woodson's textbook; or *under a hat*, as was the case for the enslaved Richard Parker of Virginia, who kept his copy of the *Webster Blueback Speller* on his head, under a hat, and hidden from public view; or literally *under the earth*, as Mandy Jones recalled of the pit schools in the woods surrounding the Mississippi plantation on which she was enslaved.[56] Orbiting at the margins of the American School has always been a veiled black educational world, where fugitive pedagogy was a critical part of content and form.

One way of looking at these individuated scenarios might be to see them as isolated acts of what some call everyday resistance, or infrapolitics.[57] Another might see these scenarios as story elements of a more general narrative of black education and the politics therein, which transcend any particular act or event.[58] This book follows the latter line of thought, forwarding fugitive pedagogy as a metanarrative of black education, a new frame for seeing this history. These acts were ordered by an overarching set of political commitments sustained by black institutions and shared visions of freedom and societal transformation. They were not sporadic. They were the occasion, the main event. Fugitive pedagogy is the plot at the heart of the matter—the story and the scheme.

The Case of Carter G. Woodson

The heritage of black education stands at the center of Woodson's life, but this can only be fully appreciated after a reframing of his intellectual contributions in more expansive terms. The collective memory of Woodson that has extended into the twenty-first century was made possible largely because of his partnerships with other educators and the work of teachers and students who gave life to his ideas by putting them into practice. It was Woodson's deep entrenchment within the networks of black teachers as a rank-and-file member, and then as a thought-leader, that made what Pero Dagbovie termed "the early Black history movement" so iconic.[59]

There is no intent here to suggest that Woodson represents all things about black education in any singular fashion; nor do I wish to add him as a third fountainhead of knowledge to the lingering Booker T. Washington-versus-W. E. B. Du Bois binary (because despite scholarship that moves beyond this binary, it persists as a dominant paradigmatic framing in discourse, public and academic). To challenge any impulse for reading this book in such a way, I consistently position Woodson in relation to a broader network of black schoolteachers and education scholars who were his contemporaries and predecessors, thus demonstrating how Woodson inherited a tradition and then played a crucial role in expanding it.

Likewise, fugitive pedagogy is not an essentialist categorical theory about all black teachers—surely there are deviations, but they are not the concern here. This book is a recuperation of a set of politics and relations that were both ubiquitous and a preeminent aspect of black educational heritage. By my assessment, it represents the best in the tradition of black American teachers as a professional group. In recovering this through line in the history of black education, I have rendered Woodson's narrative and educational model as one of its greatest exemplars. And it is one of broad reach: temporally, geographically, and in terms of educational level.

The cast of characters in this book consists of the following: Woodson as a student, a schoolteacher, and then educational leader and theorist, as well as a host of other black educators and students—the people who taught him, the schoolteachers he partnered with, educators who put his ideas into practice, and students who recalled how his educational materials influenced their classroom experiences. This book reveals the phenomenon of fugitive pedagogy from these various perspectives.

Woodson's trajectory, as both a student and schoolteacher, and the range of his higher educational experiences were unparalleled. No other black American scholar ran the gamut of educational experiences with such breadth and depth. First taught by his formerly enslaved uncles, then by a cousin born at the end of the Civil War, Woodson went on to study at Berea College (the only mixed-race institution in the South), Lincoln University in Pennsylvania (a historically black college [HBCU]), and the University of Chicago. He studied as a graduate student at the Sorbonne and earned a master's and doctorate from the University of Chicago and Harvard University, respectively. Not only was Woodson a schoolteacher for nearly thirty years; he was also a leader among educators through his partnerships with black teacher associations at the national and local levels.

After founding the Association for the Study of Negro Life and History in 1915—an unprecedented national forum for black intellectual production and the study of race—Woodson stimulated one of the largest grassroots movements in the history of black American education. By 1931 over 80 percent of black high schools celebrated Negro History Week—an educational initiative he created in 1926, which later became Black History Month in 1976.[60] Negro History Week was also widely celebrated in elementary schools and popularly covered in the black press around the country. It was even celebrated internationally as early as 1939.[61] Woodson's alternative curricula (including textbooks, classroom decorations, and more) explicitly tied the political mission of black education to classroom content like never before. Black perceptions about education manifested through his curricular materials, shaping a refined black learning aesthetic.

Woodson influenced the interior world of black education from the margins of the American School. Having severed all formal ties with schools and universities by 1922, his relationship to the schooling apparatus from this point on was definitively antagonistic.[62] Yet from the late 1920s forward, his

influence in black schools increased. Black educators' use of ASNLH materials and their introduction of Woodson's ideas to their students were not imposed from the top down. In more than one way, they were "off script" and
grassroots in nature.

The reach of Woodson's educational program went far and wide. Black college students formed historical societies and called themselves "the Wood-
sonians," in San Diego, California, during the 1930s.[63] Teachers infused their
curricula with content and activities outlined in Woodson's *Journal of Negro
History* and the *Negro History Bulletin*. A group of elementary students in
Virginia interviewed formerly enslaved people in their community and engaged in reflexive writing assignments about this experience—what they
learned, how they felt, and what this meant for their own identities as black
youth.[64] Teachers piled into churches and school gymnasiums for teacher
association meetings to hear Woodson speak about the politics of black
education and the relationship between distortions in curriculum and physical violence black people experienced in the world. It is important to note
that while Woodson's strongest connections with black teachers were certainly in the South, because black people overwhelmingly lived in this region, his educational project was not just a southern phenomenon. Black
teachers in such northern and midwestern states as New Jersey, New York,
Massachusetts, Illinois, and Missouri (many of whom were southern migrants) also introduced Negro History Week to their students.

Woodson developed language to name how school curriculum cultivated
antiblackness and racism as a social competence among students and thus
structured behavioral phenomena along the same lines. This was a novel philosophical contribution in its own right. Woodson named race as operative
in knowledge and the American Curriculum's system of representation,
thus pulling it out into the open and making it accountable to critique. These
ideas were expressed through speeches and newspaper articles that became
Woodson's iconic book in 1933, *The Mis-education of the Negro*—a book
that maintains popular circulation in the contemporary moment.

Black American teachers praised Woodson for his curricular interventions.
To them, he was a "Schoolmaster to His Race."[65] They endorsed his critical
perspective that the American School was a principal site for reproducing the
suffering of black people, which tapped at the core of their consciousness as
educators engaging in the work of freedom. Woodson argued that the social

function of schools—including its logics, curricular infrastructure, and procedural practices—hinged on the belief that the Negro was "a negligible factor in the thought of the world." By Woodson's assessment, "there would be no lynching if it did not start in the schoolroom."[66] Therefore, education was about more than jobs and general academic skill sets. It was inherently political. The work of black teachers and students, therefore, demanded a fugitive relationship to the American School. Even as their work was being carried out in the formal structure of the American School, it could be fundamentally set against it. Woodson urged black educators to be clear about these distinctions.

Using the case of Woodson and his expansive educational narrative, this work presents a rigorous attempt to "piece out the reality" of fugitive pedagogy in black classrooms and communities. An attempt to get closer to what it looked and felt like in motion. When I encounter scenarios like 2,500 teachers packing into a chapel to hear Woodson speak, some of whom had to stand on chairs outside windows on a hot day in Georgia, I am forced to stop and think about affect in a serious way.[67] I am compelled to linger with the kind of purpose and feeling that might be shaping this moment in the professional life of black teachers, given all the competing factors we know to be contouring their worlds—the promise and the peril.

On Historical Methods and Black Study

Black Americans' pursuit of education was an integral part "of our spiritual strivings," as Du Bois made clear in 1903.[68] Yet traditional methods of history and storytelling prove to be insufficient when one considers the political and spiritual underpinnings of black people's struggle for education. It was not just education for functional, utilitarian purposes or the goals of citizenship. Even in the case of Booker T. Washington's iconic Tuskegee model of practical education or Nannie Helen Burroughs's training school for girls, the immediate utilitarian objectives were never the heart of the matter. Singular disciplinary modes pose a challenge when trying to name the affective underpinnings of the story and its deeper conceptual significance.[69] Even as *Fugitive Pedagogy* relies primarily on historical methodology, an awareness of the kinds of erasure and violence inscribed in archival records demands a breaking of form.[70] My vigilance of this reality informs the kinds of sources

I seek out, the pace of my interpretation of the archival record, and how and when I use different historical materials in telling this story.

This book relies on a patchwork of sources given the limitations of available archival materials and, quite frankly, their scarcity as it pertains to black teachers and students. I include materials from formal archives and, at times, materials shared from the personal collections of individual people or relevant unprocessed materials I learned about during passing conversations with generous yet often underresourced archivists at HBCUs. I privilege materials that feature the voices of black American people on the topic of schooling and black life—a collective choir of criticism that can intentionally be held alongside narratives found in educational records, newspaper accounts, textbooks, and materials in Woodson's personal papers. To this end, I intentionally sought out the papers of dozens of prominent educators across the country, the publications and organizational records of black teacher associations, ephemera from black schools, and a range of black oral histories and autobiographies.

After years of pouring over books and records on black education, it became clear to me that black people have always been hyperaware of their bodies in relation to schooling: first in their physical exclusion and later through their racially confined educational experiences through segregation. I would also note that the entire struggle at the center of black education had to do with negotiating the racial scripts etched into black flesh in the modern world—pseudoscientific scripts and plain racist ideas having been used to "quarantine" black people at "the nether edge" of the American School as if their bodies were contaminated, some kind of contagion.[71] Putting this awareness to use, I pay close attention to matters of black embodiment in my analyses. This means being vigilant of how black people physically appear and how they function in historical scenarios—not just how they are written about but how they move and act inside of the written and spoken word (the hat on the head concealing a spelling book, the book on the lap, students adorning their bodies with costumes to reenact a slave revolt against the backdrop of Jim Crow). This is particularly important because, at times, what black people did in the context of education reveals different things than what they said or wrote. At times the two even contradict one another.

The historical transcripts and archival materials are what one theorist has likened to bones that remain of a body that once was, bones that bespeak flesh that has seemingly passed on from the material world.[72] Yet these written and spoken "facts" located in archives are not all that is essential to the story. Like the bones that signify departed flesh, I am suggesting that a student bearing witness to their teachers' secret use of Woodson's textbook indexes more than a benign moment of teacher improvisation, more than just a clever instructional move. Likewise, any analysis of a scenario portraying a black child being taught by their formerly enslaved relative—it seems to me—must have a rigorous accounting for more than the procedural aspects of this pedagogical experience. Wrestling with the invisible factors at work in these scenarios is also the work of the scholar. Some absences in the historical record are "so stressed, so ornate, so planned, they call attention to themselves," as Toni Morrison has written. Even as they are not explicitly spelled out, "these invisible things are not necessarily 'not there.'"[73]

I am also interested in feeling—black feeling. "Facts, in social science . . . are elusive things," W. E. B. Du Bois observed, "emotions, loves, hates, were facts." And "in the cold, bare facts of history, so much was omitted from the complete picture." Researchers working to preserve and analyze human experiences, he wrote, must strive to "piece out the reality" of the past as best we can.[74] It demands, for instance, that we strive to make sense of the coded meaning of a former student likening Negro History Week celebrations along with other school rituals and norms to "a kind of freemasonry" of the race.[75] The depth of this—of a student coming to think of race, or more precisely blackness, as secret society and school as a site of this initiation—has phenomenological implications and offers more than descriptive detail. Likewise, while there are several clear-cut pieces of historical information recovered from the interview transcript of McGee's student, paired with documents from Webster Parish's educational records and census data—these facts only tell us so much about that particular encounter. Concerned with more than the deed, this book tarries with the ideas and emotions that prompted McGee's quiet act of resistance. It lingers with the meaning this action held for McGee as well as the pupils sitting at their desks, studying her.

Black student voices provide crucial information as to what happened in the private spaces of black teachers' classrooms. Yet they rarely appear in formal school records. We are only able to enter McGee's classroom because her former student bore witness to what she did and how it affected him. For these reasons, *Fugitive Pedagogy* privileges black voice in relationship to institutional records and formal documents, the same way it moves beyond the familiar frames of desegregation and narratives of separate and unequal. While these histories are central to understanding the political-economic context, these institutional and ideological frames often obscure the human experience of black teachers and students on the ground. They do well to capture the persecution but very little to appreciate the art of black teaching. This is a story that can only be understood through bone and flesh, an accounting of recorded knowledge and gestures toward black feeling and understandings in otherwise places.

The sightings are extensive, tucked away in plain sight. The fugitive slave; the literate slave; the slave "learning as a means of escape," as Woodson put it; the teacher secretly reading from the textbook that documents these very origins of fugitive pedagogy, which thus becomes a doubling of the latter— these were all black flight manifesting in content and form. Irrespective of what came before and what happened alongside these clandestine educational activities, the relational dynamics between black learning, flight, and the surveillance of black life prefigured the educational agenda inherited by the freedpeople and their schools, then Jim Crow teachers and their students.

The phenomenon of black education was entrenched in the deepest realms of black American life. It was always in crisis; always teetering between strife and a hope and prayer. It is from this liminal space that *Fugitive Pedagogy* was dug up and written.

What Is to Come

The chapters in this book explore the realities of fugitive pedagogy at varying levels in black school life: individual experience, institutional culture, curriculum development, theoretical perspective, teacher practice, and student witnessing. Across six chapters, I argue that a veiled educational world was initiated during slavery and critical parts of black education continued to happen through covert means post-Emancipation and, furthermore, that it is often in these fugitive acts that we locate education at its highest calling. The case of Carter G. Woodson is emblematic of this phenomenon. He is a central figure that allows us to trace the broader atmospheres of black educational heritage.

Chapter 1 paints a new portrait of Woodson, paying close attention to his foundational years as a student. We find him witnessing the educational world around him before he sets on a path to become a schoolteacher, following in the footsteps of his formerly enslaved relatives who were his first educators. Chapter 2 charts a clear path from Woodson's work as a teacher to his founding of the Association for the Study of Negro Life and History. While likely a familiar story to many, when read through the lens of fugitive pedagogy, we see this organization as an institutional embodiment of a much more extensive legacy of dissident politics among black schoolteachers. Previous studies of Woodson position his time in the classroom as a prologue to what is often implied to be the more important parts of his story. These chapters, instead, reveal Woodson's early years to be of enormous consequence. Woodson's journey as a student and teacher left great marks on him and, in many ways, prefigured the scholar and educational leader he became.

There have always been bodies of educational criticism in relationship to formal structures of the American School. These are theoretical perspectives in tension with orthodox models of schooling. Black teachers have a distinct tradition within this genre of theory.[76] They have historically produced a body of educational criticism on schooling and black life that can and should be studied on its own terms.[77] Woodson, like many of his contemporaries, emerged out of this tradition. Chapters 3 and 4 illuminate these intellectual acts by putting Woodson's theoretical ideas and textbooks in conversation with a broader legacy of educational criticism among black teachers and scholars. These teachers developed new scripts of knowledge as well as conceptual language to analyze schooling and power in the context of black psychic and social life. This intellectual work was done at the margins of the American School, even as it made its way into the classrooms and professional world of teachers. Chapter 3 reveals how Woodson's ideas in *The Mis-education of the Negro* were informed by his growing awareness and criticism of white imperialism in the African Diaspora and a vigilance of the role white philanthropy played in black education in the United States and on the African continent. Thus, I situate *Mis-education* as a decolonial text on schooling and black life. Building from this, Chapter 4 offers a thematic reading of Woodson's curriculum development in relation to black schoolteachers who published textbooks before him. I elevate key themes that cut across these texts published between 1890 and 1922.

Chapters 5 and 6 are companion chapters. They reflect the shared vulnerability of black teachers and students as well as their shared participation in fugitive pedagogy. Chapter 5 reveals black teachers strategically partnering with Woodson and putting his ideas into practice as an explicit critique of a school structure that was hostile to their very existence. Chapter 6 elevates the voices of students, allowing them to narrate what they saw happen in their educational worlds—just as Woodson appears in earlier chapters bearing witness to his education context. We learn how these students came to understand the significance of Woodson's program as a critique of the violence they experienced in the world and the American School. These students speak explicitly of how their regular routines were altered or concealed in the presence of white authorities. More than empty vessels to be filled, black students are discovered to be conscious participants, dissident learners.

The book ends with a conclusion that meditates on the important role of black educators within any liberatory vision and, in particular, their importance to the field of Black Studies. Woodson, again, becomes a bridge for thinking through the relationship between the history of black education and the emergence of Black Studies in the late sixties, nearly two decades after his death. I assert that fugitive pedagogy is the origin story of black education and, likewise, of Black Studies. When looking at the two histories alongside one another, it becomes clear that we inherit the tradition of black study in the post–Civil Rights context because it passed through black schoolteachers. Well before it was implanted at mainstream white American universities, the protocols of black study were honed in the private spaces of black teachers' classrooms and the institutions they built and sustained. We find that former students of black teachers are well represented among the first cohort of scholars to develop Black Studies protocols in the academy.

Collectively, these chapters render a collage of fugitive pedagogy, no linear account but instead a thematic assemblage of its key parts in the form of one particular narrative. Through this case of Woodson, we see the origin story of black education reappearing in educational content and form across time. Fugitive pedagogy was inherited and put to use by teachers and students of Woodson's generation and those thereafter. This is to say, black people have perpetually had to exist within yet against the American School given their violent conscription into its symbolic and structural order. At its most basic level, this has been the meaning of *black*education when the two words face each other: two embattled words, merged together, long used side by side, emplotted with both a bitter and beautiful history of ideas and relation. *Fugitive Pedagogy* reveals the heritage of *black*education to be a plot of perpetual escape, always striving toward a world where what is known to be human is not premised on the subjection of black life. Always striving toward a time when black life is not distorted as "a negligible factor in the thought of the world."[78]

1

Between Coffle and Classroom: Carter G. Woodson as a Student and Teacher, 1875–1912

Carter G. Woodson's first teachers were former slaves. Born in 1875, Woodson and his peers were part of the first generation to learn on the *other side* of slavery. They inherited the black educational traditions of their forebears, however. Woodson's teachers were also family: two uncles and a first cousin, who held dear the subversive aspirations of their people prior to Emancipation. Woodson's years spent in the classroom as both student and teacher served as the prologue to his emergence as "the father of Black History." More than this, his socialization in this black educational world shaped the very questions that he would later take up and the political messages of social transformation that characterized his life's work as a historian and educational leader. Witnessing the lived experiences of his teachers taught him as much as the curricular content, if not more. Through their lives and pedagogy, he developed a studied perspective on the distinct vocational demands of being a black teacher.

By his midthirties, Woodson had studied and taught across the United States, Europe, and Asia. He received his doctorate in history from Harvard at the age of thirty-seven. The journey of learning under the tutelage of his formerly enslaved relatives to becoming one of the most conspicuously educated black Americans in the twentieth century brought Woodson personal and intellectual conundrums along the way. Most notably, his life was consumed by his unrelenting critique of the American School and the racist foundations of Western knowledge. Focusing on Woodson's development from student to teacher clarifies how the traditions inherited from his first teachers—that of fugitive pedagogy—intensified as well as took on new meaning after his professional initiation into the highest orders of knowledge. Like other black scholars in the Jim Crow years, feelings of alienation were often explained through remembrance of the racial logics of slavery. Woodson's work continued the mission of his first teachers, since black freedom itself continued to be incomplete. Fugitive pedagogy persisted as part of a protracted struggle waged in the material and symbolic realms in which schools figured significantly.

The Origin Story of Black Education

Before Emancipation, the enslaved had to gain their education by "snatching learning in forbidden fields," as Woodson characterized it. The black abolitionist and teacher Francis Ellen Watkins Harper explained that some tried "to steal a little from the book. And put words together, and learn by hook or crook." Acquiring knowledge was a criminal act. As Frederick Douglass's master put it, a slave who learned to read and write against the will of his master was tantamount to "running away with himself."[1] Stealing one's self in this way meant that the literate slave was a fugitive slave: to secretly acquire literacy—for religious, practical, and intellectual ends (or, perhaps, especially as leisurely activity)—was akin to black flight from the sites of their enslavement.

Antiliteracy laws targeting black people were older than the United States itself. The first law of this kind was a slave code enacted in 1740 in reaction to the Stono Slave Rebellion of 1739 in South Carolina. This code, which was meant to improve surveillance of the enslaved, listed writing among other illegal activities.[2] Black people's disallowance from the realm of educational opportunity anteceded the birth of the nation. This prohibition was absorbed into the dominant ideology of the nation, even as American common schools were established after American independence for the purpose of training a responsible citizenry; thus, conceptions of citizenship emerged as a metonym for whiteness. The antiblack sentiments that justified slavery justified excluding black Americans from citizenship and from schools—this antagonism was not an anomaly but was, in fact, a structural feature.[3]

Antiliteracy laws and the intellectual surveillance that accompanied them left great marks on the politics of black education. They enforced the idea that blacks were outside the social contract of American society—inconceivable as fully human, citizen, or student.[4] Many enslaved and free blacks subverted these legal mandates by acquiring literacy through fugitive tactics—leaving a mark of equal or greater consequence. While the overwhelming majority of blacks were illiterate under slavery, approximately 10 percent learned to read and/or write; suggesting that literate slaves were not so unusual as to be unknown to other blacks.[5] These literate slaves were recognized as leaders with a practical skill set that benefitted their community.[6]

How did the 10 percent of blacks who learned to read and write in the South before Emancipation gain the gift of literacy? As Woodson recounted time and again in his writings: "Negroes themselves . . . stole away to secret places at night to study." The historical record documents black Americans climbing into holes in the ground under the cover of night, attending schools run by free blacks, "playing school" with white children, "stealin' a meetin'" in the woods, and trading food for lessons, among other covert means. In her remarkable narrative of black education in the antebellum South and early in Emancipation, Heather Williams reveals that black people were self-taught and their own biggest advocates for education, in slavery and in freedom.[7]

Frederick Douglass, raised in Maryland between the 1820s and 1830s, represents the best-known example of learning in secret. Left alone to look after the master's house, he employed his own version of fugitive pedagogy. He spent his time "writing in the spaces left in Master Thomas's copy book, copying what he had written." Douglass wrote in the margins of the *Webster Spelling Book*, populating these in-between spaces with words he appropriated and mimicked, turning them toward his own semantic and political ends. Woodson's nearby home state of Virginia passed laws prohibiting education for enslaved *and* free blacks as early as 1819. This legal precedent was reinforced through subsequent acts passed in Virginia leading up to Emancipation. In April 1831, for instance, an act was passed declaring "that all meetings of free negroes or mulattoes, at any schoolhouse, church, meetinghouse or other place for teaching them reading or writing, either in the day or night, under whatever pretext, shall be deemed and considered as an unlawful assembly." The law then authorized whippings "at the discretion of any justice of the peace, not exceeding twenty lashes."[8] Such legislation, and the sentiments of antiliteracy ideology, became nearly universal in the South. When the Civil War began, black Americans challenged the prohibition of their mental elevation. Their efforts to learn expanded in formal and public ways; they initiated "native schools" in the Contraband Camps, which prefigured the Freedmen's Bureau schools, and then the first public school system in the US South.

With the end of the Civil War came "jubilee," as the formerly enslaved described the biblical time of freedom.[9] No longer in bondage, black people across the South performed their first acts of freedom by occupying the classroom. Booker T. Washington recalled a "whole race trying to go to school," and he noted: "Few were too young, and none were too old, to make the attempt to learn. As fast as any kind of teachers could be secured, not only were day-schools filled, but night schools as well."[10] The rush to the schoolhouse transcended any single location. Washington's narrative described blacks' quest for education throughout all the Southern states.[11]

Once legally permitted to become educated in the postbellum South, black Americans continued to experience violence and other forms of opposition to their efforts. Yet they continued to resist in the best ways they knew how.[12] Even as black education developed institutionally through the endeavors of blacks themselves and also in conjunction with white northern church denominations and philanthropists, black Americans nonetheless pursued critical parts of their educational lives in secret. As a class of political actors, black students and teachers emerged as persuasive advocates in fund-raising for their respective institutions. And like black preachers, teachers (or, more expansively, Negroes "who had some learning") were important leaders in black communities, not just because of their professional status but also as stokers and caretakers of the freedom dreams that helped initiate their escape from bondage.[13] Black Americans shared an "equal rights" vision that remained unfulfilled. This vision fueled the emergence of black equal rights leagues and other organizational entities representative of black life during Reconstruction and the decades to follow. Black teachers' associations reflected this collective drive on the part of a segment of leaders who signified the living history presented in Carter G. Woodson's first classrooms.

Black people's fugitive pedagogy lent itself to an origin story of black freedom. It was a central part of the general strike initiated by the absconded slaves who refused the political economic arrangement of slavery when they fled the plantations during the war. As a framework for learning, it contested ideas of black inferiority, while rejecting the superexploitation and ownership of black people as fungible laborers. The black schools and teachers after the war, by their very existence, symbolized the refutation of a knowledge realm that debased them, educational institutions that excluded them, and curricula that portrayed them as always already subjugated and "narratively condemned."[14] Fugitive pedagogy framed black educational life from the time of slavery through Jim Crow as a narrative plot that transcended the limited world in which black folks found themselves. It became more than a teaching method—more than utilitarian skills to be learned. Instead teaching and learning themselves continued to be "a means of escape," as Woodson wrote. Education would guide blacks in pursuit of a new world and a new way of being; it was a total critique of the current order. Black Americans passed this narrative on as a panacea for social ills, and it heavily informed both politics and values after Emancipation. Carried over from slavery, fugitive pedagogy reflected the general story of black people's shared past and present. In the postbellum era, black Americans continued to live their educational lives through the frame of this origin story.[15] It continued to structure the relationship between education and the black political struggle more broadly. Woodson himself contributed to this long memory of education's role in black America's quest for freedom and justice.

The Pedagogy of Woodson's Family History

Woodson first learned of the origins of fugitive pedagogy from his parents. His mother and father, Anne Eliza (Riddle) and James Henry Woodson, were formerly enslaved. Woodson proudly described his father as "a fugitive [who] rushed to the invading troops" to escape bondage after physically assaulting his owner in a struggle to avoid being whipped. Woodson's mother, Anne, was eleven years old when she pleaded to be sold instead of her mother and younger siblings. Perhaps if she could entice a high enough bid, her financially challenged master would avoid splitting up what remained of her family. This was the prayer she clung to as she journeyed to the auction block in Richmond, Virginia. The bids placed for Anne were too low. Instead, her mother and two youngest brothers were sold at the price of $1900.[16] Anne shared this story with Woodson in his youth, recounting how she, in shackles, passed before the statue of George Washington on a horse, pointing to the South.

The enslaved interpreted this posture to be President Washington's "command to carry the Negroes down South."[17] Whether or not the bronze representation of Washington signaled the fate of black life, Anne's recalling this experience to Woodson was layered with encoded meanings. As the monumental figure of the nation cast a shadow over their worlds, the enslaved

George Washington Equestrian Monument in Richmond, Virginia, erected in 1858. Virginia State Capitol History Project.

people *read* this statue as illustrative of slavery's violent intrusion on black sociality. It signaled dispossession, the sale of black flesh as commodity, and the nation's collusion with black subjugation. The racial life of this statue continued to accrue meaning. Jefferson Davis would take his oath as president of the Confederate States of America in front of this statue in February 1862, and the image of this monument was placed at the center of the Confederacy's official seal. Anne passed the statue in chains, with a *coerced* willingness to sell herself. The lack of protection that triangulates between Anne's decision, the representation of the first US president, and the sale of her brothers and mother was knowledge embedded in context, stories that shaped Woodson's deference to his first teachers. This was a story that left an impression on Woodson. It framed how he came to know his uncles as teachers and freedmen.

When the war ended, Anne's brothers, John and James Riddle, hurried to the freedmen's schools. These two men, Woodson's uncles, would become his first teachers in a one-room schoolhouse in the years after Reconstruction. Woodson later told how James and John "availed themselves of the first opportunities to study in the schools for freedmen after the general emancipation." This site of study emerged as a place for a new self-fashioning. These brothers' pursuit of study was no benign endeavor. Their first act of freedom was informed by the plot of black education that began in the time of slavery.[18]

The Freedmen's Bureau made great strides to expand the schooling initiatives started by blacks in the state of Virginia, beginning in the summer of 1865. This federal agency absorbed educational activities initiated by the formerly enslaved themselves, leading to the region's first public education system. The bureau oversaw these efforts in Virginia until June 1870. Following Virginia's readmission to statehood, the Freedmen's Bureau withdrew from the state, and the former white planter class worked to regain authority. During this five-year period, however, approximately 50,000 black students learned or enhanced their literacy skills in Freedmen's Bureau schools. John and James were among this group. Woodson recalled that his uncle John became the first black person in Buckingham County, Virginia, to secure a first-class teaching certificate.[19]

While the educational opportunities for black Americans in Virginia expanded dramatically following the Civil War, it was not without violent white opposition. Black schools, and churches used for educational activities, were routinely burned, and teachers in the Virginia's freedpeople's schools were subject to various forms of terror (including evictions, social isolation, and mob violence).[20] While Woodson's uncles were privileged to attend school, the antiblack sentiments that drove antiliteracy laws of years past continued to contour violent white opposition. John and James were sorely aware that their educational opportunities were as precarious as their newly acquired status as *freed*men. Black education was the subject of violent white protest when Woodson's uncles began to learn in the Freedmen's schools, and it persisted during Woodson's years as a student during the 1880s and early 1890s, when the days of the Freedmen's Bureau were long gone.

Citizenship rights gained by blacks in the years following Emancipation continued to be gutted, and the white planter class worked diligently to re-inscribe a racial hierarchy reminiscent of the Old South.[21] Francis G. Ruffin of Virginia, a former Confederate colonel and later a major political voice and editor of Richmond's *Dispatch* newspaper, published a report in 1889 arguing that Negro education was a futile public program. In *The Cost and Outcome of Negro Education in Virginia: Respectfully Addressed to the White People of the State,* Ruffin outlined his views on the matter as a southern Democrat. White Virginians were burdened with the expense of educating blacks, he argued, despite past efforts proving ineffective for helping blacks to achieve better conduct and higher morals. The formerly enslaved deteriorated even further post-Emancipation. They were still no more "fitted . . . for the dis-charge of civil and social duties" than they had been before useless attempts at their mental elevation. Ruffin relied on emerging social science research to explain how black people's capacity to learn became regressive at the stage of puberty, at which point their capacity for mental development became se-verely inhibited. To further substantiate his claims, Ruffin cites statistical data to paint a narrative of black criminality. The figures outline a dispro-portionate rate of black crime in Virginia from 1871 to 1889 as evidence that Negro education was ineffective or, worse, that there was a causal relation-ship between increased education and increased black social vice. Similarly, he cites the number of black children born out of wedlock and black prac-tices of religious worship, among many other indicators that, for him, proved that black education did more harm than good. Ruffin concluded, "It appears then that in the 19 years of public free schools there has been no develop-ment of religious, intellectual, moral or industrial advancement in the ne-groes; rather a falling back in all these attributes . . . 'you cannot gather grapes of thorns or figs of thistles,' nor convert an African into a Caucasian by 'les-sons taught in school books,' or by any process; and therefore the attempt should cease." This clouded the air of public discourse, even as Woodson learned and strove under the direction of his emancipated teachers. To the left of Ruffin were the likes of General Samuel Armstrong, founder of the Hampton Institute in Virginia. Armstrong advocated for black education as long as it centered on industrial and agricultural training, and he widely disseminated these ideas among white educational leaders in the state and

across the country. Armstrong believed that blacks were morally and culturally bankrupt, though mentally capable.[22]

Persistent discursive and physical assaults against black educational efforts
fueled the demand for fugitive learning practices. The subversive disposition
of formerly enslaved people continued to structure the politics at the heart
of black attempts at learning. Woodson's uncles' strides at learning in the
freedpeople's schools and their teaching him in the one-room schoolhouse
were a freedom-seeking project, over and against a dominant social order that
hailed the Negro as the most degraded form of the human species, as incapable
of citizenship and incapable of achieving the highest forms of human development and civilization.

James and John embodied the dialectic of black educational heritage. Their
lives were marked by both the coffle and the classroom, providing an implicit
signification of what was politically at stake in black education. Black
schooling remained an active negation of dominant white public opinion.
Woodson was initiated into a tradition of learning that was fundamentally set
against the dominant norms of the American social order. He and his first
teachers, like black students and educators across the country, were striving
within this liminal existence. They were situated between black attempts to
put their dreams of freedom into practice and the realities of white restrictions imposed on their attempts to know the world and themselves *otherwise.*

Woodson's early educational development is characterized by a striking
intimacy between the home and the schoolhouse. Just as his gift of literacy
acquired through school served a functional purpose in the home, the stories of his family shaped how he interpreted the meaning of his uncles' life
and their work. Woodson wrote about these uncle-teachers and his parents'
enslavement on multiple occasions. As a student, he witnessed the shared vulnerability of black people through the story of his teachers and family. These
first encounters taught Woodson more than just reading, writing, and arithmetic. He also inherited a political orientation to schooling informed by the
lived history of the teachers standing before him. The kinship and intertwined
lineage between Woodson and his first teachers made him aware of their
shared vulnerability as black people, a vulnerability that was bound up in the
constraints placed on their educational strivings.

Standing before Woodson in the one-room schoolhouse was one uncle who
had been sold with his grandmother and his eldest uncle, who stayed on the

plantation. Here, Woodson encountered the project of black education. His formerly enslaved uncles, like his mother, were marked by memories of "the chattel principle" being enacted on their bodies.[23] The coffle was living history when these brothers taught in their classroom. Woodson's early education offers important lessons, especially when the material and the symbolic are collapsed. To comprehend the educational life world I am calling *black educational heritage* or any conceptual understanding of it, we must look beyond (or beneath) what is spoken and written in the historical record and attend to affect and embodied meaning that are often hidden in context. The bodies of these first teachers were meaning in motion. Their subjectivities communicated embodied knowledge to their students: they were flesh-as-former-commodity: once property, now teaching as an act of self-possession. Teaching for these formerly enslaved men was an act of unmaking the terms of their relation to the *word* and *world*. It challenged a knowledge system that marked them as beneath the threshold of human history and disrupted a social order that functioned on these antiblack ideas. Woodson's uncles, in their flesh, embodied the fugitive demands that were at the center of black education from its inception. Their teaching and his learning were about an insistence on black humanity—an assertion that was always already fugitive.

Woodson's family struggled to survive. He recalled days when his mother "had her breakfast and did not know where she would find her dinner." Their family had very little by way of material possessions. Some Saturday nights Woodson had to "retire early . . . that [his] mother might wash out the only clothing that [he] had." This way he would have something clean to wear the following day for church. The farm's crops yielded little money, but the food cultivated on the land went a long way to help sustain their large family. Woodson's mother bore nine children, two of whom died in infancy. His father was a skilled brick mason and secured scattered work laying the foundations for houses and building stone walls and chimneys. The money earned from this labor is what primarily supported their family financially.[24] A meager beginning, filled with serious work on a six-acre family farm, mostly of deadened land, was a key characteristic of his early childhood in New Canton, Buckingham County, Virginia. This required that the children work to help maintain the family. Woodson was a man of the soil.[25] He also worked as a garbage boy before the age of twelve, helping drive a wagon to collect waste in his hometown.[26]

Education was highly valued in their household, but Woodson often missed school because of his responsibilities on the farm. Their economic vulnerability required such sacrifice, as was the case for many black Americans living in the politically economic regressive times of the post-Reconstruction South. Truancy, however, did not equate to indifference. For most of Woodson's childhood, the small school for black children in New Canton was only opened five months of the year. Even during these months, however, his attendance was scattered. On days when the weather was fair, he often stayed home to work. If it rained or snowed, he went to school.

Despite his inconsistent attendance, Woodson developed a love for learning. This passion was enhanced as he realized the practical implications it had for his role in the family. Woodson's father relied on him to read newspapers aloud. While James Woodson was illiterate, his son's command of the written word allowed him to engage with literate culture and interrogate the political affairs of their world as represented in the press. This practice of communal literacy was an important feature of education's liberatory function in black communities before and after Emancipation. Reading gave Woodson a sense of purpose and usefulness. It also exposed him to broader atmospheres of the world he lived in, beyond the rural context of the farm he lived on or the coal mines he would later work in as a teenager.[27]

The *McGuffey's Reader*: An Early Encounter with the American School's System of Representation

There were few books in Woodson's world as a young boy, but he did recall a meaningful encounter with an old *McGuffey's Reader* around the age of twelve. *McGuffey's* was a moral primer, providing reading material that emphasized the kinds of values and character traits that were widely held as essential for being a good student and citizen. *McGuffey's* was widely used for instruction in spelling at the grammar school stage in Virginia. The book included general overviews of punctuation and pronunciation; then the bulk of the text consisted of "selections in prose and poetry" through which students were exposed to widely accepted moral ideals and an expanding vocabulary, the most difficult words being accompanied by definitions.[28]

One story, on "Consequences of Idleness" and the "Advantages of Industry," stuck with him. It featured two contrasting characters, Charles Bullard and George Jones. Charles studied hard and respected his parents and teachers. George never took his schoolwork seriously and was not respectful to his peers or teachers. Charles graduated from college, becoming a "credit" to his family and community. George, on the other hand, became just the opposite. Woodson recalled this story offering a road map for his life, something to which he could aspire. At twelve years old, he read this story and decided he would strive to be like Charles Bullard, although he admitted to being "more George Jones than Charles Bullard" at times, recalling several incidents when he misbehaved in school. Woodson was a fast learner, often finishing assignments before his classmates. Because there were no spare books around to occupy his time, "he amused himself by cutting up." When this happened, his uncles "appl[ied] the birch," sometimes twice in one day. His mother would then give him a whipping at home "for having already deserved two." Surely, these experiences invited more laughter in retrospect than they did in real time.[29]

McGuffey's did not discuss race in explicit fashion, yet racial ideas were operative even when hidden in plain sight. The absence of black or Native American people in the stories, poems, and illustrations mapped onto a larger political context where these groups were obscured within the official knowledge of schools, and one in which European and Euro-American "exploration" and imperialism were assumed to be benevolent and inevitable.[30] While Africa appears three times in the reader, these are passages referring to elephants, giraffes, and coffee. Africa is a place where animals are found, where the coffee bean is indigenous, but there are no people there, no life, just a place brought into the known world through white exploration. An illustration depicting a coffee crop field also includes native Africans working; however, they are not mentioned in the narrative. They simply serve as props to a story about the exotic coffee bean. In discussing the giraffe, the primer takes care to note, "Le Vaillant (the celebrated French traveler and naturalist) was the first who gave us any exact account of the form and habits of the giraffe" based on his explorations in South Africa.[31]

There is no way to fully comprehend what Woodson made of this text at such a young age. Did he realize or ponder how this schoolbook failed to engage the realities of his life, beyond generic lessons of morality? Nonetheless, as evidenced by his favorable recollection of Charles Bullard and George Jones, this primer still offered him a learning opportunity. Primers like *McGuffey's* cultivated ideological investment in the nation, a belief in the United States as a superior civilization, and the assumption that (American and European) imperialism was necessary for advancing human civilization. Ironically, this text helped set Woodson on a path for higher learning and a trajectory of citizenship within the ranks of American empire building.

This text also planted seeds for topics Woodson would interrogate later in life: the occlusion of Africa and the Negro in texts about the world, the tendency to present them with no interiority. The primer was an extension of the imperialism of the day and failed to provide its most vulnerable students with the language and understanding to know the violence of what was presented as casual explorations of the world by Europeans and Euro-Americans. It offered no semantics for understanding the violence undergirding the small suggestion that life forms indigenous to the African continent were only "known" after European contact. Tragic as it is, such texts were clung to by students like Woodson, who extrapolated, as best they could, lessons they could use in a world in which they were searching for opportunity and life beyond subjection.

The Coal Mines and Communal Learning

By the age of seventeen, Woodson had gained knowledge of arithmetic, history, geography, and spelling under his uncles' tutelage. While these academic lessons were essential for establishing an academic foundation, he also learned fundamental ideals about the meaning of education in his life as a black child.[32] He remained at his uncles' school in New Canton until about 1892. In search of work opportunities, he left home to join two of his older brothers in building the railroad from Thurmond to Mt. Hope in Fayette County, West Virginia, and eventually working in the coal mines.[33] Opportunities for work were scarce in Buckingham County, Virginia, and the paths for academic growth were few. Fayette County, however, presented access to new labor opportunities and unexpected academic experiences.

Woodson's years in the coal mines presented an organic exposure to black American history and a route to teaching. Many of the black coal miners were formerly enslaved and illiterate. Among them was Oliver Jones, a man who welcomed his colaborers into his home during the evenings to fellowship.

Having learned that Woodson could read, Jones hired him to serve as a reader for their group, offering him fruits and desserts in exchange for his gift of literacy. This responsibility had a profound impact on Woodson's life. More than just a reader, he often served as a lay researcher.[34] These fellowship gatherings after long days in the coal mines became Woodson's inaugural classroom. Like his first teachers, Woodson's first students were also formerly enslaved men. Their curriculum was a patchwork consisting of books by black American authors, black newspapers, mainstream newspapers, and the knowledge these men carried from their own lived experiences.

Again, the young Woodson was required to lean on the inherited practice of "communal literacy," just as he did when reading to his father—a practice he maintained through his early twenties. By reading to and for others, Woodson made it possible for those around him to engage with ideas and interact with the written word. Literacy was never primarily an individualized, antisocial endeavor in the context of black life; it was largely a social act at the center of black political struggle. Literacy acts held great cultural and political significance, derived from the time of slavery.[35] Writing of communal literacy, one scholar notes: "Literacy education for African Americans was not an isolated or individualistic endeavor, but a communal one. . . . [Black] families viewed literacy as an inheritance that is passed on to strengthen future generations and [that gave] them opportunities in a hostile environment."[36] Others have illuminated these communal aspects of black literacy practices through the narratives of black Civil War troops. Some of these men taught one another to read in their camps and even in infirmaries among the wounded soldiers.[37] Woodson came to know education to be a communal endeavor. He inherited this cultural norm from both his family and the Civil War veterans and former slaves he labored alongside in the coal mines.

Oliver Jones's home was "all but a reading room." Some of the most exciting books he read focused on black soldiers on the American battlefront, from the Revolutionary War to the Civil War. "The history of the race was discussed frequently" in this parlor-turned-classroom. As a result, Woodson recalled that his "interest in penetrating the past of the race was deepened and intensified" during his time with this group. If a veteran came out as a candidate for some public office, Woodson would look them up in books and identify what battles they fought in. The black veterans weighed these candidates' narratives against their own recollections of the war.[38] Through the stories of these former slaves, Woodson learned that black people, too, were living, breathing history. Despite their technical illiteracy, they had the capacity to read the world and speak truth to power.

Communal literacy taught Woodson that black education was inherently tied to a larger goal of black American group development as opposed to individual achievement. It also exposed him to counternarratives of history, sowing seeds that bore fruit in his strident critiques of the American School's curriculum years later. The tension between the *McGuffey's* primer and the kinds of books he read in Oliver Jones's parlor reflects a disjunction Woodson continued to grapple with throughout his life.

The origins of Woodson's pedagogy lie in these first encounters with the political life of black education: his formerly enslaved uncles teaching him as they worked to forge a new human vision of the world that included those who were once property; his mother's testimony about the shared vulnerability of black people and its integration into the symbolics of the nation; black coal miners listening to him read aloud while offering criticisms of written words they themselves could not decipher. These were his first lessons in teaching, "the fundamentals," so to speak. Woodson inherited a moral orientation to education that was cultivated by his first teachers and students. He came to know the demands of black education to be intimately tied to the legacies of slavery. More than this, he learned that the function of education for black people was seeking collective redress in a world that continued to be hostile to their very existence.

Woodson's time with this group of coal miners ended in 1895 when he left to pursue his secondary education at the Frederick Douglass School in Huntington, West Virginia—a school named, like many others, for the fugitive slave who became the leading voice on black political issues post-Emancipation. Woodson's education would again be under the leadership of a relative.[39] His first cousin and namesake, Carter H. Barnett, born in 1865 just after the Civil War, was a teacher and then principal at the Douglass School starting in the early 1890s until 1900.[40] Woodson's father and Barnett's mother were siblings, and both of these young men had been named for their grandfather. Barnett was well connected in the local community. Not only was he a respected educator; he was also a political voice as the editor of the *West Virginia Spokesman*, a local newspaper he published.[41] More than this, Barnett was one of the earliest members of the black teacher association in this state, which was founded in 1891. The organization was formed out of a reading circle of black teachers in Charleston, West Virginia. These teachers believed they could better advocate for their professional group and students by forming an association. The group consisted of "teachers and race leaders."[42] Thus, Barnett, who Woodson described as a "scholarly" man was active in building black institutions that advanced the cause of black American education and political life; he was also the second black person to graduate from Denison University in Ohio in 1892, and the first to play on its baseball team.[43] Through Barnett, Woodson learned that the work of black educators was not confined to the walls of the schoolhouse or the mandates of West Virginia's educational officials. These cousins shared more than their given name. Barnett modeled the kind of schoolteacher Woodson would become, and both eventually shared the alienating experience of navigating white institutions of higher learning.

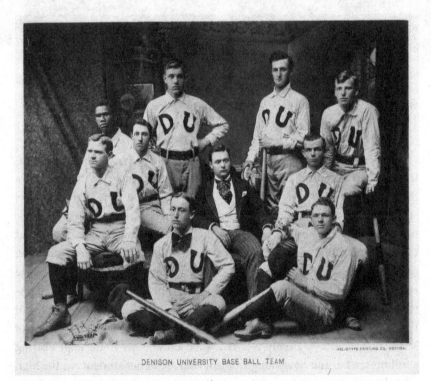

DENISON UNIVERSITY BASE BALL TEAM

Denison University Baseball Team yearbook photo, 1890–1891; Carter Barnett (far left). Denison University, *The Adytum: Yearbook* (Press of Advocate Printing Co., Newark, O., 1891), 84.

Students of the Frederick Douglass School (Huntington, West Virginia, c. 1896);
Carter G. Woodson (top row, fourth from the left), Carter H. Barnett (far-right corner).
West Virginia State University Archives and Special Collections.

The high school program at the Douglass School was recently established when Woodson arrived there in 1895, and its structure grew from a
one-room school to a six-room brick building, though the majority of its
students were still in the lower grades.[44] A tattered photo provides a glimpse
into the atmosphere of this school. Principal Carter Barnett stands with hat
in hand, and to his right is a group of nearly fifty small children standing
on the school's steps, all dressed in carefully adorned formal clothes: some
noticeably too big, others outgrown, and a few picture-perfect. All look intently at the camera in front of them seeking to record some memory of
their mission in the moment. Standing in the back of the crowd is a group of
seven young adults—a twenty-year-old Woodson, another young man wearing
a full mustache, and five young women, who are either students in the high
school program or teachers. All are distinguished in demeanor and sartorial
presentation. Their collective self-fashioning is intentional and a political

statement in its own right—the ruffled collars, dark suits, long dresses, and accented shoulders were an outward expression of a shared inner striving. And their "weak wings beat against their barriers," to borrow from W. E. B. Du Bois, "barriers of caste, of youth, of life; at last, in dangerous moments, against everything that opposed even a whim."[45]

Woodson was one of two graduates in May 1896, finishing his coursework in less than two years.[46] A week after Woodson's final days of high school, the same newspaper that announced his graduation would also report the news of a landmark Supreme Court ruling: *Plessy v. Ferguson*. Woodson graduated from high school at the very moment that the legal era of Jim Crow was ushered in, judicially stratifying society along racial lines of separate and unequal.[47]

Off to College: Woodson as a Student-Teacher

Woodson enrolled at Berea College and began teaching during his first year out of high school. His collegiate experience was unconventional: most of his coursework was completed as a part-time student; he was only in residence for two quarters between 1897 and 1898; and he attended Lincoln University, a historically black college in Pennsylvania, during the fall of 1897.[48] Woodson's academic performance at Lincoln was stellar: he was among the top academic performers in the school's sophomore cohort.[49] Why he chose to return to Berea is unclear, but the flexibility of teaching full-time while furthering his studies may have appealed to him. Shortly after his return from Lincoln, he began teaching at a rural school in Winona, Fayette County, West Virginia. He became president of the deacon board at First Baptist Church of Winona, where he taught Sunday school. Like other black American teachers who taught at school and church, Woodson taught many of his students on weekdays and Sundays.[50]

Berea was the only college in the South to offer admission to both black and white students, though Woodson enrolled when the percentage of black students at the school declined as the administration focused on attracting white students, following the preference of school benefactors. Berea had no black faculty in Woodson's time, and white faculty actively resisted demands from black students and alumni to hire black American professors.[51]

Woodson's success as a teacher landed him a job as the principal at his former high school. Ironically, he was hired to replace his cousin, Carter Barnett, whose political advocacy put him at odds with local white leaders. Urging blacks to move beyond blind loyalty to the Republican Party, Barnett ran a slate of independent black candidates for office, using his newspaper as a platform to garner support. Barnett was fired and Woodson became principal in 1900; the school board's white leadership was likely unaware of Woodson's relationship to Barnett.[52] Barnett's firing taught Woodson lessons about the vulnerability of black educators under the control of white authority in Jim Crow schools, a lesson that Woodson would be reminded of time and time again in the years to come.[53] Despite these political constraints, Woodson excelled as principal of Douglass High from 1900 to 1903. He established a library, invited prominent leaders to speak, and established a strong school culture shaped by civic duty and cultural practices formalized in the black church.

Woodson's promise as an educator showed in his strong performance on teacher certification exams. In 1901, he was examined across twenty subjects (from drawing and theory of teaching to physics and Latin) to become a certified teacher in West Virginia. Woodson averaged 91 percent with no grade under 82 percent across all categories.[54] Yet his success as a school leader required more than the knowledge assessed in these exams.

Woodson created a school culture at Douglass that invited community engagement and cultivated a strong sense of identity. Public events attracted considerable attention for students' oratorical performances. These formal occasions staged by Woodson, the Douglass schoolteachers, and students stood in stark contrast to dominant narratives of black pathology. Even so, white spectatorship revealed the proliferation of racist attitudes. In 1901, a local reporter noted that Douglass School graduates' "words were pronounced with scarcely any thing of the usual African cadence and could be heard in all parts of the hall." The keynote speech given by Reverend J. E. Bullock addressed the theme of being "Co-laborers with God." The white reporter noted the "rich and musical" cadence of Bullock's voice, his "brown skin and striking historical appearance," while offering no specific content of the speaker's message, except to say that the speech could have been better appreciated by a more "cultured and critical audience" than the black families, community members, students, and teachers assembled.[55] These insults masquerading as compliments reveal the antiblack perception of even the most "respectable" black people in the local white imagination.

While the students' remarks on their academic striving and success caught the interest of paternalistic local whites, they did little to dispel deep-seated ideas about black cultural inferiority. In fact, the students' success was attributed to the stellar leadership of the white superintendent of black schools. The reporter suggested that "Professor Cole" (the white superintendent) and the nameless "teachers in charge of the colored school" were to be congratulated. Woodson goes unmentioned, though he was the leader of the school and likely the organizer of the commencement exercises at hand.

After the assassination of President William McKinley in September 1901, Woodson led a memorial service. Students sang and spoke on aspects of the president's life and leadership.[56] The school also contributed to the statewide McKinley Memorial Fund to build a monument in honor of the president.[57] This same academic year, Woodson successfully appealed to local school authorities and citizens for support in establishing a school library.[58] The commencement of May 1902 was more elaborate than the previous year's. The ceremony, filled with orations, songs, and a keynote by Woodson, drew a large crowd from the local community. Woodson's sister Bessie, one of the graduates, delivered a speech on Patrick Henry.[59] Her rendition of Henry's declaration "Give me liberty or give me death" stirred passionate sentiments in the crowd. The rhetoric deployed of the American Revolution had long been appropriated by black Americans. In the antebellum era, such words "offered black abolitionists an opportunity to present themselves as equal men whose struggle mirrored that of American Revolutionaries."[60] Bessie's oration referenced traditions older than the Emancipation era.

While working full-time as the principal of Douglass, Woodson made steady progress as a student at Berea through its extension education program. In the summer of 1902, he took courses at the University of Chicago, and in spring of 1903 he was awarded an AB degree in literature from Berea.[61]

In the same year, the twenty-seven-year-old Woodson saw Booker T. Washington in Kentucky. Washington's ideas about race relations and the political economy of black labor in the South appealed to Woodson, whose work on his family's farm, on the railroad, and in the coal mines gave him personal insight into the realities of agricultural and industrial work. Booker T. Washington's message of black industry and self-determination as a means for better living conditions seems to have struck a chord with Woodson. And to be clear, Washington's reputation preceded him in Woodson's imagination. Black teachers in West Virginia recognized Washington's work at Tuskegee as a meaningful contribution to black American education, even making him an honorary member of the West Virginia State Teachers Association.[62]

Reflecting on this encounter years later, Woodson recalled that Washington told a "joke" that "was a bit of a prophecy." A man claiming to have been to hell is asked what he saw there. "Every white man had a Negro," he responds, "holding the Negro between him and the fire." The punch line, Woodson observes, drew a "tremendous outburst of laughter" and "vociferous applause" from the audience. Just as things grew quiet, "an old-time Negro" called out, "Hush yer mouf, boy!" Still more laughter ensued. Woodson sees this "droll" remark as the "compliment of an illiterate but thinking Negro who could see much further into the future" than the better educated. The old man, who "had been through the fiery furnace of slavery," wisely "feared that there might be ahead the ordeal of serfdom." Reflecting back in 1934, Woodson writes: "Little did I think at that time that I would live long enough to see myself in this veritable hell. This is exactly where the Negro is today in the present crisis. Throughout the country, wherever I find Negroes in conspicuous numbers, somebody is holding one between him and the fire." For Woodson, this "hell" is more than lynchings and riots: "He who thinks of the Negroes only when some of them have been lynched or mobbed has not begun to tackle the real problems; and he will never accomplish much in the uplift of the race. If you will get from between the other fellow and the fire he cannot burn you."[63]

Washington's educational program was controversial: it accommodated white supremacy, endorsing segregation and complying with the racial division of labor in the postbellum South. He argued that blacks should build their economic base through self-help instead of focusing on political agitation. He clashed with a growing faction of black American thinkers who found his gradualist approach offensive and called for immediate action toward racial equality and justice. Tensions were volatile. Washington's presence in Boston in 1903 incited a "miniature riot" resulting in a police officer being stabbed; among the dissenters was the black Bostonian William Monroe Trotter, one of Washington's fiercest critics.[64] In April of this same year, W. E. B. Du Bois's *The Souls of Black Folk* was published, in which he also critiqued Washington, arguing that he faced a "triple paradox." Washington "is striving nobly to make Negro artisans business men and property-owners," Du Bois observed, "but it is utterly impossible, under modern competitive methods, for workingmen and property-owners to defend their rights and exist without the right of suffrage." Secondly, Washington insisted "on thrift and self-respect, but at the same time counsels a silent submission to civic inferiority such as is bound to sap the manhood of any race in the long run." And finally, Washington advocated "common-school and industrial training, and depreciates institutions of higher learning; but neither the Negro common-schools, nor Tuskegee itself, could remain open a day were it not for teachers trained in Negro colleges, or trained by their graduates."[65]

Despite these critiques of Washington, Woodson found his vision compelling, especially his interest in creating black institutions and taking a pragmatic approach to navigating a society overdetermined by white supremacy. While sympathetic to Washington, Woodson would be far less accommodating of white benefactors and political allies. He would commit his life to creating and sustaining black institutions while maintaining a consistent suspicion of white paternalism.

The Conundrum of Black Learning in the Heart of American Empire

Woodson's years at Berea took place against the backdrop of the Spanish-American War. In 1898, the summer after his sophomore semester at Lincoln, the United States defeated Spain and took control of Cuba, Puerto Rico, Guam, and the Philippines. Teachers from the United States were hired to transform education in the Philippines, with the first cohort arriving in 1901. This educational commission was an extension of American empire, directly tied to the internal colonial education forming in the US South, where white educational authorities sought to impose school models that trained black Americans to be a servant class and permanent second-class citizens.[66] As one historian has argued, "the distension of public schooling for the purpose of crafting degrees of citizenship at home [referring particularly to black and Native American education] and the proliferation of American economic power through empire-building projects both at home and abroad were more intimately intertwined than is usually recognized."[67]

Officials governing education in the Philippines built on the model of industrial education implemented at the Hampton Institute and Washington's Tuskegee, as well as colonial education at Native American boarding schools. Fred Atkinson, the first general superintendent of education in the Philippines, visited Hampton, Tuskegee, and the Carlisle Institute to prepare for his work in the newly acquired US territory. He was impressed by the model of education taken up in these schools and became committed to not "overdoing the matter of higher education and unfitting the Filipino for practical work." The model of education he desired for the Filipino natives was "an agricultural and industrial one, after the pattern of our Tuskegee institute at home."[68] The similarity in the tools of domination being applied at home and abroad led some black Americans like T. Thomas Fortune, owner of a black newspaper called the *New York Age*, to declare in 1903 that black Americans and Filipinos were political companions. "For it is construed that we stand largely where they stand," Fortune argued, "outside of the American Constitution, but under the American flag. The hazards of war make strange bedfellows, but none stranger than this of the Afro-American and Filipino peoples."[69]

By the end of 1903 Woodson secured a position as a teacher in the Philippines through the US Department of Insular Affairs, and he held this position until the beginning of 1907.[70] Woodson was likely enamored with the rare chance to exercise his civic identity as an American citizen. He was also motivated by the opportunity to travel the world and to receive a significantly higher salary. Black teachers were paid less than their white colleagues in the US South, so the chance to teach abroad at a higher salary was particularly appealing. In the 1902–1903 school year Woodson was paid a monthly salary of $65 in West Virginia, which meant he made no more than $780 dollars a year.[71] His first-year salary in the Philippines was $1200.[72] This marked significant progress from his time working in the coal mines less than ten years prior.

At least fourteen black American teachers worked in the Philippines. They were an insignificant portion of the thousands of American teachers working on the island. Yet their presence is surprising, given that some officials held strong reservations about hiring black educators. Responding to Woodson's application, the governor-general of the islands and future US president William Howard Taft observed that Filipinos despised having Negro teachers and that hiring them was generally "bad policy."[73] White teachers brought their homegrown racism to the islands, at times referring to Filipino natives as "niggers."[74] Even so, Woodson's application was accepted. Perhaps his coursework at Chicago made him appealing; the superintendent of education in the Philippines was David P. Barrows, an anthropologist from the University of Chicago.

Barrows was suspicious of the educational program he inherited, particularly its overemphasis on manual labor. He suggested that many Americans advocating for this model planned to advance an exploitive agenda, developing "a great body of unskilled labor, dependent for living upon its daily wage, willing to work in great gangs, submissive to the rough handling of the 'boss'."[75] Universal education was essential for the Filipino people to have a popular government, Barrows suggested. He hoped to use common schooling to adapt American educational and political values to the Filipino context, cultivating civic investment in the national project among the masses. Due to the language barrier, it was impractical for American educators to teach at the primary levels. Therefore, Filipinos taught students for the first few years, while Americans taught more advanced grade levels, training many Filipinos to be teachers but also providing industrial education.

Woodson arrived in the Philippines via ship and was assigned to a school in Licab, Nueva Ecija, halfway through the 1903–1904 school year. He was later promoted to a supervisor position in June 1904 and transferred to Pangasinan.[76] But Woodson's transfer took place only after an altercation ensued between him and a white government clerk who publicly insulted him. The transfer was put into place after Woodson filed a formal complaint.[77] In Pangasinan he was responsible for overseeing the operations of all the schools in his division, including such tasks as identifying new Filipino teachers based on their performance in the schools, fixing salaries, testing the efficiency of American teachers, distributing supplies, keeping records of school property, and tracking attendance.[78]

In later years, Woodson wrote little about his international teaching, in keeping with his general reluctance to write about his own life. In particular, he says little about the relationship between this educational program and its ties to the larger program of American imperialism. In these early years, Woodson's primary quarrel was against antiblack oppression within the United States. He would not fully see the links between imperialism abroad and black oppression at home until years later, when he saw that he "committed some of these errors himself" in his decades of teaching.[79]

Woodson's time in the Philippines did teach him to value the culture and customs of students. He later wrote of a businessman who came to the Philippines and taught better than educators with degrees from "institutions like Harvard, Yale, Columbia, and Chicago." He did not use the prescribed books "because they were not adapted to the needs of the children." He did not teach them about people like George Washington, because they had never heard of him. "This real educator," wrote Woodson, "taught them about their own hero, José Rizal, who gave his life as a martyr for the freedom of his country." Rizal was a Filipino nationalist whose literary works were credited with helping spark the Philippine Revolution the led to Filipino independence from the Spanish. However, Rizal was executed by the colonialist before the US acquisition of the island.[80]

Chicago and Harvard: Confined at the Margins of Higher Learning

While managing his responsibilities as a district supervisor, Woodson took courses by mail through the University of Chicago. His heavy course load in French suggests that he was planning for travel to France and the need for an additional language for the graduate programs he intended to pursue. He learned to speak French and Spanish while abroad.[81] Before returning to the United States, Woodson traveled to Egypt and various countries in Asia and Europe. At the Sorbonne (University of Paris), he took a semester of courses on various aspects of French political and religious history.[82] He then enrolled full-time at the University of Chicago in the autumn quarter of 1907, remaining in residence until the summer of 1908. The university required him to take undergrad courses because his degree from Berea was deemed insufficient.[83] In March 1908, Woodson received a bachelor of arts in history, his second undergraduate degree.

He had already begun work on his master's: in February, he planned to write his master's thesis on the development of the Negro church and its relationship to black American life. He struggled to find statistics on black churches across states, their financial status, or other records showing the breadth and depth of these institutions. Seeking mentorship, he wrote to W. E. B. Du Bois.[84] At the time, Du Bois was a professor at Atlanta University and the only black PhD in history, having earned his degree from Harvard in 1895. Du Bois had written on the black church in *The Philadelphia Negro* (1899) and in his edited volume *The Negro Church* (1903). It is unclear how Du Bois responded to this query; but even as a master's student, Woodson's research interest in Negro life and history was formalizing. Already, he was forced to confront the challenge of recuperating subjugated knowledge about black life in an academic structure that saw little value in such sources and scholarship. Over the summer, he struggled to settle on a thesis topic. Despite his interest in the black church, he considered writing on "the separation of West Virginia from the Old Dominion."[85] Either this study was not approved, or he was unable to secure adequate sources to support the academic project. A couple of weeks later, his thesis on "the policy of France in the War of Austrian Succession" was accepted on August 28, 1908, earning him a master of arts in romance language and literature.[86]

Wasting no time, Woodson wrote to the Graduate School of Arts and Sciences at Harvard University just before earning his master's degree to inquire about enrolling in their doctoral program. He likely applied because Du Bois, the only black American with a doctorate in history, had received his PhD there. Woodson submitted an application on September 12 and received an acceptance letter in less than two weeks.[87] As he applied, Woodson was anxious, unsure of the precise admissions requirements. He had already taken a year and half of graduate courses between the University of Chicago and the University of Paris (not to mention two college degrees). "I can read German. I speak, read, and write French and Spanish freely. . . . How much more must I do there?" he asked the dean of Harvard's graduate division.[88]

It is interesting to note that Woodson misrepresented a portion of his early academic résumé in his Harvard application. While on other occasions he proudly disclosed that he graduated in less than two years from Douglass High School, Woodson intentionally concealed this fact on his paper application. Perhaps he was self-conscious that this might raise undue suspicion about his academic pedigree: the recognized norm for high school was four years, despite the reality that African American schools struggled to obtain resources and teachers to provide the same course offerings and standardized structure. When listing "high schools or other preparatory schools attended, and periods of attendance," Woodson wrote: "Douglass High School, Huntington, W.V. 4 years." This was a small but intentional cover-up, especially given that he was required to complete an additional undergraduate degree at Chicago.[89]

While a student at Harvard, Woodson witnessed the blatant dismissal of black life and history, forcing him to realize that the whitewashing of human history was shaped at the highest academic levels, in the sites where official knowledge was produced.[90] He arrived having taken many courses on American and European history, European languages, educational psychology, and a French course on the colonization of North Africa. He had been inundated with what were deemed the canons of knowledge pertaining to the modern world. This extensive coursework suggested that human history was a story of white people and their exploits. His original doctoral advisor, Professor Edward Channing, openly challenged the idea that black people played any significant role in American history. Channing went as far as to say that Negroes were a people with no history at all. This motivated Woodson to ask Professor Albert Bushnell Hart to serve as his dissertation advisor. Hart had served in the same capacity for W. E. B. Du Bois, and Woodson believed he may have been less conservative in his racial politics than Channing, who believed that blacks in Africa and America were inferior "in race stamina and race achievement" and that any academic accomplishments made by Du Bois, Woodson, and later Charles H. Wesley were attributed to their mixed-race ancestry. For, in his eyes, they were "much more white than negro." Yet Hart also believed blacks were an inferior race, though he was not opposed to their educational uplift.[91] Beyond the specific racist ideas of Woodson's Harvard professors, there was a much broader antiblack epistemology undergirding the historical profession. The dominant school of thought on American slavery, for instance, was shaped by the thinking of Ulrich B. Phillips, who praised slaveowners and insisted that brutality was of little significance and that, overall, slavery was a positive influence on the black race, given their dark African background. Phillips was the student of William A. Dunning, who argued that Reconstruction was corrupted by radical Republicans and unqualified freedmen in leadership. The Dunning school of thought on Reconstruction fundamentally justified black disenfranchisement.[92]

Woodson's difficulties in graduate school went further than the antiblack ideas of his professors. After a full year of coursework, he was unsure whether he would complete the PhD at Harvard. He was not permitted to take his examinations and was denied a fellowship for the following year, preventing him from starting his dissertation research. Feeling discouraged, he reapplied for a job in the Philippines and got as far as Seattle before abandoning the journey. Instead, he accepted a job teaching in Washington, DC, where he would study to retake his exams and continue the process of researching and writing.[93]

Washington, DC, and Black Institutional Life

Woodson felt out of place on arriving in DC, having primarily lived in Virginia and West Virginia.[94] His "hayseed clothes," as he called them, betrayed his rural background and made him stand out and the target of many jokes. He was also unaccustomed to the costs of living. Woodson recalled his first time getting a haircut and learning that the price was more expensive than what he had in his pocket. This caused quite the stir between him and the barber, though they eventually became good friends.[95] While initially an outsider—and from no established family name—Woodson earned his status among the who's who of the city.

His immersion in DC's black institutional life helped him find his way during his first ten years in the city. He was an active member of the NAACP. In 1911, he was initiated into Sigma Pi Phi (the Boulé), the first fraternity founded for black American men.[96] Born and raised Baptist, Woodson was a member of DC's Shiloh Baptist Church. He also joined Omega Psi Phi, an intercollegiate fraternity founded at Howard University in 1911.[97] Woodson's active membership in black institutions was characteristic of many black schoolteachers' lives.

This interior world of autonomous black institutions forged a counterpublic sphere, where black Americans set out to address the social ills they faced in society as they struggled for intellectual, political, and social elevation for the race.[98] Despite the clenching grip of Jim Crow and its antiblack social policies, during the late nineteenth and early twentieth century, black American communities across the country blossomed with new social structures as they worked to build a world as free people. This period known as "the Nadir," between the end of Reconstruction and the beginning of the First World War, witnessed the growth of what the Black Studies scholar Imani Perry calls "black associationalism": the "forming and joining of associations for nearly every venture, from entertainment and education to religion and commerce." Associationalism was a broad trend in American social and civil life at the time, and "black associationalism was likewise robust, though behind a veil."[99] Washington, DC, was a representative place for this expansion in black institutions and organizations, due in large part to the magnitude of Howard University.

Being a member of these organizations was more than an official stamp of pedigree and social status. It meant retreat from the racial hostilities of the American public sphere. It also meant close proximity to key political figures and intellectuals, access to conversations about local and national black political agendas, and connection to other people with a shared commitment to addressing racial injustice.[100]

Many of the leaders in the organizations Woodson joined had ties to the local educational system. For instance, many of Woodson's co-initiates into the Epsilon Boulé of Sigma Pi Phi fraternity were past or present teachers at the prestigious M Street High School. Judge Robert Terrell was a past principal of M Street and the first black judge in the District of Columbia; Garnet Wilkinson was a teacher at M Street; Kelly Miller taught at M Street before becoming professor of sociology at Howard; Roscoe Bruce became the assistant superintendent of colored schools. All of these men were among the nineteen initiates with whom Woodson joined the Boulé in February 1911. Edward Williams, the sitting principal of M Street School, was also an initiate of this group.[101] After teaching at multiple schools during his first couple of years in DC, Woodson followed his fraternity brothers and began teaching at the M Street School in October 1911.[102]

The intersection between black American education and black associationalism underscores the kind of advocacy base formed in black communities to support matters of schooling and other social and civic affairs. This was the kind of life world black educators functioned within. It extended far beyond the classroom but was always linked to it. The role of black American

First row: Ernest E. Just, Charles I. West, Kelley Miller, John F. Francis, Robert Terrell, James A. Cobb. Second row: A. H. Glenn, E. French Tyson, E. C. Williams, Garnet C. Wilkinson, Milton Francis, Carter G. Woodson, Arthur S. Gray. Third row: William C. McNeill, G. S. Wormley, Haley Douglass, Alfonso O. Stafford, Arthur M. Curtis, Roscoe C. Bruce.

1911 initiates of Epsilon Boulé of Sigma Pi Phi Fraternity. Reproduced from Charles H. Wesley, *History of Sigma Pi Phi* (Washington, DC: Association for the Study of Negro Life and History, 1954).

educators during this period must be understood in relationship to a host of other institutions. Black teachers' professional identities were shaped by much more than their school affiliations. Woodson was emblematic of this reality.

The professional and intellectual atmosphere Woodson experienced as an M Street faculty member provided necessary refuge from the academic hostility of his graduate school experience. Being a member of this faculty offered Woodson both a supplement to and reassuring critique of the higher learning offered in the hallowed halls of Harvard. Woodson's outlook as an educator was powerfully enhanced by this school environment. He taught history, French, Spanish, and English. The relationships built with his colleagues and the social and civic activity in the local community expanded his world in profound ways. Teaching at M Street was arguably just as important as his time teaching in the coal mines and earning his advanced degrees.

Teaching at Washington's M Street School

M Street High School, in Washington, DC, later named Paul Laurence Dunbar High School in 1916, offered a premiere education by all standards. It was originally founded in 1870 as the Preparatory High School for Negro Youth. After the first year, Mary J. Patterson, the first black American woman

Anna Julia Cooper, the author of *A Voice from the South*. Documenting the American South, University of North Carolina at Chapel Hill.

to receive a college degree (Oberlin, 1862) was appointed as the school's principal.[103] She was the first of a long line of impressively educated black Americans to serve as the principal of this institution.[104] These educational leaders did a remarkable job at establishing a strong academic culture at the school. As early as 1899 "the pupils of the M Street High School scored higher than the students of the white Eastern and Western high schools on standardized tests in English and general subjects. Of the thirty faculty at the time, twenty 'had degrees from top-flight Northern colleges and universities and five others had graduated from Howard.'"

When Anna Julia Cooper inherited this school as principal in 1901, there was a firmly established academic culture. Cooper, who held strong views about politics, gender equality, and black education, had already authored her famous book, *A Voice from the South: By a Black Woman of the South*, in 1892. As principal, she strategically appealed to elite schools in the New England area to secure scholarships and admissions for M Street graduates. Her leadership intimidated local white authorities, likely because the school was outpacing white educational norms in the area. Cooper refused to submit to the trend of industrial education that was sweeping the nation as a dominant model for black education. In the 1902–1903 school year, she invited W. E. B. Du Bois as a guest speaker. He emphasized that efforts were made in the United States to restrict the curriculum of black students to a lower set of standards than those held for white students. Cooper would eventually be fired in 1906, and many community members came to her defense. Though no longer principal, she continued teaching Latin at M Street and would be one of Woodson's colleagues when he arrived.[105]

Woodson joined M Street's faculty in 1911 under the principalship of Edward Christopher Williams, a former librarian and instructor at Western Reserve. At this critical phase of Woodson's development as a schoolteacher and scholar, he found himself situated in the bastion of black academic excellence.[106] Several of the school's alumni had already gone to Harvard, where Woodson was actively working towards his PhD. Furthermore, while graduate degrees were not required of the faculty, the school had numerous teachers with advanced degrees in liberal arts, law, and medicine. The teachers at the school were impressive beyond their credentials. For instance, Nevalle Thomas had traveled in the Middle East, often drawing on his knowledge from travel to give stirring lectures during his classes on ancient history. His class was a favorite among many students. Thomas was also a local activist, an involved member of the NAACP who would eventually serve as president of the local branch.[107] Woodson was also an active member of the organization.[108] Years later, Thomas and Woodson were both outspoken following DC's race riot of 1919. They celebrated black community members for fighting back with dignity against the onslaught of white mob violence.

M Street graduates went on to do amazing things, from innovation in medicine to political activism and institution building. Graduates included leaders like Nannie Helen Burroughs, who founded DC's National Training School for Women and Girls (a private school supported by the National

Baptist Convention) in 1909.[109] The academic achievement of M Street students was simply in a class of its own. In the class of 1911, which graduated just before Woodson was hired, nearly every student planned to continue their education, either at a normal school or at one of several elite colleges, including "Howard University, Fisk University, Drexel Institute, Oberlin College, Dartmouth College, Brown University, the University of Pennsylvania, Syracuse University, and Amherst College."[110] Charles Hamilton Houston, the valedictorian in 1911, was later known as "the man who killed Jim Crow"— he successfully argued a number of landmark court cases and was instrumental to the black American Civil Rights struggle because of the legal strategies he developed and taught at Howard Law School. His commencement address focused on the life and work of the literary giant Paul Laurence Dunbar, for whom the school would be renamed a few years later.[111]

While there was much to be celebrated about M Street School, it still faced the structural inequities characteristic of black education during Jim Crow. M Street's facilities were dated, and the school was not allowed to rent local facilities for sports competitions, even as this courtesy was permitted to white schools in DC.[112] There were also struggles over the curriculum of the school, as shown in the case of Anna Julia Cooper's principalship. Curriculum struggles would continue to be the case as it pertained to the lack of formal representation of black life and culture.[113] The school was severely overcrowded when Woodson arrived. There were 32 teachers working on a full-time basis with twenty-two classrooms. The total number of seats in the school was 612 while there were 684 students enrolled. Many students had to sit in the assembly hall to study during school hours.[114] Woodson spent part of the day monitoring students and keeping them on task in the auditorium. Of no celebrity status, without the prestigious title of *Dr.* before his name, Woodson sat before this group of students hard at work, demanding order in the assembly hall as they all studied.[115] He often encountered students who were not in his class in this way.

"Now if Jane will stop talking to Liza, we might get some studying done in this room." These were the words one student recalled from her first encounter with Woodson at M Street. It was early in the fall semester, and a group of ninth-grade girls had been directed to study in the assembly hall. Jessie Roy, one of the students in this group, was both new to high school and unacquainted with Woodson, who sat in front of the auditorium. Woodson himself was deep in study along with the students.

"Who is he?" Jessie asked in the form of a note she scribbled on a sheet of paper, showing it to the girl sitting closest to her.

"He is Mr. Carter G. Woodson, my French teacher," her friend wrote back.

"Nice, isn't he?" I queried.

"Yes," came the reply.

Only years later did Roy learn what caused Woodson to be so focused on the papers and books in front of him while he was supposed to be supervising the students. Long afterward, she realized Woodson was likely "studying about the history of some noteworthy Negro, or about the race as a whole."[116]

Rayford W. Logan, who would later earn a PhD in history from Harvard, took French literature as a high school senior in 1912–1913 with the now Dr. Woodson and would become one of his closest protégées in later years. Logan recalled that Woodson was a "serious, stern, almost dour disciplinarian" who was meticulous as an instructor. His memory of Woodson "seated erect at his desk" resonates with that of William M. Cobb, who was a freshman when he encountered Woodson in 1917 at what was then Dunbar High School. During passing periods, Woodson stood outside of his door "so posed, the quiet, unsmiling dignity of his figure commanded good order." Cobb described Woodson as having a "reserved, independent demeanor."[117] Student accounts of Woodson paint a portrait of him as a stern educator who had a rigid passion for both his teaching and scholarship. Despite his authoritative disposition, students admired him. As Jessie H. Roy recounted, Woodson was a no-nonsense kind of teacher, yet there always lingered a "twinkle in his eyes."[118]

These accounts demonstrate the discipline Woodson maintained to complete his doctoral work while meeting the demands of being a public school teacher. While teaching, he conducted research at the Library of Congress. Despite his success at M Street, he faced difficulty in completing his doctoral journey. The first draft of his dissertation was rejected. He rewrote the manuscript, and after a severe delay, his dissertation titled "The Disruption of Virginia" was approved in the spring of 1912. After his committee did not pass him on his examinations in American history, he retook his exams and passed only after Professor Hart had been removed from the committee.[119]

Woodson's Journey through Black Educational Heritage

By the time he completed his doctorate at Harvard, Woodson had been thoroughly initiated into a knowledge system that narratively condemned black people, that did not consider them historical subjects. For nearly thirty-five years, he had studied the languages, histories, and expressive cultures of American and European societies. He had studied romance languages and medieval and modern histories, and he had taught them in schools. What did it mean to have undergone this entire formal system of learning in the American School, comprising decades of sustained study, without ever encountering himself or his people in the system of knowledge deemed to be the highest truths about the world and humanity?

Yet among Woodson's contemporaries, there was perhaps no other individual with such intimate knowledge of the range of educational experience in black life—from the rural, postslavery South to the urban context of DC and higher education at a black college and the most elite white schools, at home and abroad. He could recall his years in Oliver Jones's parlor-turned-classroom; his mother's recollection of his family's commodification as slaves; his uncles' everyday defiance of southern white hostility toward the idea of black education, first in the Freedmen's classrooms where they learned to read and then by teaching the first legally emancipated generation of black children in the South. These experiences stretched his view of the world, giving him a much wider aperture for interrogating the function of education in black life.

Without question, Woodson knew black people had a history and culture, that they had contributed in significant ways to US history. The child and student of former slaves, he had listened intently to the stories of Civil War veterans who fought nobly for their emancipation, had labored alongside black men and women striving to build a world premised on the human dignity of their communities and their students. All of this was disavowed in his educational trajectory. The knowledge Woodson witnessed and knew to be true was studiously disfigured in the official knowledge of schooling and the United States' public imagination. He had seen with his own eyes the things his Harvard professors distorted. The intensity of this disjuncture had been cultivated in Woodson in a way that very few others, if any, had experienced.

From this point forward, Woodson would bear witness to these distortions in knowledge, writing the Negro into the story of humanity and "denaturalizing" the accepted scientific ideas and cultural scripts that rendered black people invisible and subhuman.[120] His attack on Western knowledge and the schools that were its institutional embodiment was especially powerful because he knew both so well. The depth of his immersion in this knowledge and these schools fueled the urgency and intensity of his work to negate them.

2

"The Association . . . Is Standing Like the Watchman on the Wall": Fugitive Pedagogy and Black Institutional Life

The Association for the study of the Negro is standing like the watchman on the wall, ever mindful of what calamities we have suffered from misinterpretation in the past and looking out with a scrutinizing eye for everything indicative of a similar attack.

—CARTER G. WOODSON (1936)

When we think of the wealth of America; when we remember the number of foundations today which have sums that they do not know how to use, it is no credit to the nation that they helped Woodson so little. Many of them of course will declare that they were willing to help, but that Woodson was not exactly to be "trusted"; he would not come to heel when whistled to, and fawn. Their willingness to help was therefore always accompanied by a desire, unobtrusively, of course, to control or at least direct in general lines the work which Woodson was doing. This Woodson absolutely and definitively refused to allow.

—W. E. B. DU BOIS (1950)

The year 1915 was spiteful. It marked the half-century anniversary of black emancipation in the United States, which came with the passing of the Thirteenth Amendment in 1865. The anniversary, already sullied by the apartheid conditions of Jim Crow, became even more a travesty when *The Birth of a Nation* first premiered as *The Clansman* in California on January 1, 1915. President Woodrow Wilson screened the film at the White House on February 18, two days before President Abraham Lincoln's birthday and a month before the fiftieth anniversary of his assassination. It was released as *The Birth of a Nation* in New York on March 2. The most popular and innovatively produced and directed film to ever come before the American public centered on denigrating the image of black people while portraying the Ku Klux Klan as protectors and saviors of the nation. The film epitomized at least two key features of America's Progressive Era: great technological innovation and the condemnation of blackness.[1] African Americans around the country exerted great energy on their fiftieth anniversary of Emancipation organizing and protesting against "the slanderous film," as *The Crisis* magazine dubbed it.[2] The lynching of fifty-six black Americans in 1915 also marked this milestone, a 10 percent increase from the previous two years, based on the recorded number of incidents.[3] The question and meaning of black freedom, black progress, and black life concerned all black Americans living during this low point in the race's history. Studying the past and how it structured the present and futures could not have been more important than on this occasion commemorating fifty years on the other side of slavery.

On September 9, 1915, Carter G. Woodson founded the Association for the Study of Negro Life and History. He founded the Association with a distinct mission—to transform the representation of black life and culture in Western knowledge (and in doing so, transform knowledge itself)—however, the political ethos embedded within this mission resonated with the many black institutions that preceded it. Black institutions were a vital line of defense for African American social and political life. They were centers of refuge, sites for alternative education and political advocacy, and, more generally, a web of networks forming a counterpublic to address the needs of a civically estranged people.[4] Antiblack exclusion partly triggered the formation of these institutions, but to assume that this is the sole reason for their emergence or that they mimicked the aims and ideals of the white public sphere, where black inclusion hinged on domination, would be a mistake. Similar to the Invisible Institution, where black Americans engaged in independent religious worship, clandestine schools during slavery, and colored conventions that began during the antebellum period, there continued to be covert objectives at the center of black institutional life post-Emancipation.[5]

Woodson's Association was unprecedented. It is the first and longest-running academic organization devoted to the study of race; and its ancillary publications—the *Journal of Negro History* and the *Negro History Bulletin*—produced a body of knowledge that challenged, and eventually transformed, established schools of thought in the American academy. This organization is essential to the story of black education. While no brick-and-mortar school, the ASNLH symbolized something much greater: an institution

founded by a black schoolteacher with the intent of rewriting the epistemological order, the basis of all curricula and school models. Black educators,
especially teachers in primary through secondary schools, formed a critical
base within the organization's membership and, by the 1930s, one of its
most reliable sources of financial support.

While much has been written about the Association's unmatched success
in popularizing black history, much less has been written about the central
role of schoolteachers and their pedagogical insights in the building and sustaining of this organization. To appreciate Woodson's work through the
ASNLH requires a new accounting of its emergence. This chapter explores
the Association's contextual development, how it emerged in Woodson's mind
as a forty-year-old schoolteacher, Harvard PhD, and the child and student of
former slaves. Doing so reveals the Association to be a product of the escape
practices in black teachers' pedagogy as well as intellectual traditions endemic
to their professional world.

Black Teachers Challenging the Scripts of Knowledge

Woodson completed his PhD in 1912 while continuing his work as a teacher
and becoming further immersed in the social and civic activities of DC's
black community.[6] These two aspects of his life were deeply intertwined. In
1914 Woodson joined the prestigious American Negro Academy (ANA), a
national organization committed to studying issues pertaining to black
people, though its core membership, never totaling more than twenty-seven,
was Washington based.[7] A small group of elite men, including Alexander
Crummell, Kelly Miller, and Paul Laurence Dunbar, founded the ANA in
1897 on the heels of *Plessy v. Ferguson*. Members of this organization shared
concerns about black education. Arturo Schomburg, the famous Afro-Latino
bibliophile and Black Renaissance thinker, joined the ANA the same year as
Woodson. Schomburg made a reputation for being outspoken in his critiques
of school curricula's omission of black life. In July 1913, he gave a lecture entitled "Racial Integrity: A Plea for the Establishment of a Chair of Negro
History in Our Schools and Colleges" before a teachers' summer school at
the Cheyney Institute, a historically black school for educators. Schomburg's
address circulated among the ANA membership, and Woodson kept a copy
of the pamphlet for his personal library.[8] Challenging racist ideas and in-

cluding the study of black life in schools also concerned the ANA founder and educator Richard Robert Wright, a former slave and Atlanta University's first valedictorian in 1876. Almost two decades prior to Schomburg's plea, Wright published an essay in *The A. M. E. Church Review* entitled "The Possibilities of the Negro Teacher," outlining the need for black educators to develop textbooks and teaching methods tailored to the needs of black schools and students. In 1912, the Washington, DC, teacher Leila Amos Pendleton—like other black educators, such as Silas X. Floyd of Georgia and Edward A. Johnson of North Carolina before her—wrote a textbook. Pendleton's *A Narrative of the Negro* regularly appeared in the recommended books section of the NAACP's *The Crisis* for nearly a decade.[9] Woodson published his first book, *The Education of the Negro Prior to 1861*, in spring of 1915, during a time of deep introspection for black Americans and the country as a whole.

Where had we come as a nation, and what was the experience of black people in the journey? What was the meaning of Negro freedom fifty years after Emancipation? While pondering such queries, black teachers in Washington, DC, grew hyperaware and critical of the overwhelming absence of black cultural knowledge and history in school curricula. They did what they could to squeeze aspects of Negro history into their schools, recognizing the birthdays of important figures like Phillis Wheatley and holding regular celebrations of Douglass Day. But in June 1915, Roscoe C. Bruce, the assistant superintendent of colored schools and co-initiate into Sigma Pi Phi with Woodson, made a special appeal to DC's board of education:

> In the teaching of American history in the elementary schools and in the high schools reference is more and more made by our teachers to the place of the American Negro in that history, to the part which he has played in American life. Two of our teachers—Principal John W. Cromwell, of Crummell School, and Dr. C.G. Woodson, of M Street High School—have written important volumes that in their fields should constitute sources for the use of our teachers. It gives our children and youth a sense of pride in the stock from which they sprang, an honorable self-confidence, a faith in the future and its possibilities, to know what men and woman of Negro blood have actually done, whether in the fields or in the schoolroom or in the war for the building of America.

Bruce asked the board of education: "Can it be that all the generals, all the statesmen, all the men of letters were white men? Is there not danger that our colored children and youth will be overwhelmed with what I may call the prestige of the white man?"[10] These questions were personally and professionally motivated. Bruce was the son of a formerly enslaved father who became the second black American elected to the US Senate during Reconstruction and a mother who was a teacher and a leader in the National Association of Colored Women. He knew the answers to his questions.[11] Before the time of the New Negro and the Black Renaissance on the horizon, teachers raised questions about black heritage and identity against that which was imposed as official knowledge in the American School. Woodson participated in these conversations with his DC colleagues during the months preceding his summer travel to Chicago, where he founded the ASNLH in September.

Building a "Historical Alliance" on the Fiftieth Anniversary of Negro Emancipation

Woodson conducted research in Chicago during the summer of 1915. Washington, DC, public schools were on holiday, so he was relieved from his usual teaching responsibilities at M Street School. It was also the perfect place to spread the word about his first book, *The Education of the Negro Prior to 1861.* The former Memphis teacher Ida B. Wells-Barnett, also a black journalist and founding member of the NAACP, hosted Woodson for a public lecture in her capacity as president of the Committee of Fifteen on Unity among the Race. The event took place at the organization's reading room on August 8. In promoting the event, Wells-Barnett noted, "Mr. Woodson is the second man of color to receive the degree of Ph.D. from Harvard University," and he had authored "one of the finest books written on the race." She ensured black Chicago they were in for "a literary treat." Woodson spoke on "the uplift of the Negro prior to 1861, and its bearings on problems of today."[12] He provided an exhaustive study of black education prior to the Civil War: the private efforts of black people to educate themselves, support offered by sympathetic whites, and the systematic obstruction of black attempts at education through antiliteracy laws in the South. This book framed the early formation of the strained relationship between black people and the schooling apparatus of the United States—a topic that Wells-Barnett knew intimately, having been fired as a teacher for exposing a sex scandal involving white school officials in Memphis and black women teachers two decades prior.[13]

Two weeks after Woodson's lecture, Chicago hosted the Illinois Half-Century of Negro Freedom Exposition, from August 22 through September 16. Woodson actively participated in the exposition. When not conducting research at the University of Chicago, he worked at a booth at the exposition, displaying books about the Negro and selling printed photographs of historical black figures, such as Frederick Douglass, Sojourner Truth, and Paul Laurence Dunbar.[14] Years later Woodson distributed similar photographs to schools across the country through the ASNLH, bringing before the eyes of students a visual narrative that reframed the story of black history and culture, one that represented black people as political actors and historical subjects, a people situated in a continuum of struggle for freedom and who produced a beautify literary and expressive culture based in their experiences.[15]

Woodson wrote to Jesse E. Moorland, a minister and civic leader in Washington, DC, during the third week of August, proclaiming, "Something must be done to save the records of the Negro that posterity may know the whole truth." Funds needed to be raised to collect and publish materials related to the history of black people, that a "historical alliance" might be formed. Woodson appealed to Moorland to serve as secretary-treasurer of the organization. Moorland was geographically close to Woodson, so regular communication would not be an issue, and Moorland had relevant experience for this endeavor, having donated an extensive collection of books on the Negro to establish Howard University's research library. Moorland responded and encouraged him to wait and begin this work in DC, through a partnership with Howard University.[16] Woodson moved forward with his plans, acting out of urgency and, likely, some suspicion of doing the work under the direction of a black college controlled by white leaders. Woodson planned for white scholars to be involved—having been in conversation with the sociologist Robert Park of the University of Chicago about supporting this effort—but he insisted on black autonomy from the beginning.[17]

On September 9, 1915, Woodson and four others staying at the Wabash Avenue Colored YMCA had, what seemed to some, an "impromptu meeting" that led to the founding of the Association for the Study of Negro Life and History. Those present included George C. Hall (physician), Alexander

Jackson (executive secretary of the Wabash YMCA), William B. Hartgrove (Washington, DC, schoolteacher), and James E. Stamps (Yale graduate student in economics).[18] Jackson, a sophomore at Harvard when Woodson sat for his qualifying examinations as a doctoral student, hosted the meeting in his office at the Wabash YMCA.[19]

The YMCA opened two years prior to this historic meeting, providing a vibrant environment for the exchange of intellectual and political ideas.[20] Over the course of the summer, Woodson regularly participated in discussions with others passing through the space. Many conversations quickly turned into small groups of people listening to "his stories and philosophies."[21] James Stamps, a graduate student in economics at the time, recalled Woodson attracting audiences in common rooms. Visitors "loved [Woodson's] wit, his humor, and even his sarcasm."[22] Conversations were ongoing leading up to the September 9 meeting, as Woodson meditated on the idea. When Robert Park invited Woodson to join a study group focusing on folklore just weeks prior, Woodson declined, sharing that "something else was taking shape in his mind."[23] While appearing impromptu to the other founding members, Woodson had been plotting well before. The rapport established among the men boarding and working at the YMCA presented a unique opportunity for Woodson to begin laying the framework for the organization he imagined. Furthermore, the occasion of this summer, structured by black feelings attached to the commemoration of Negro freedom and, simultaneously, the outrage at the heightened public disavowing of black life warranted such an endeavor. This vexing set of circumstances stoked Woodson's conviction.

When Woodson and his associates convened their discussion about "the historical alliance" on September 9, *The Birth of a Nation* provided evidence of the need for such an organization. Woodson and his fellow lodgers at the YMCA discussed the controversial film during their many conversations that summer.[24] It symbolized a general disdain for black life, not only in the laws of the land but also at a sentient level in the national culture. The film's central ideas reflected the ideological structure of the American School and the knowledge system that formed its curricular foundation. Deeply familiar with this reality as a teacher and historian, Woodson was convinced that something must be done, that the Negro would not become "a negligible factor in the thought of the world." From its inception, the Association held a pedagogical vision that accounted for the learning experiences of students in schools. Woodson "pointed out what an organization which would report continuously true historical achievement of the Negro would mean to the old and young," James Stamps recalled. Such an intellectual project would be key in "changing the image of the Negro," but it would also "arouse the youth to study for achievement."[25]

Upon returning to Washington, DC, Woodson took on the bulk of the work in executing the plan agreed on in Chicago. He quickly incorporated the Association in DC on December 2, 1915.[26] Woodson did this even as he assumed his responsibilities as a teacher. The historian Charles Wesley recalled years later that it was from Woodson's "small school teacher's salary that the first steps were undertaken in 1915."[27] Black teachers always gave more than what they were technically paid to do, because *the work* of black teachers far exceeded the description of their job on paper. Woodson's trajectory as a student, teacher, and Harvard-trained historian all positioned him to act on an impulse shared by black teachers for decades.

Woodson's building of the Association resonated with the local work done by black teachers in Washington to challenge local standards in the school curriculum. In November 1915 Roscoe C. Bruce coordinated a teachers' institute comprising professional development seminars for black educators in the city, acting on the concerns raised in his report to DC's board of education in June. W. E. B. Du Bois gave one of the keynote addresses, taking as his subject "Outlines of Negro History." The following day Du Bois led a workshop for high school teachers on "Sources and Methods in Negro History." Du Bois was widely known as the editor of *The Crisis* magazine. He had also visited the teachers and students of M Street on at least one previous occasion, when Anna Julia Cooper served as principal. Du Bois held personal ties to Woodson and a number of other educators in Washington as president of the American Negro Academy.

Woodson participated in the ongoing conversation about the history of the race in the seminars organized by black teachers in Washington, DC, while producing the first issue of the Association's *Journal of Negro History*, published in January 1916. Black teachers made important scholarly contributions to the inaugural issue of the journal. Not only was it published by Woodson from his post at M Street, but his colleagues Jessie Fauset and Mary Church Terrell contributed book reviews that were included in the issue; William Hartgrove, ASNLH founder and DC teacher, contributed an essay on the story on a black mother and daughter's struggle for education and their lives as teachers; the issue also featured a review of the ANA member and DC principal John Cromwell's textbook. What's more, the last page began with a dedication to Booker T. Washington, who died on November 14, 1915. Woodson's editor's note observed, "In the death of Booker T. Washington the field of history lost one of its greatest figures. He will be remembered mainly as an educational reformer, a man of vision, who had the will power to make his dreams come true." But Washington also made important contributions to the study of black life. His autobiography was "a long chapter of the story of a rising race." His textbook, *Story of the Negro,* and his book *Frederick Douglass* gave "the Negro a larger place in history."[28] As evident by the circumstances surrounding it founding, as well as the heavy involvement of black teachers in the first issue of the *Journal,* Woodson's Association was a product of the intellectual and political culture at the center of black teachers' professional world, an academic culture that was particularly pronounced in DC's black public schools.

Black teachers planned additional professional development seminars during the spring semester, building on the work done in the previous months. Woodson himself facilitated a workshop in March 1916 on "History and Civics."[29] It is important to note that less than a mile away from M Street School, Howard University's leadership denied a proposal for a course "dealing with Negro problems" during this same month. The academic executive committee rejected the proposal, which had been prepared by black faculty members, including Kelly Miller, because they felt it "inexpedient to establish a course in Negro problems at this time."[30] The committee also rejected a course proposal by Professor Alain Locke during June of the previous year on "inter-racial relations." Black faculty members at Howard continued to be censored in their teachings and course offerings. The university's first course in Negro history arrived three years later, when Woodson took the knowledge he had been developing as a high school teacher and implanted it in Howard University's curriculum.

In 1916, the name of the M Street School was changed to honor the memory of the poet and ANA founder Paul Laurence Dunbar, exactly ten years after his death. Black teachers increasingly used Dunbar's poetry to incorporate a black literary culture into their schools. Around the country, teachers and students identified Dunbar as the chosen bard of black schools, both studying his poetry and naming their schools after him, making Dunbar one of the most popular names for black schools across the country—along with others such as Douglass, Washington, Wheatley, and Lincoln. The change from M Street to Dunbar High School happening on the heels of the Association's founding, and the Association's founding taking place amid a series of ongoing conversations about including black life and culture in DC's school curriculum, is no small coincidence.

The Association for the Study of Negro Life and History was an institutional embodiment of an idea widely held by black teachers. Woodson, being among this body, led the charge by giving a name to something that was a shared mission, and he created an institution where the work could be nurtured and flourish. To give an account of the Association's emergence is to recognize how Woodson was uniquely positioned to lead such as organization. It also calls attention to the social web of ideas and institutions and people to which Woodson was connected. This broader educational world gave meaning to the Association and aided in its development.

Building while Teaching and the Red Summer of 1919

Between 1915 and 1919 Woodson continued his work in the public schools of DC while building up the Association. He left Dunbar High School in the spring of 1918 to serve as interim principal at Armstrong Vocational High School, the former principal having left for active military service. The United States had fully entered World War I when Woodson arrived, and he found Armstrong facing a crisis because so many of its students were enlisting. While Dunbar had an issue with overenrollment, Armstrong faced severe underenrollment. In previous years Armstrong's enrollment approached nine hundred students; by June 1918 the enrollment was less than half of this.[31] Woodson's post at Armstrong ended the following year after he accepted a position as dean of Howard University's School of Liberal Arts, professor of history, and head of its graduate faculty.[32] The school inaugurated its graduate program in the autumn of 1919. Woodson entered the academy for the first time after teaching in DC public schools for ten years.

The summer of Woodson's transition to Howard was memorable to say the least. It was the Red Summer of 1919, where violent riots broke out around the country. White mobs targeted black Americans in northern and southern cities, as long-standing racial tensions became exacerbated by the aftermath of the war. The riots began in the South. "The returning Negro soldier was, . . . for the South, an object of contempt," explained Woodson. "The very uniform on a Negro was to the southerner like a red rag thrown in the face of a bull." What Woodson referred to as "post-war down-with-the-Negro propaganda" spread all over the country, taking hold even in the nation's capital, which had long been "southernized." On July 19, after exaggerated news reports that three "Negro thugs" attacked a white woman, mobs of white men in uniform began attacking black people walking on the streets.

Writing in his textbook to students two years later, Woodson recalled, "Negroes were pulled from vehicles and street cars and beaten into unconsciousness. One was thus taken possession of by the mob and beaten unmercifully right in front of the White House, where the President [Woodrow Wilson] must have heard his groans but has not yet uttered a word of protest." With his own eyes, Woodson saw how "negroes were shot and left to die on the streets." When traveling home on this day, Woodson found himself in the midst of a white mob pursuing a black man at the intersection of Eighth Street and Pennsylvania Avenue. He recorded the memory of this encounter in *The Negro in Our History,* titling it: "A Lynching in Washington."

> A large mob swept down Pennsylvania Avenue pursuing a Negro yelling for mercy, while another mob at the debouchment of Eighth Street had caught a Negro whom they conveniently adjusted for execution and shot while the author, walking briskly as possible to escape the same fate himself, heard the harassing groans of the Negro. To be sure that their murderous task was well done a leader yelled to the executioners, "Did you get him?" The reply was, "Yes, we got him."

The lack of police response outraged black members of the community. Having long been overpoliced and underprotected, black Washingtonians "made extensive preparation for the retaliatory onslaught of the whites." Woodson recounted, "This mob had misjudged the Washington Negroes. . . . Weapons were bought, houses were barricaded, and high powered automobiles were armored for touring the city late in the night."[33]

This encounter reinforced something Woodson already knew. His elevated social status as a black teacher, and soon-to-be professor, did not shield him from the violent realities of white aggression and antiblack violence. In fact, teachers had long been prime targets of racial violence as enfleshed representations of black aspiration and progress. In an antiblack world, achievement and criminality could be equivalent transgressions. Woodson understood the violence of 1919 as a nodal point in a continuum, where after slavery black people continued to be met by white hostility and violence. They were "no longer valuables attached to owners, as horses and cattle," Woodson explained to students reading his textbook. No longer valuable as property to be owned and perceived only as a problem, or merely excess and a threat to white security, "there was little to restrain the degraded class from murdering them in communities where few white men had any conception of the blacks as persons entitled to life, liberty, and the pursuit of happiness."[34]

The Red Summer of 1919 represented a crisis, not only of the physical realm but also a manifestation of deeply encoded ideas in the system of knowledge about who and what the Negro was and was not, in the United States and in the world. Having witnessed this lynching four years after the release of *The Birth of a Nation* and the founding of the Association, Woodson understood his mission to rewrite the epistemological order to be of enormous implications. Redefining the meaning of black life and culture in the story of human civilization was a mission to redefine knowledge itself, offering a transformed interpretation of what it meant to be human—a system of knowledge not premised on black death and dying.

Five students enrolled in Woodson's first graduate course at Howard in autumn of 1919. Among them was Arnett Lindsay, who recounted the "characteristically frank manner" in which Woodson laid out the requirements for the MA degree. Woodson professed that "any student would be dropped automatically with no opportunity to make up any deficiency unless the minimum grade of [a] B was maintained in every required subject." According to Lindsay, Woodson offer students a "new and acceptable form of history" in this class, an approach to history that took into account social conditions of the periods they studied and that attended to black life and culture.[35]

Woodson's History 30: The Negro in American History was one of the first courses on black history and culture to be offered in an American university. It stood in stark contrast to the expansive number of Howard University courses focusing on European history, which constituted eleven of the twenty-one course offerings. The objective of History 30 was to "connect with the movements in our history such factors as slavery, abolition, colonization and the compromises leading up to the conflict of the North and South. It will also treat the status of the free Negro, the program of the Civil War, the drama of Reconstruction, efforts of racial adjustment, and the struggle of the Negro for social justice." Even in the description for his survey courses on US history, Woodson outlined that his courses would attend to major historical events; how they "affected the whole country and especially the Negro will be carefully studied."[36]

Woodson brought great passion to the classroom, which complemented his high academic expectations. His "retentive memory enabled him to cite sources accurately and quote verbatim from documents, narratives and other historical materials." The blatant denial of black achievement throughout his own formal training as a historian engendered this enthusiasm.[37] Woodson's lectures were a rebellion against the Eurocentric narratives of human history that prevailed in the American School—a curricular orientation he had been forced to submerge himself in as a scholar in pursuit of higher learning. He gave a stirring lecture on the Boston Massacre and the martyrdom of Crispus Attucks, a historical event his Harvard professor spoke of only in "the most facetious fashion."[38] The death of Attucks, Woodson explained, held deep conceptual significance for the question of American independence, despite its distortion and omission in mainstream history courses and textbooks of the time. He invited students to consider the relationship between Attucks's experiences as a slave and his sacrifice for the nation's pursuit of freedom. "Having experienced as a slave what oppression means," Woodson observed, Attucks "was among the first who dared to resist [the] soldiers who were brought to Boston to crush in the bosom of the patriots that rapidly developing courage to fight for independence."[39] The person who knew the true meaning of freedom was he whose enslavement had formed the substance of the American ideals of liberty. Attucks—and black life and culture more broadly—offered a counterpoint for thinking about the deeper meanings of freedom in the vexing political context of the United States.

Lindsay was the only student of the original group to successfully complete the MA degree. His thesis was accepted, and he passed his oral examination in May 1920. Lindsay was the first and only graduate student formally advised by Woodson. At the close of his examination, Woodson waited until the other faculty bid their congratulations and then turned to Lindsay and wittily shared, "You have more sense than I thought you had": a statement characteristic of Woodson's style of communication and sense of humor yet an obvious gesture to congratulate Lindsay on his achievement. This expression of how proud he was of the young scholar symbolized Woodson's broader vision of the work, developing students who committed to reconstructing a collective vision of the world and black people's place within it. Woodson published Lindsay's thesis, "Diplomatic Relations between the United States and Great Britain Bearing on the Return of Negro Slaves, 1783–1828," in the *Journal of Negro History*. This was easily the highest praise he could offer.[40]

While his time at Howard was historic in many ways, Woodson resigned shortly after Lindsay's final exams. A strained relationship with the school's white president, James Stanley Durkee, caused his departure. By Woodson's assessment, Durkee was unfit to run any institution, let alone a black university. Woodson refused to comply with Durkee's requests that he monitor his colleagues' attendance in chapel. Conflict arose again after Woodson began offering continuing education classes for black teachers without the president's knowledge. They clashed yet again after Woodson publicly critiqued Durkee for removing books from the library that he interpreted as having communist leanings. Howard, like many other schools, had a long history of censorship. Faculty and students were also forbidden "to make statements to the public press concerning the policy of the Board or the management of the University without prior consultation with University authorities."[41] Durkee gave Woodson an ultimatum: write a formal letter of apology for his insubordination or his job would be terminated. Woodson refused to apologize, despite recommendations by some of his black peers to find a middle ground with Durkee. His time teaching at Howard ended after one year.[42] Woodson carried a long memory of black educators being fired or pushed out for holding political and intellectual views that conflicted with their white superiors. He witnessed this when his cousin and former high school principal, Charles Barnett, was fired in 1900. Woodson's M Street colleague Anna Julia Cooper met the same fate. And there were plenty of others who came before and after.

Woodson *privately* expressed the full extent of his disdain for Durkee to Jesse Moorland just before he resigned. He also aired his frustration with Moorland and other black Americans who seemed to insist on "interracial cooperation" at any cost.

"You have a weakness for good-for-nothing white people who because of your broken down theory that in the Negro schools the best of the two races may be united," wrote Woodson. Yet "this has never been true, is not now true, and will never be so until the Negroes have made such progress as to be recognized as the equals of whites." Plenty of excellent black scholars taught at Howard were more qualified to lead the school than Durkee. Despite this fact, and it being a black university, Durkee and other white faculty received preferential treatment and greater respect simply because they were white. "If well educated Negroes cannot remain at Howard University without losing their self respect, what hope is there for the Negro youth?" He elaborated on this critique of white paternalism: "There is not in Howard University, including the President, a single white man who has made an impression in any field. There are at Howard, however, several Negroes whose scholarship is known at home and abroad. What is the propriety then in subjecting the philosopher of Athens to the barbarian of Sparta?"[43] Some believed that Durkee would help raise funds for the school among wealthy whites; however, Woodson believed this to be a sad excuse for not appointing a more capable black leader. Woodson expressed deep frustration about the stronghold white racial liberals held over black education, many of whom were ineffective and blatantly racist. Their model of "interracial cooperation," according to Woodson, was a "farce of racial manipulation in which the Negro is a figurehead."[44]

Woodson left Howard and accepted a position as dean at West Virginia State College in 1920. He joined the faculty at West Virginia to help his friend John Davis reorganize the school's academic program with the understanding that his time there would be short. Woodson's primary goal would then be developing the work of the ASNLH.[45] After one year, he transitioned into the full-time role as director of research for the Association and the editor of its *Journal of Negro History.*[46]

Teaching at the university level made up a short portion of Woodson's time as an educator—approximately two years between Howard and West Virginia combined. His experience as a teacher was overwhelmingly in the public schools of West Virginia, the Philippines, and DC, between the 1890s and 1919. Woodson's affinity for the development of black youth and his familiarity with the racially stratified education system in the United States significantly informed his pedagogy as an educator of the people, which now expanded beyond previous institutional constraints. These decades of teaching greatly informed Woodson's research agenda and the universe of intellectual activity that constituted the Association's program. While Woodson physically exited the classroom at the opening of the 1920s, this marked the beginning stages of his work constructing an alternative universe of intellectual activity focused on studying black life.

From the "Historical Alliance" to the "Watchman on the Wall"

To characterize an institution as fugitive might seem ironic. Institutions generally denote formality and restrictions, some bounded set of protocols. This is partly true. Of interest here, however, is the phenomenon of black educators crafting institutional personas that made them palatable to the white gaze, even as they transcended these public personas within the interior of their institutions. This was the case for Woodson's Association, as it was for most black institutions during Jim Crow. The black counterpublic sphere embodied Paul Laurence Dunbar's imperative that "we wear the mask"—and in particular, "the mask that grins and lies." A black interior life always existed behind this veil. By necessity, fugitive pedagogy was part and parcel of the social infrastructure of black educational institutions, as they were forced to function within the constraints of the American social order and its antiblack antagonisms.[47]

Woodson was well aware of the tightrope black educators had to walk to advance their causes. Yet even as he tried to account for white surveillance in the American School, many white academics and white racial progressives found his efforts to be extreme and an impediment to their version of interracial cooperation. Walter Daykin, a sociologist from the University of Iowa, critiqued the work of the Association as part of a wider range of "devices" used to "facilitate Negro ethno-centrism." He observed, "Negroes are urged to appeal to boards of education for the adoption of Negro history text books, or to induce libraries and schools to purchase Negro literature and pictures of notable men of the race." But all the scholarship produced by Woodson and other scholars involved in this movement were "compiling data in order to interpret world history from a racial point of view. These historians are partisan, and often record data with the conscious purpose of gaining converts to the Negro's cause." Daykin argued that "Negro historical writings are further characterized by racial biases, moralizations, and rationalizations."[48] According to scholars like Daykin—who published this critique in *Social Forces,* a well-established sociological journal—scholarship by black thinkers tended to be militant and overly subjective, especially if it pertained to matters of race explicitly. This critique from white scholars and philanthropists persisted during the developmental years of the Association. As such, Woodson became increasingly transparent in expressing his thoughts on the matter of white paternalism and control. The evolution of the Association through the 1920s and 1930s reflected this.

In the beginning Woodson intentionally employed discourse that invited the support of potential white allies as a means of advancing the cause of the Association. He insisted on pursuing white philanthropic dollars and access to opportunities for expanding the work of the Association even as he refused white control over its agenda. Woodson assembled an interracial executive board during the early years of the Association. He included key people who would be important advocates for securing funding and developmental opportunities—people such as Robert Park of the University of Chicago, Thomas Jesse Jones of the Phelps Stokes Fund, and Albert Bushnell Hart of Harvard's History Department. This would serve the interest of the organization well, until tensions rose between Woodson and white benefactors, beginning as early as 1922.

The first major philanthropic contribution came from Julius Rosenwald in 1917 with a $100 pledge per quarter for the *Journal of Negro History.*[49] Rosenwald's contributions would be the largest sum of money donated from a single source to the ASNLH until five years later when the Carnegie Corporation pledged $25,000 over the course of five years to cover the debt and overhead expenses, and soon thereafter the Laura Spelman Rockefeller Memorial gave $25,000 to finance five years of research.[50] As observed by the historians August Meier and Elliott Rudwick, it was the relationship that Woodson developed with J. Franklin Jameson, the editor of the *American Historical Review* and director of the Department of Historical Research at the Carnegie Institution of Washington, that helped stimulate this successful fund-raising campaign.[51] Jameson wrote letters to white funders advocating on Woodson's behalf, emphasizing "the unusual opportunity that is presented, when a colored man competently qualified, and who has the confidence of his race, is ready to embark upon this line of investigation."[52] While

Woodson's degrees from Chicago and Harvard were not enough to earn him a faculty appointment in a mainstream American university—and there is no evidence that Woodson had such a desire—these affiliations did make it easier for him to form relationships with elite white intellectuals and benefactors.

In 1922, just after securing the Carnegie research grant, Albert Bushnell Hart publicly resigned after Woodson refused to accept Hart's recommendation for how the money should be spent. Hart's resignation as an established white scholar from Harvard was no small matter. It was a loud statement of disapproval by someone that was positioned as one of the white scholars who helped legitimize the Association in the minds of white funders. Julius Rosenwald, who also served on the board, deputized his secretary to look into the matter, having already heard reports that Woodson leaned "toward the radical side." Thomas Jesse Jones, who had been placed on the board in 1916 as a representative of the Phelps Stokes Fund, did not resign like Hart but was instead dismissed from the board by Woodson, after Jones worked to block a black man named Max Yergan from being readmitted to South Africa, where he worked for the YMCA (see Chapter 3). Jones, too, would claim that Woodson pushed him off because he desired to "place radicals in charge." The board being assembled by Woodson, Jones assessed, was more likely "to stir up prejudice rather than promote scientific study."[53]

Woodson did what he could to sustain relationships with white funders over the years, yet his resistance and controlling demeanor led to their decline by the early 1930s. By this point his efforts to walk the racial tightrope were no longer sustainable. In 1932 Woodson wrote to Benjamin Brawley regarding his refusal to participate in an encyclopedia project on Negro history sponsored by the Phelps Stokes Fund, after he and Du Bois were initially excluded from the project. Woodson stressed that he was "in no way opposed to interracial cooperation. . . . The program of the Association for the Study of Negro Life and History, however is conceived of by Negroes; and liberal minded members of the other race assist us in the only natural way of helping us to help ourselves." He was committed to the idea that philanthropists should not dictate the research agenda of black scholars and their intellectual work. The impact of this scholarship was too consequential.[54] Black scholars continued to face challenges surrounding what research white funders would sponsor and unfair restrictions imposed on the kinds of black scholarship white publishers would print.[55] As W. E. B. Du Bois observed, the "willingness [of white funders] to help was therefore always accompanied by a desire, unobtrusively, of course, to control or at least direct in general lines the work which Woodson was doing. This Woodson absolutely and definitively refused to allow."[56]

Woodson also resisted funders' request that the ASNLH be based at a black college. Many of these schools were beholden to white boards and funders, and Woodson was highly critical of this.[57] His best attempt at saving face among white philanthropy was by maintaining an executive board that was made up of both blacks and whites, similar to the NAACP and the National Urban League, and by publicly proclaiming his commitments to interracial cooperation. However, this balancing act went out the window by the 1930s once he was completely cut off by white philanthropists and estranged among some of his elite black peers, of whom he was often quite critical for failing to make what he believed to be necessary sacrifices for the race. As Meier and Rudwick keenly observed, "His final rejection of a philanthropy-sponsored connection with a Negro university was symbolized by his recruitment of the presidents of land-grant and lesser collegiate institutions for his council."[58] This included educational leaders like Mary McLeod Bethune of Bethune-Cookman College and H. Councill Trenholm of Alabama State Teachers College. Interestingly enough, it was through these figures that Woodson deepened his connection to black teachers' associations, therefore developing a vigorous, symbiotic relationship between the work of the ASNLH and the work of teachers in the classroom. Leaders such as Bethune, Trenholm, and Luther Porter Jackson (of Virginia State University) were major figures in the professional world of black teachers, all having served as presidents of a state or national black teachers' association. They all served on the executive council of the ASNLH by the early 1930s. This marked a definitive shift in the trajectory of the Association, particularly as the Great Depression set in.

The Association's funding now came from smaller contributions made by a broader body of dedicated members, and especially black teachers. The income of the ASNLH dropped tremendously during the early years of the Depression, but by 1940 Woodson shared that "it has gradually increased until it is now about two-thirds of what it was during the most prosperous years of the undertaking. . . . The success thus achieved is a credit to the Negro race and serves as eloquent evidence of that capacity of the Negro for self help. . . . It is fortunate that the Association for the Study of Negro Life and History is obtaining its income in small amounts from a larger number of people."[59] The broad base investment in the ASNLH by large numbers of black people across the country was a greater affirmation of the Association's work than any single contribution from a rich white benefactor.

While in 1915 Woodson conceptualized the Association as a "historical alliance" on paper, by the 1930s he employed more combative language to characterize the organization's mission. In 1936 Woodson explained that "the Association for the study of the Negro is standing like the watchman on the wall, ever mindful of what calamities we have suffered from misinterpretation in the past and looking out with a scrutinizing eye for everything indicative of a similar attack."[60] The transition in language—from the "historical alliance" to "the watchman on the wall"—betrays political objectives that had always been at the heart of the Association's mission when it emerged from Washington, DC, teachers' rebuke against the racist curriculum in the public schools and as black people protested the release of *The Birth of a Nation*. Woodson had always intended for the Association's work to be weaponized against the calamities black people suffered because of the antiblack ideas encoded in the American imagination, which animated events like the Red Summer of 1919.

The political ideas and critiques found in *The Mis-education of the Negro* (see Chapter 3) were not altogether new developments in Woodson's thinking when he published the text in 1933. They cannot be explained away as a bitter rupture with his prior thinking due to his alienation among white philanthropists. Funding challenges surely frustrated him, but these ideas were always there and at the core of Woodson's worldview when the Association was founded—even if they were kept private. The recent discovery of Woodson's unpublished manuscript from 1921 reveals that his ideas expressed in *Mis-education* were consistent with his thinking during the early years of the Association. Woodson likely chose not to publish the manuscript, now titled *Carter G. Woodson's Appeal,* because it would not have been well received by white funders and racial liberals of the time.[61] Seeing no pragmatic function in attempting to save face among white liberals a decade later, however, Woodson removed the mask.

Fugitive pedagogy helps clarify the move from a masked persona of the "historical alliance"—a coming together that always had a deeper plot embedded within it that transcended the objective goals of *doing* history—as well as the move to characterize the Association as "the watchman on the wall."

What began for Woodson in his uncles' one-room schoolhouse had evolved into demands for black self-knowledge, an educational program that could motivate students to have racial pride and that celebrated historical acts of resistance modeled by black people in the United States and beyond. Schooling continued to be a site where black Americans worked to forge new paths toward the promise of freedom, in that black freedom continued to be curtailed in the twentieth century. The plot Woodson inherited from his formerly enslaved uncles persisted; it was a set of educational politics that black teachers and students continued to be initiated into. The travestied nature of black freedom seventy years after Emancipation meant that there continued to be a demand for fugitive practices of teaching and learning. Black education continued to be set against the order of things. The Association, "standing like the watchman on the wall," was an institutional embodiment of this phenomenon.

The ASNLH as an "Insurgent Intellectual Network"

The ASNLH was a rebellion against established schools of thought in the American School at every level, from the primary grades through the university. The Association and its members treated black life and culture as a legitimate area of study and, in the process, named race in explicit terms, therefore making it accountable to critique. More than this, they boldly asserted that black intellectuals were qualified to do this work.

A great deal of experimentation took place within the organization during the 1920s, pertaining to structure, membership, and educational programming. The ASNLH was distinct from other traditional academic organizations, including the American Negro Academy.[62] As the lead member of an ad hoc committee in the ANA, Woodson attempted to reform its membership policies. The membership of this organization was very controlled, never exceeding twenty-seven and Anna Julia Cooper was the only woman ever admitted before it dissolved in the late 1920s.[63] Woodson envisioned the ANA having a broader reach within black communities, thus increasing its relevance and sustainability. While unable to meaningfully change the social politics and membership structure of the ANA, Woodson took what he learned from these experiences to enhance how he approached membership in the Association. He recognized the importance of engaging the academic elite and the black masses for any meaningful educational program for the race.[64] Unlike mainstream white academic organizations or the ANA, Woodson's Association engaged communities across social rank and rooted itself in schools, communities, and other black social and civic organizations. The Association's vision cut across the various class and intraracial sectors of black America. Woodson's years of experience as a schoolteacher and his humble beginnings in the coal mines likely informed this inclusive program, one built around communities as opposed to academic affiliation. For instance, the ASNLH structured it branches, which began forming in the 1920s, based on cities as opposed to colleges or universities. They essentially functioned as study groups of local scholars (formally trained and otherwise) who actively promoted black study in the local communities and schools. This practice continued to set the organization apart from other academic associations into the twenty-first century.

The Association was an intellectual project with black Americans across age, class, and gender in mind. The inclusion of gender here is a careful assertion, despite the gendered conventions of the time. The centrality of women in the Association—for instance, with Mary McLeod Bethune being the president for the last fifteen years of Woodson's life—played a major role in advancing the Association's mission. Furthermore, in that black teachers formed a core base of the ASNLH, women were extremely important. Black women made up the majority of the teaching profession from the first decade of the twentieth century. In 1900 black women teachers accounted for 86.7 percent of black women professionals, compared to less than 25 percent of black men professionals. By 1910 black women made up 22,547 of the 29,772 black American teachers, more than 75 percent of the profession. This trend persisted in the decades to come.[65]

By the end of the 1920s, Woodson's organization made substantial progress in expanding the reach of his educational program. While the first wave of scholarship published by the Association was a bit inaccessible to lay readers and grade level students, this academic research eventually informed the textbooks and school curricula developed in years that followed. By 1929 more than one hundred schools, junior high through college, were using his textbook, *The Negro in Our History*, published through the ASNLH's press, the

Associated Publishers, Inc., which was established in 1921.[66] Woodson's annual reports track the work he did across the country to garner interest in the ASNLH. "Wherever there is a call to encourage a school or a club to do more for the study of Negro life and history, the Director generally responds," explained Woodson. He traveled to different cities and gave stirring talks, which often led to the establishment of "local clubs to co-operate with this national organization."[67] The clubs Woodson referred to are the early formation of ASNLH branches, which formed under the Extensions Division of the Association. According to membership data around 1928, there were over 1,600 dues-paying members of the Association—representing forty states, with approximately 34 international members (see table 2.1).[68] On the occasion of the Association's twenty-fifth anniversary in 1940, Woodson proudly noted that "the important achievements [had] been the promotion of actual research which has given the public twenty-seven monographs of Negro life and history, the collection of five thousand manuscripts bearing on the Negro, the inauguration of Negro History Week [in 1926], and the founding of the *Negro History Bulletin* [in 1937]."[69]

The ASNLH was distinct from other traditional academic organizations. One historian traced the various moving parts of Woodson's educational program to show how each part informed the other.

> Through his effort to reach the masses of the black people in the United States, Woodson had worked out a remarkable program within the Association where every program matched something else within the organization. The pictures Woodson obtained for use in the *Bulletin* were blown up to larger size and sold individually. The articles in the *Bulletin* were transferred to the encyclopedia file. Negro History Week was advertised in the *Bulletin*, and during Negro History Week extra issues of the *Bulletin* were printed for promotional circulation, thus adding new subscribers each year. In the later years young and unpublished scholars were published in the *Bulletin* before moving up to the now-prestigious *Journal*. This gave the *Bulletin* a steady stream of articles and provided the younger historians and writers an opportunity to publish.[70]

Woodson built on the social infrastructure of black communities to drive forward his vision of an educational model that centered black cultural life.

Table 2.1. Association for the Study of Negro Life and History Membership, c. 1928

Association for the Study of Negro Life and History Membership, 1928			
Alabama	38	Pennsylvania	129
Arkansas	10	Rhode Island	2
California	14	South Carolina	19
Colorado	2	Tennessee	29
Connecticut	16	Texas	28
Delaware	8	Virginia	98
Florida	29	Washington	7
Georgia	46	Washington, DC	183
Illinois	51	West Virginia	94
Indiana	22	Wisconsin	2
Iowa	6	Total United States	1,567
Kansas	13		
Kentucky	54	**International Members**	
Louisiana	12	Africa	5
Maine	5	Australia	1
Maryland	57	British West Indies	3
Massachusetts	43	Canada	4
Michigan	32	Canal Zone	1
Minnesota	7	Central America	1
Mississippi	14	China	2
Missouri	109	Cuba	2
Nebraska	3	England	7
Nevada	2	Germany	1
New Hampshire	1	Haiti	1
New Jersey	29	Ireland	1
New Mexico	2	Italy	1
New York	181	Portugal	1
North Carolina	85	Switzerland	1
Ohio	67	Virgin Islands	2
Oklahoma	16	Total International	34
Oregon	2		

Total ASNLH Members 1,601

Source: "An Appeal for More Members of the ASNLH," c. 1928, box 1, folder 31, Woodson Collection, Emory University.

The ASNLH annual meetings brought together professional scholars and ordinary community members, which reflected "a genuine interest on the Director's part in influencing a large black public, and it presented a way of interesting them in their history."[71] This broad public was reflected in the academic program of the Association's annual conference, where black churches, schools, and artists were directly engaged. As the Woodson biographer Patricia Romero observed, "The programs of these early meetings deviated from those of the other historical societies. After or preceding each session a musical selection was rendered by a local singer or church group. This was very much in keeping with the tradition within the Negro society of the time and probably was not considered unusual by most of those in attendance."[72]

Much of this local organizing work was done by black teachers. The historian John Hope Franklin observed this during his first meeting of the Association in 1936, in Petersburg, Virginia: "It was not merely a program of college and university professors, but there were large numbers of teachers, of high schools and elementary schools as well," Franklin recounted. "And, he always had, as he did that week, a day set aside for the discussion of the dissemination of information in the schools. And there was a time during the program when schoolteachers as well as students participated in it."[73]

Woodson likened the ASNLH to a "free reference bureau," regularly responding to academic questions about black life and culture, providing written feedback on projects being taken up by black scholars around the country. Woodson personally helped teachers develop units of study to present to their local school authorities.[74] Wilhelmina Crosson, an English teacher in Boston, highlighted Woodson's responsiveness and willingness to engage community members with educational questions. "I could write to him at any time when I was delving into the history of the race," Crosson recounted, "and a letter would come back with many references and it always ended with remember, 'Boston was the birthplace of liberty. I am sure you will find this at the library on Harvard's campus.'"[75]

The sacrifices black Americans made to support the ASNLH should not be taken lightly. The fact that Woodson's educational program expanded most dramatically during the 1930s—the years of the Great Depression—speaks volumes to the impact his work had among black communities and how it nurtured black people's aspiration in hard times. Clarke Leo Smith Jr. was a student at West Virginia State during the 1930s and heard about Woodson's work through the school's president, John Davis. In a letter to Woodson, Smith wrote, "You do not know me but I have met you many times through your books." President Davis's remarks about Woodson caused the student to be "moved to tears." He enclosed two dollars with his letter to "aid [Woodson] in a small way to further [his] great work." Smith's family sent him this money for "laundry and miscellaneous articles." However, Smith declared, "If you can give your life for the advancement of Negro History, certainly I can give this small sum which is all I have to offer." Smith's testimony is one of many examples of the investments ordinary black people made in the Association's educational project and the powerful role word of mouth and partnering with black institutions played in carrying forward the Association's work.[76]

The emotional investment placed in the work of the Association by a broad base of black people carried over to financial support and their committed time to help sustain the organization, despite wavering support from major white donors. In this way, the association was an "insurgent intellectual network," as characterized by the historical sociologist Aldon Morris. Pushed to the margins of the mainstream academic society—meaning excluded from learned societies, disciplinary associations, and opportunities to publish with mainstream presses and journals—black scholars created academic pathways outside of the American academy.[77] The Association was an academic counterpublic sustained by the resources black people gave of their poverty, and its scholarship provided counteranalyses to dominant schools of thought upheld by preeminent white scholars.

"Schoolmaster to His Race": The Association's Influence as an Insurgent Intellectual Network

The Association allowed Woodson to serve as a surrogate mentor to educators, scholars, and community leaders around the country. The Civil Rights activist and community leader Dorothy Height emphasized the influence of Woodson's communal pedagogy in her life and that of the students she worked with as director of DC's Phyllis Wheatley YWCA. Height began in this position in 1939. The YWCA was in close walking distance to Woodson's office, where he lived alone, so he often took his meals with the Wheatley house residents. The conversations with Woodson over dinner were times when Height "truly received a liberal arts education," as she put it. Height learned of Woodson before meeting him; her mother gifted her one of his books for Christmas years before. After reading the book, Height recalled: "I would ask my mother, you know, 'Is this really true?' and she said, 'Yes.'

And then, to meet Dr. Woodson, himself, and have him reinforce it meant a lot to me." Years later, after she and Woodson became friends, he too gave her a book as a Christmas gift. Once "when I was moving," Height recounted, "I went to clear my bookcase, and a book by Du Bois with a little card fell out. . . . And on the card it said, 'Merry Christmas, Dorothy. C.G. Woodson.' And I cherished it as if it were gold, because here was a man who really helped me to understand more about who I was and who my people are, but also made his knowledge something that has stirred all of us."[78]

This strong commitment to community engagement was a central part of the pedagogy that drove Woodson's educational program. The residents of the Wheatley home explained that they always welcomed Woodson's presence because he was a "great philosopher and teacher." Woodson "would engage in stimulating conversations with the young women as they passed, tarried and listened to learn from the experiences of his full rich life." They recalled him to be "a fountainhead of knowledge of our history and racial heritage, together with an interesting store of anecdotes of wit and humor."[79]

Wilhelmina Crosson of Boston recalled similar encounters. "I see him now as though it were yesterday," she wrote, "seated in the Victorian chair in the Baldwin Memorial Library of the League of Women saying to a group of youngsters 'If you do not learn about the history of your race you will become a negligible factor in the thought of the world. Learn about the black man; his achievements were many. Be proud of your race!'"[80] Out-of-school spaces were always important sites of black pedagogy—first the coal mines, then Woodson's Sunday school classroom, and sites like the Wheatley home, black newspapers, and even his Association. Woodson's conviction to support the educational development of black people, particularly as it pertained to their racial and political identities, pushed him to operate in this way. It shaped the way he moved through the world and how he engaged young people in the community he lived in and in the places to which he traveled.

Black schoolteachers characterized Woodson as a "schoolmaster to his race."[81] Jessie Roy, Woodson's former student at M Street, became a teacher herself. When writing her second book on "Negro pioneers," Roy barely had to go to the Library of Congress to conduct research, because Woodson made himself available as a resource. Roy would simply go to Woodson's office and, as she put it, "sit for hours, spellbound, while one of the greatest masters of history told us in simple, clear language, facts and dates concerning the char-

"Dr. Carter G. Woodson Presents *The Picture Poetry Book* and *The Child's Story of the Negro* to Thurston Ferbee and Lois Grey," "The Saturday Morning Art Class," *Negro History Bulletin* 5, no. 7 (April 1942): 158. Used with the permission of the Association for the Study of African American Life and History, www.asalh.org.

acters about whom he wanted us to write." Woodson occasionally allowed Roy and her colleague, Geneva C. Turner, to accompany him to dinner at the YWCA to continue their studies or return to his office to study late into the night. According to Roy, "Socrates in his hey-day never had two more devoted students."[82] Woodson wrote the introduction to *Pioneers of Long Ago*, and his Associated Publishers, Inc., published it. He assured readers that these authors had written the book in a manner that maintained academic integrity and that was "suitable for children on the lower levels in the public schools."[83]

Teacher education and development was a major function of the Association's activities. Woodson desired to empower teachers, who were then to go on and shape the minds of young people in the classroom. Teachers needed to be equipped with knowledge that had the power to transform their self-perceptions and enhance their moral orientation to their work. As developing scholars themselves, black educators needed opportunities to expand their imaginations about black life. How else could they inspire black students to conceive of new possibilities for their collective futures? Woodson responded to teachers from around the country, sending them Negro history kits and posters for their classrooms, as well as filling book orders. These exchanges were made possible because of Woodson's involvement in the professional network of teachers, including as a life member of the American Teachers Association (ATA), founded in 1904 as the National Association of Teachers in Colored Schools, the umbrella organization for the state black teachers' associations across the nation.[84]

Well aware of black scholars' alienation in the mainstream American academy, Woodson actively mentored the next generation of knowledge producers on black life and culture. The Association provided space to mentor emerging scholars pursuing advanced degrees in the social sciences and humanities, even offering financial support for some of these students, beginning with Alrutheus A. Taylor's fellowship in 1922. With this support Taylor pursued his MA degree at Harvard, where he later received his PhD in 1936. Rayford W. Logan, Woodson's former student at M Street who also received a PhD in history from Harvard, received financial support from the Association in the early 1930s. Other notable scholars in this group were Charles H. Wesley, Lorenzo J. Greene, Luther Porter Jackson, Zora Neal Hurston, Lawrence Reddick, Langston Hughes, and Myra Colson Callis.[85] These fellowship opportunities and grants fell under the ASNLH's Department of Research, which was established in 1922 with the contributions made by Carnegie and the Laura Spelman Rockefeller Memorial Fund.[86] Woodson used this funding to support black scholars pursuing formal training in the academy and to conduct independent research in the field. Hurston credited Woodson and the ASNLH for funding her to travel to Alabama to gather information about the last group of Africans illegally brought to the United States through the transatlantic slave trade in 1861. In addition to archival research, Hurston conducted an extensive oral history with Cudjo Lewis, the last living member of this group.[87]

The historian Alrutheus A. Taylor described how "[Woodson] aided serious students . . . to secure funds wherewith to finance advanced study; he has assisted candidates to develop doctoral dissertations; he has given scholars encouragement and support in post-doctoral investigations; he has helped scholars to edit their work; and he has secured for others the use of facilities which were otherwise closed to them." Reinforcing this point, Lorenzo Greene explained that "Dr. Woodson's office was a training school for me, like those assistants who preceded me. . . . He gave me invaluable preparation in research." Of the fourteen black Americans awarded a PhD in history by 1940, eight of them had been mentored in some way by Woodson.[88] Operating at the margins of the American academy, the Association supported scholars to work around the strictures that prohibited black people from conducting research or that sought to undermine their work. The exclusion of black scholars from the academy created barriers not only for their individual achievement, but it also stifled discovery and production of knowledge about black life. These barriers helped to manufacture and maintain the racialized silences and gaps in knowledge. Operating as an insurgent intellectual network, the Association helped mitigate these challenges and created an intellectual public for black study to be nourished and appreciated.

By serving as "the watchman on the wall" the ASNLH took on the responsibility of meeting the needs of junior black scholars as best it could. Its academic ventures reflected the dialectic forged between antiblack mechanisms of exclusion and control in the academy and the subversive intellectual practices employed by black people to navigate these constraints. The insurgent activity of the Association was an institutional embodiment of fugitive pedagogy. Black scholars developed research networks independent of mainstream social science, historical, and literary networks while providing "counteranalyses to those of the mainstream." Black scholars "were not embraced by mainstream networks, nor did they receive nurturing resources from those networks."[89] Furthermore, in addition to this alienation, the insurgency of black intellectual networks, like Woodson's Association, was a response to the perpetual violence and dishonor black Americans faced under Jim Crow.

Members of insurgent intellectual networks were ever mindful of how forthcoming they could be about the full intentions of their academic agendas. This reflects the sociality of many black institutions in the early twentieth century, and particularly so for the network of scholars who found intellectual refuge in Woodson's Association. Fugitive pedagogy manifested in black institutions, especially when we consider the rebellious practices that formed within their interior.

*   *   *

The ASNLH was a complex social institution forced to show multiple faces. Negotiating power in the context of Jim Crow required black institutional leaders to work around the racist ideas that were pervasive in the public ethos and the American academy. This sociopolitical context demanded a very distinct kind of black performance in order to achieve the support of funders and academic opportunities, whereby the larger goals and mission of black institutions might be masked by an expressed set of goals that were compliant with the desires of white racial liberals. Despite what at times appeared to be a defanged public-facing message, the urgency of the work taken up by the ASNLH struck a familiar chord with black teachers and communities. Its political implications—beyond publicly expressed statements—were obvious to them. The mission of the Association was not just about the collection and dissemination of facts on black life. It was about telling a greater truth than the myths on which the known world was built: a plot to know the world and the meaning of humanity on new terms.

Black Americans flocked to Woodson's educational program, the black masses and the intellectual elite. Malcolm X, an organic intellectual, pointed to Woodson's scholarship as integral to the development of his political consciousness while imprisoned. He recalled, "Carter G. Woodson's Negro History opened my eyes about black empires before the black slave was brought to the United States, and the early Negro struggles for freedom."[90] Mary McLeod Bethune, the renowned educator and political leader, wrote that she simply "believed in Carter Woodson because he stirred the dormant pride in the souls of thousands ignorant or unmindful of our glorious heritage."[91] W. E. B. Du Bois, who had a strained relationship with Woodson, nominated him for the NAACP Spingarn Medal, which Woodson received in 1926. Years later, Du Bois identified Woodson's successful popularization of Negro History Week during the Black Renaissance as "the single greatest accomplishment" in the movement "for the advancement of art and literature."[92]

Despite his accomplishments, Woodson and the ASNLH largely existed in the shadows of the mainstream intellectual world. In elegiac fashion, Du Bois assessed, "No white university ever recognized [Woodson's] work; no white scientific society ever honored him. Perhaps this was his greatest reward."[93]

3

A Language We Can See a Future In: Black Educational Criticism as Theory in Its Own Right

Woodson . . . looked at the entire educational system and he said that it is set up in such a way as to motivate white students by telling them that they had done everything and to de-motivate black students by telling them that they had done nothing. So the question that we have been running away from is the body of knowledge in the university and schools itself. It is not any other extraneous factor. It is the body of knowledge. It is the system of representation.

—SYLVIA WYNTER, "Race and Our Biocentric Belief System" (2000)

To give something a name is to make it discernible and therefore accountable to critique and study. Black Americans struggled with how to talk and think about the education predicament they found themselves in and the systems of knowledge that structured their realities. Their pursuit of language and understanding produced a distinct body of educational criticism, one that analyzed the relationship between education and black life and exposed how education factored into black people's suffering as well as their struggle for freedom and justice. A way of speaking and knowing emerged from the interstices of black people's alienation within and resistance to the American School. Mining this language provides revelatory insight about the intricacies of black life in the social phenomena of education and study, a heritage comprising black people's experience in education as well as their interpretations of said experiences.[1]

Black educational criticism is theory in its own right. The very idea of "snatching a lesson" or "stealin a meetin'," as some enslaved people called it, was more than descriptive of "what" they did in a procedural sense to obtain education.[2] A deeper reading might attend to the values that motivated enslaved people to secretly learn ("the why"). It might also contemplate the ritualistic nature of the covert act, signified by the various idioms used to describe it (e.g., "steal away to learn," "catch a lesson," "stealin a meetin'," etc.). Similarly, Frederick Douglass's assertion in his autobiography that "knowledge unfits a child to be a slave" gestures toward a distinct set of ideas about education in the minds of black people in bondage, ideas conceptualized in relationship to their particular experiences as a people who could be bought and sold, because blackness was coterminous with slaveness in the modern world.[3] Black Americans carried politics and values into Emancipation cultivated during slavery; the same was true for conceptual ideas pertaining to education. This formed the basis of a continuing intellectual tradition.

Black educational criticism, often referred to as black educational thought, was part and parcel of fugitive pedagogy, providing theories of education and counteranalyses of the American School from below.[4] The educational criticism of black people was fundamentally counterhegemonic in its assertion that they were rational subjects, and because the ideas embedded within it challenged the racial hierarchy of slavery and then Jim Crow. This body of educational theory disrupted fundamental myths shaping human sociality.

Naming "Mis-education": A Conceptual Breakthrough in Black Educational Criticism

Carter G. Woodson published *The Mis-education of the Negro* in 1933. This text represents a quintessential example of this theoretical tradition. Woodson's central idea, "mis-education," became a lasting fixture in black vernacular culture as a shorthand critique of white supremacist ideas propagated by Western imperialist indoctrination, especially in the context of schools.[5] Naming "mis-education" invited a suspicion of normative educational values and for black people to think outside of dominant conceptions of schooling, which reproduced ideas and social practices rooted in white supremacy. Woodson's polemical text provides a window into a long body of educational criticism by black thinkers wrestling with first questions, fundamental lines of inquiry that set out to name and interpret urgent matters in black experience, that struck at the root of the crisis.

The curriculum of the American School, Woodson argued, produced impoverished perspectives of black culture and history and therefore, too, degraded representations of black people in the national culture. These distortions operated as authoritative knowledge, as naturalized "scientific" facts. Woodson argued, "The thought of the inferiority of the Negro is drilled into him in almost every class he enters and in almost every book he studies."[6] The American Curriculum inspired white students by telling them that their race—referring to a homogenous white identity, beyond ethnic and national difference—was responsible for all notable progress in the world. The semantics embedded in this curricular orientation, its very narrative structure, intended diminished aspirations for black students and to demotivate them from challenging their current state of subjugation. The motivation of white students and white achievement was premised on the debasement of black students and black achievement, in the same way that whiteness accrued its value in an antiblack world through the negation of other racialized groups, most notably black people as the modern analog of the slave (speaking, here, in ideological and curricular terms). Woodson continued: "The oppressor . . . teaches the Negro that he has no worth-while past, that his race has done nothing significant since the beginning of time, and that there is no evidence that he will ever achieve anything great."[7] The American Curriculum narrated black life as a past of nothingness and in proleptic fashion suggested that nothing was likely to change for their future. Woodson's critique of mis-education named the racialized gaps in "official knowledge" of schools.[8] More than mere oversight, he insisted, these gaps were carefully manufactured, a knowledge system constructed by those in power who deemed African-descendant people as outside of history, outside of human time—trailing behind "the great march of human civilization," as one textbook author put it (see Chapter 4).

A shared antipathy for black people as well as their culture and history within the American School ecology, Woodson recognized, made black teaching and learning urgent tasks of a distinct kind. He argued that the sustained erasure of black cultural and political achievements from knowledge animated the physical violence and precarity experienced by black people. Mis-education was an assault on black life in the psychic and physical realm, its violence manifested discursively and materially. Time and again he asserted, "There would be no lynching if it did not start in the schoolroom." Addressing the violent erasure of black life in the canons of knowledge was a critical first step in developing a liberatory program of education. What we come to know and say about the world, the stories we tell and study, manifests in all other aspects of our lives. Antiblack curricular violence and the physical violence black people experienced were symbiotic. Addressing the material conditions of black life required upending black people's condemnation in the symbolic order. This was the heart of Woodson's theoretical argument.

Mis-education, like the more expansive body of black educational criticism, cannot be fully appreciated through the mainstream white progressive educational theories of Woodson's contemporary moment; nor can they be confined to the false dichotomy of the Booker T. Washington and W. E. B. Du Bois debate on industrial versus classical education.[9] Furthermore, distilling theory from black educational criticism demands close reading of the words put forward by black thinkers alongside their deeds and practices of negotiating the constraints of the American School. Therefore, my reading of *Mis-education* is couched in a broader analysis of Woodson's actions on the ground during the early 1930s and the exchange of ideas between him and his contemporaries. Furthermore, this tradition of educational criticism represented by Woodson in the United States resonates with that of other educators and thinkers in the African Diaspora. Generating new language to talk about blackness, power, and technologies of schooling represents a distinct line in black intellectual history that transcends the United States, representing a critical feature of black diasporic consciousness.

"Blind to the Negro": Imitation and the Illegibility of the Black Condition

Woodson was concerned with the *mis*-education of black people, not that they were *un*-educated. Theoretically speaking, those blacks who were "highly educated" were the major source of his concern. Woodson's critique was less about access to education in general and more about exposure to hegemonic curricula and indoctrination into white ruling-class ideology. This conflict is revealed in the opening scenario of this book taken from Tessie McGee's classroom in 1930s rural Louisiana.

In secretly reading from Woodson's textbook, McGee undermined the racist curriculum adopted by the state's board of education. According to the state-adopted textbook, "Not only are almost all the civilized nations of to-day of the white race, but throughout all the historic ages this race has taken the lead and has been foremost in the world's progress."[10] While access to schooling was still a major issue for black Americans during the 1930s, Woodson's concern was the epistemological underpinnings of education provided to those who made it past these barriers. Two years prior to publishing *Mis-education,* Woodson reflected on his own life, explaining in the *Negro World* newspaper that it took him twenty years after completing his doctorate at Harvard University to recover from his thorough initiation into the Western world's highest orders of knowledge.[11]

"Imitation" emerged as a key trope in Woodson's development of mis-education as a theory of antiblackness in the American School. The implantation of hegemonic white ideology and curriculum in the context of black education created vexing conditions. It offered black learners no social analysis to develop critical perspectives on the oppressive conditions surrounding them and taught nothing of the continuum of struggle black students inherited. The curriculum did just the opposite. It allowed students to internalize racial myths that reproduced their oppression—or, at best, it left them to figure out a way forward with no resources or conceptual knowledge to assist them in imagining beyond the limitations of Jim Crow.

Woodson's critique of imitation extended from a belief that ideas shaping school content ultimately informed process. Questions about ideology and knowledge, so deeply bound up in power relations, should come before or be made an integral part of the institutional development of black education. Woodson was less concerned with the debate surrounding industrial versus classical education or integration versus segregation. As Woodson asserted in *Mis-education,* attempting to choose a side within these binaries was "how we missed the mark." At a conceptual level, he raised questions toward the stories and ideas about the world that formed the bases of the knowledge system, which then instructed curriculum content and pedagogical practice. What was the human vision within education, and in what ways were black students allowed to see themselves within that vision?

The term *imitation* or some variation of the word shows up more than twenty-three times in *Mis-education.* "The chief difficulty with the education of the Negro," Woodson asserted, "is that it has been largely imitation resulting in the enslavement of his mind." As a consequence of this imitation, black Americans were taught to revere the history and achievements of the white race and thus aspire to whiteness—or the symbolic forms of achievement outlined in white historical narratives. This raised ethical concerns for Woodson, not only because of the racial implications but also on the grounds of what was just and moral. "What advantage is it to the Negro student of history to devote all of his time to courses bearing on such despots as Alexander the Great, Caesar, and Napoleon, or to the record of those nations whose outstanding achievement has been rapine, plunder, and murder for world power?" What did it mean for a persecuted people to look to the stories of those who killed and stole for power as a source of their enlightenment? It was backward to romanticize the history and ethics of a group that has dominated and enslaved to conquer the world. What's more, it was self-destructive to internalize the very system of representation structured through and on one's own subjection.[12]

The impact of such indoctrination was debilitating, and it alienated black people from their own realities. "When a Negro has finished his education in our schools . . . he has been equipped to begin the life of an Americanized or Europeanized white man," wrote Woodson, "but before he steps from the threshold of his alma mater he is told by his teachers that he must go back to his own people *from whom he has been estranged by a vision of ideals* which in his disillusionment he will realize that he cannot attain."[13] The formal protocols of the American School taught black students to negate their own cultural and racialized identities, despite the fact that they would never be interpreted as white by the larger society.

At the heart of the American School was a "vision of ideals" that estranged black learners. These ideals were primed for the experience of an "Americanized or Europeanized white man." Ultimately, this estrangement was an impediment to black people's vision of their own historically situated subjectivities and the world in which they found themselves.

In an undated manuscript, Woodson elaborated on his critique of mimicry in black education: "The Negro is merely shoved out through the back door of the school provided for the needs of other Americans and ordered to imitate from afar the best he can what is going on in the main show."[14] This analysis of the conditions of black education not only critiqued it as a flawed assimilationist program but also denotes the violence of black exclusion from the mainstream public sphere vis-à-vis mainstream schooling. Black students were excluded—better yet, "shoved out through the back door"—from the main show, or the citizenship project of schooling offered to white students, and instead expected to mimic these programs in the confined space carved out for them at the margins of the American School, reflective of their alienated status as degraded citizens, as substudents. Blacks were forced to construct an educational program that attempted to replicate whiteness, with no interrogation of how and why they were excluded from this structure of power, or "the main show," to begin with. A preoccupation with imitation and mimicry foreclosed the possibility of imagining an alternative model of schooling that moved beyond the hegemonic norms of white ruling-class ideology. "The education of any people should begin with the people themselves," Woodson argued, "but Negroes thus trained have been dreaming about the ancients of Europe and about those who have tried to imitate them."[15] This critique of imitation was a caution toward internalizing a fascination with European and Euro-American culture and values that diminished the possibilities of a positive black self-image and a critique of white supremacy.

The American School lacked the resources to equip black people with the knowledge and skills necessary to develop their race, precisely because it distorted the reality of the black condition, both past and present. As a result, students became estranged from the masses of their race. They were taught not to see the realities of their worlds. Woodson argued that "the leading facts of the history of the world should be studied by all, but of what advantage is it to the Negro student of history to devote all of his time to courses bearing on such despots as Alexander the Great, Caesar, and Napoleon[?] . . . Why not take up economics as reflected by the Negroes of today and work out some remedy for their lack of capital, the absence of cooperative enterprise, and the short life of their establishments." He again targeted the most prestigious white institutions to suggest that the apex of the United States' elite education was insufficient: "Institutions like Harvard, Yale and Columbia are not going to do these things, and educators influenced by them to the extent that they become *blind to the Negro* will never serve the race efficiently."[16]

Having spent many critical years of his own life in these elite universities as a student, Woodson spoke from experience. As opposed to preparing them for the work of freedom and social transformation, dominant scripts of knowledge more likely forced black students to become "blind to the Negro." The American Curriculum, even in the most elite contexts, rendered black people and their oppression illegible. The absence of sustained attention to the history of violence and exploitation that structured black life in the modern world, or black people's unceasing resistance to these assaults, underdeveloped black people's ability to see and know themselves as a historically situated people or the depths of their human struggle.

Taking Woodson's critique of mimicry seriously, we find that mis-education theoretically names the coconfiguration of knowledge canonization, power, and antiblackness as a political mandate of white supremacy. Black education was forced to mimic hegemonic ideas of schooling without any critical interrogation of its reliance on dominant epistemology—a knowledge system that informed the racial order of society and its debasement of black people in its conceptual understanding of what it meant to be human. According to Woodson, this imitation of hegemonic schooling ran the risk of developing a false consciousness among black people; it cultivated aspirations of whiteness and its markers of power while rendering invisible the black condition as abject, dispossessed, and unfree.

In response, Woodson advocated for an educational program that challenged the distortions of black life in the American School. He called for *rigorous sight* of the black condition—a more exhaustive knowledge about the historical construction of antiblack ideas, an awareness of how these ideas were practiced in schools and society, and deep study of expansive narratives about the social and political life of African descendant people in the world. Woodson argued that race (and blackness in particular) needed to be named explicitly in the process of study, for it had implications for all aspects of our social order. As such "the Negro" as well as "Negro life and history" made race/blackness a hermeneutic for the process study, and a realm of experience for excavating a submerged body of knowledge. Education, Woodson professed, must give black students new ideational resources to parse through their realities, resources for imagining the world anew.

An Appeal for Rigorous Sight in Black Education

A central objective of education must be to support students in thinking critically about their social and historical realities. This required a conceptual engagement with black Americans' lived experiences, a practice of study that developed a disciplined and vigilant mode of intellectual inquiry into power and antiblackness, as well as the life and culture of black people—what I am calling *rigorous sight*. A learning objective emerging from the critique of mis-education, which caused one "to become blind to the Negro." Rigorous sight is presented here as a matter of pragmatism, to name something that is par-adigmatic in Woodson's writing and actions, though not explicitly stated in *Mis-education*, or at least not in the most coherent fashion.

Through the development of rigorous sight, Woodson believed black people would recognize that they were oppressed, how that oppression was main-tained, and what systems facilitated their subjugation. Writing a year after the release of *Mis-education*, he insisted, "If conditions around the Negro child are undesirable or even intolerable I would not try to hide these things from him. I would inform him accordingly just as soon as he developed *the power to see* and observe things for himself." Students needed to have an awareness of the injustice surrounding them and be informed that those things were systemically and historically derived. They needed sup-port to interrogate these realities. Teachers needed "to show wherein these conditions have resulted from unsound policies and unwise methods."[17] A conceptual understanding of black Americans' oppressed conditions should be a critical objective of schooling—this is what it meant "to think" as Woodson often retorted.

Woodson anticipated that not all black people agreed with him on this matter. "Several mis-educated Negroes themselves contend that the study of the Negro by children would bring before them the race problem prema-turely," Woodson observed. These individuals "urge that the study of the race be deferred until they reach advanced work in the college or university."[18] He disagreed with the idea that matters of race and the racial history were developmentally inappropriate for primary and secondary school students: "These misguided teachers ignore the fact that the race question is being brought before black and white children daily in their homes, in the streets, through the press and on the rostrum." He asked, "How, then, can the school ignore the duty of teaching the truth while these other agencies are playing up falsehood?"[19] In a Jim Crow society built on racial chattel slavery, race structured every aspect of experience. There was no outside of race.

Mis-education cultivated a desire to forget the racial history of the United States. Those who believed that "the Negro should cease to remember that he was once held a slave, that he has been oppressed, and even that he is a

Negro" contributed to the distortion of black life. While some blacks were ashamed and invested in forgetting this past, "the traducer . . . keeps before the public such aspects of this history as will justify the present oppression of the race."[20] The absence of a deep study of the past concealed the functions of white supremacy. This concealment was of no benefit to black people.

Woodson likened this intentional effort at disremembering racial oppression in classrooms to the policing of knowledge among enslaved people by plantation overseers and masters. "This was accomplished during the days of slavery by restricting the assembly of Negroes to certain times and places and compelling them to meet in the presence of a stipulated number of the 'wisest and discreetest men of the community.'" The surveillance of black intellectual life was a carryover from slavery, reflecting a set of enduring relations that structured black experiences of schooling. Elaborating on this critique, he offered, "These supervisors of the conduct of Negroes would prevent them from learning the truth which might make them 'unruly' or ambitious to become free."[21]

Learning for black students was a distinct task. It demanded a critical lens of black people's collective oppression and, more specifically, the functionality of those systems and ideas that sustained their oppression needed to be named and rigorously studied. This political imperative of black education was to be calibrated from the primary school level and beyond. As Mary McLeod Bethune echoed just three years later at the annual meeting of the ASNLH, there was a need for "interpreters" to translate the findings of scholarship on Negro life and history to meet the needs of the masses, and particularly black youth.[22] Sheltering black students from the realities of antiblackness underdeveloped their potential to effectively resist and think beyond the structures built on their suffering. It impeded any true understanding of black cultural life, which had long been a critique of this domination.

Black Americans' struggles for freedom required an educational program that studiously engaged the realities of their world in all of its forms—material, psychic, and social. Recognizing this, Woodson demanded an education in pursuit of rigorous sight. This meant developing protocols of study that deeply engaged the realities of black suffering and black people's continued struggle for social transformation.

Woodson's theory marked a historic shift in black educational criticism. For so long black people's primary quarrel in education centered on access. Access to literacy, access to professional training, access to higher education and citizenship. Surely, people before Woodson identified the need to talk about black history and achievement; however, Woodson's naming of the wide-ranging impacts of the racist distortions in curricula was new territory. This clarity achieved by *Mis-education* was a conceptual breakthrough. It was new language for a new world.

The Role of White Paternalism in Sustaining Mis-education

Efforts to cultivate a rigorous sight in black people had long been suppressed. This was evident during the time of slavery through the criminalization of black literacy as well as the surveilling of black gatherings. Post-Emancipation this suppression took on new form as black education became included in the American School in nefarious ways. Woodson argued, "Starting out after the Civil War, the opponents of freedom and social justice decided to work out a program which would enslave the Negroes' mind inasmuch as the freedom of body had to be conceded. It was well understood that if by the teaching of history the white man could be further assured of his superiority and the Negro could be made to feel that he had always been a failure and that the subjection of his will to some other race is necessary the freedman, then, would still be a slave."[23] Alongside the absence of black life and culture in curriculum, Woodson also critiqued the implicit message that black people were incapable of thinking for themselves. This idea that black people lacked the capacity for reason—what the Cameroonian philosopher Achille Mmembe refers to as "the Western consciousness of Blackness"—was used to justify white paternalism and the persistence of racial domination.[24] Mis-education aimed to facilitate black submission to white control because, as curricula revealed, black people lacked the capacity for self-determination as evident by the absence of any meaningful contribution on their part to the development of human civilization.

Recent scholars have provided similar analysis of black education in the first days of Emancipation, looking particularly to the freedmen's schools managed by white northerners and missionary aid societies. The content of textbooks provided for freedmen's schools after the Civil War positioned blacks as indebted to white patriots for their freedom. One historian observed, Northern whites were "paternalistic caretakers" and blacks were portrayed as a "benighted people" in need of moral guidance and direction.[25] No mention is made of the colored soldiers who enlisted and fought for the Union and their freedom. The freedpeople received only representations of Northern whites as heroic saviors who sacrificed their lives for black emancipation. Textbooks like *Advice to Freedmen, Friendly Counsels for Freedmen, Plain Counsels for Freedmen,* and *John Freeman and His Family* demanded that the formerly enslaved kneel in humble appreciation. Another observed, "The burden of debt, duty, and gratitude foisted onto the newly emancipated in exchange or repayment for their freedom is established in the stories of origin that open these textbooks." There was an outsized representation of white sacrifice for black emancipation and a peculiar absence of black people having done anything to free themselves: "The blood of warring brothers and mothers' sons that stained the war-torn landscape of the United States granted the enslaved freedom, but the blood regularly spilt at the whipping post or drawn by the cat-o'-nine-tails in the field, the 200,000 black soldiers who fought for the Union . . . failed to be included in the accounts of slavery's demise."[26] Through these narrative and ideological frames, white benevolence was the primary means to black salvation.

Echoing Woodson's critique of the American School's *confined* inclusion of black people, these scholars demonstrate how deference to white paternalism became engrained in black education at the curricular level in the first days of Emancipation. Such narratives presented no opportunity for black students to interrogate white supremacy and erased any semblance of black historical subjectivity in the struggle for their freedom. They were props in a heroic tale of white paternalism, brought out of the benevolent institution of slavery by the goodwill of the (white) Union soldiers. They were to be perpetual wards of white benevolence.

As an apparatus of power, these early structures of black education—speaking strictly in a top-down sense—staged a processional from slavery to freedom that inducted blacks into a system of indebtedness to white paternalism, curtailing any explicit ethical commitment to challenging whiteness or antiblack domination. Woodson declared that the post-Emancipation curriculum offered to black schools "did not take the Negro into consideration except to condemn or pity him." To the extent that those who benefitted from black people's oppression continued to control their education, mis-education would persist.

Woodson's critique of white control over black education extended from an intimate awareness of how white educational funders and leaders manipulated the development of black schools. He witnessed this phenomenon early on with the firing of his cousin Carter Barnett from Douglass High School in 1900, and likely well before then. By the 1930s Woodson had more than enough evidence that white paternalism and ideological manipulation were two sides of the same coin, and both definitive characteristics of black schooling at a systemic level. "Negroes have no control over their education and have little voice in their other affairs pertaining thereto," Woodson argued. "In a few cases Negroes have been chosen as members of public boards of education, and some have been appointed members of private boards, but these Negroes are always such a small minority that they do not figure in the final working out of the educational program. The education of the Negroes, then, the most important thing in the uplift of the Negroes, is almost entirely in the hands of those who have enslaved them and now segregate them."[27] Woodson argued that freedom and justice would not be realized through an education constructed and controlled by the very class of people whose privilege relied on the subjugation of black people.

Just any education controlled by black people, however, was not sufficient to bring about rigorous sight in black students either. Woodson made this point clear, time and time again. Many black teachers, being mis-educated themselves, lacked a critical interrogation of white supremacy. "Taught from books of the same bias, trained by Caucasians of the same prejudices or by Negroes of enslaved minds, one generation of Negro teachers after another have served for no higher purpose than to do what they are told to do. In other words, a Negro teacher instructing Negro children is in many respects a white teacher thus engaged, for the program in each case is about the same."[28] As long as the dominant systems of representation continued to be the basis of black teachers' professional training and the main source of their teaching, their efforts were likely to collude with the structural program of mis-education. This was the case whether or not this collusion was intentional on the part of the teacher. To be clear, Woodson's critical assessment of an essentialized "Negro teacher" was more a matter of political representation, which served a rhetorical function. A common misreading of *Mis-education* has been to read this claim as a total dismissal of black teachers.[29] Woodson's claims were in some sense hyperbolic, but no less driven by a sincere critique.

More than a decade before publishing *Mis-education*, Woodson articulated the conundrum forged between the financial vulnerability of black Americans, white funding, and the manipulation of black education by white leaders. Thomas Jesse Jones of the Phelps Stokes Fund became a single personality embodying all the things that caused Woodson's suspicion toward white racial liberals and paternalistic philanthropy. Jones carried great influence among white funders and educational reformers during the first half of the twentieth century. He was one of many "white architects of black education," as the historian William Watkins observed.[30] Writing candidly of Jones, Woodson asserted, "Dr. Jones is detested by ninety-five percent of all Negroes who are seriously concerned with the uplift of their race. They dislike him because he is the self-made white leader of the Negro race, meddling in all affairs affecting Negroes, exercising the exclusive privilege of informing white people who is a good Negro and who is a bad one, what school is worthy of support and what not, and how Negroes should be helped and how not."[31]

While many of Woodson's black contemporaries shared his opinion, very few would publicly voice such striking critiques. Similar to his advocacy for the cultivation of rigorous sight in black students, Woodson desired for black people to recognize how white paternalism continued to prevent meaningful strides from being made in black education and, by extension, stifled black intellectualism. As the previous chapter demonstrated, this was a challenge he battled with personally in running the ASNLH.

In 1932 Woodson expressed to professor Benjamin Brawley of Howard University that Jones and white philanthropists, as "self-appointed leaders" of black education, had "set back the wheels of progress . . . for almost a generation."[32] By the 1930s, Woodson had become effectively estranged among white philanthropists. This was due to some combination of his controlling personality, particularly when it came to the work of the ASNLH, and his lack of diplomacy when dealing with the egos of white allies. Woodson was unapologetic in his critiques of their manipulative practices in a way that departed from the racial etiquette of the day.

This strained relationship with white benefactors caused friction between Woodson and other members of the black intellectual elite. Likewise, both of these groups were targets of his frustration expressed in *Mis-education*.

These frustrations came to a head when Thomas Jesse Jones and the Phelps Stokes Fund set out to develop an encyclopedia on the Negro and explicitly excluded Woodson and W. E. B. Du Bois from the project. Brawley was invited to participate, which prompted the exchange between him and Woodson. Brawley and the other scholars called on by the Phelps Stokes Fund, however, insisted that Woodson and Du Bois be included.

Giving in to this unanimous push back from the potential contributors, the Phelps Stokes Fund extended invitations to Woodson and Du Bois. Woodson adamantly refused. Du Bois, however, thought it was practical to accept the invitation and find some middle ground to ensure that they would have intellectual freedom. He appealed to Woodson in the following terms:

> Dear Sir:
>
> I was asked to act as a Committee by the Conference on Negro Encyclopedia to induce you to join us. I had hopes to see you personally but had to rush back from Washington. When I am there again, I shall talk with you. Meantime, as time is passing, I am venturing to write.
>
> I do not doubt but what you have made up your mind on this matter and that nothing I can say will change it. However, perhaps I ought to bring to your attention the motives that influenced me.
>
> I was omitted from the first call, as you were, and for similar reason. My first impulse on receiving the invitation to attend the second meeting was to refuse, as you did. Then I learned that this invitation did not come from the Phelps Stokes Fund, but was the unanimous wish of the conferees, and that if I refuse to heed it, I would be affronting them, even more than Stokes and Jones. Then, in the second place, I had to remember, as both of us from time to time are compelled to, *the enemy has the money and they are going to use it*. Our choice then is not how that money could be used best, from our point of view, but how far without great sacrifice of principle, we can keep it from being misused. By the curious combination of accident and good will, we appointed at the last meeting a Board of Directors and Incorporators, which leave out the more impossible members of the Conference. A place on the Board was left for you. If you do not accept it, that will leave us so much weaker.
>
> I hope you will see your way open to join us.
>
> Very sincerely yours,
>
> WEBD / DW[33]

Woodson was outraged at the audacity of the Phelps Stokes Fund for taking on a project that infringed on the intellectual work already being taken up by the ASNLH, but he was also frustrated by Du Bois and the others for accepting this invitation. Woodson publicly expressed his anger in the black press during the years immediately preceding the publication of *Mis-education.*

Woodson shared with Brawley how "Thomas Jesse Jones, supported by Anson Phelps Stokes, secretly circulated in 1923 a most scurrilous attack on the work of the Association among all persons who were known to contribute to its support."[34] He wanted Brawley to understand how Jones's manipulative behavior continuously undermined black leadership and black intellectual work. He symbolically represented the system of mis-education that Woodson and black institutions raised ideological warfare against.[35] Woodson made the point even more aggressively in his communication with Du Bois:

> When Stokes and Jones saw that their lopping off the support of the Association did not silence me as to what I think about Jones, Stokes approached me with a bribe. He offered me money and the use of his name to raise money, if I would come out in a statement to the effect that I had misunderstood Jones. . . . Of course, I refused to sell out; and they have been hounding me ever since. Jones has made himself the dictator of the programs of the social uplift of the Negro. Now he hopes to do the same with research.[36]

Collaborating with Jones and Phelps Stokes on such an important project that would have implications for the study of black life and culture in schools posed an ethical and ideological conflict for Woodson.

A rift developed between Woodson and the scholars who accepted the invitation made by the Phelps Stokes Fund. In his view, the initial exclusion of himself and Du Bois made clear the funder's desire for their own interests and ideology to shape the intellectual project. To this he retorted, "Proposals like these coming from without from those who have already done the race much harm should be looked upon as gifts brought by the Greek."[37] Woodson's reference to the Trojan horse in Greek mythology suggested that the terms accompanying the financial support were toxic to the intellectual project at hand. This gesture of support from Jones and Phelps Stokes was contaminated and disingenuous. In characteristically stubborn fashion, Woodson explained to his colleagues that he had nothing else to say on the matter "except that I am not interested. I never accept gifts from the Greeks. . . . the Association for the Study of Negro Life and History will bring out its ENCYCLOPEDIA AFRICANA by the end of 1933."[38] It is important to note that Woodson made mention of beginning such an effort before the Phelps Stokes Fund had taken up their encyclopedia project, having written to other potential funders about his plans to do so.[39]

The conflict surrounding this encyclopedia project surely fueled the critique of black intellectuals in *Mis-education*. Neither of the encyclopedias came to fruition, though Woodson and Du Bois both did a considerable amount of work on their respective projects. Phelps Stokes notified Du Bois in 1938 that the General Education Board decided to no longer fund the project. The young historian Rayford W. Logan, Woodson's former high school student, worked closely with Du Bois on the project. He extrapolated an important lesson from this event that echoed Woodson's sentiments: "The word of one white man could determine whether a project concerning Negroes could be approved or not."[40] Unbeknownst to Du Bois, the decision to defund the project was influenced by Jackson Davis, a white educational leader from Virginia, who believed that Du Bois's political activities compromised his scholarly abilities, a critique often made against black scholars then and now.[41]

Woodson advocated for black intellectuals to operate independent of oversight from white funders throughout the remainder of his life. He explained, "I could get aid from several white persons and foundations, but once I accepted their money they would tell me how to dot an 'i' or cross a 't.' And I don't want that."[42] Thus, the critique of white paternalism's stronghold on black education found at the heart of *Mis-education* was deeply personal for Woodson. It was informed by a long history of manipulation he witnessed from the firing of his high school principal and his challenges with the white university president at Howard University to the Phelps Stokes encyclopedia project, and there were endless other examples between these events.

White paternalism adversely affected black education well beyond the United States. This was a transnational phenomenon. Woodson offered this criticism in *Mis-education* and the broader span of his writings, his criticism having moved beyond the national context as early as the 1920s. Woodson's theoretical arguments in *Mis-education* emerged from a diasporic consciousness, which suggests that the book might be more appropriately read as a decolonial text, part of a global body of black educational criticism.

Mis-education and Woodson's Decolonial Discontents

Woodson's writings about black life and history transcended national boundaries prior to the publication of *Mis-education*, and that same transnational perspective informed this iconic book. He observed, "Much of Africa has been conquered and subjugated to save souls. How expensive has been the Negro's salvation! One of the strong arguments for slavery was that it brought the Negro into the light of salvation. And yet the Negro today is all but lost."[43] Woodson long critiqued colonial education on the African continent administered by white philanthropy.[44] Once again, Thomas Jesse Jones embodied this exploitative relationship between white funding and black education. "Jones transferred his operations to Africa," wrote Woodson. "He easily ingratiated himself into the favor of the few European agencies working for the enlightenment of the natives within the locus prescribed by economic imperialists."[45]

In expanding his critique of white philanthropy from the United States to Africa, Woodson underscored how education became an integral tool in imperialist expansion on the continent. Black people in Africa and in the United States were educated in a manner that facilitated their submission to the political system of their oppressors. Expanding this analysis in more general terms, he asserted, "The Negro, both in Africa and America, is being turned first here and there experimentally by so-called friends who in the final analysis assist the Negro merely in remaining in the dark."[46] Again, education provided by the very people who were privileged by the subjugation of black life should be looked upon as a suspicious offering.

Woodson endorsed such activists as Max Yergan and Paul Robeson and their work to challenge imperialism on the African continent, further nuancing the anti-imperialist and decolonial tone of *Mis-education*. In 1924 Woodson exposed Jones's involvement in blocking Yergan's ability to travel to South Africa, and in the 1930s he actively supported the work of Yergan and Robeson with their International Committee on African Affairs. Woodson celebrated them for "keeping before the modern world the urgent need for the redemption of Africa from the economic imperialists and the Christians cooperating with them."[47] Woodson's experience with black education in the United States gave him a perspective to interrogate the educational politics implemented on the African continent; and likewise, learning of the racial politics of education in Africa gave him a deeper understanding of what was happening at home before his own eyes. This became increasingly obvious once he learned that the same white funders were pulling the strings on both sides of the Atlantic.

Woodson's attentiveness to colonial educational practices in Africa invites one to consider the relationship between his theory of mis-education and similar theories developed by scholars motivated by a diasporic consciousness. Individual black scholars and teachers had long observed a relationship between black oppression in the United States and the domination of black people beyond the nation. Educators in the nineteenth century, such as Richard Robert Wright, Charlotte Forten Grimke, and Edward A. Johnson, are evidence of this phenomenon. To varying degrees, they reconsidered the history of Africa, drew on narratives of the Haitian Revolution when teaching school children, or challenged those who argued that African descendant people were the children of Ham to justify claims of black inferiority.[48] Woodson's *Mis-education* was an extension of this tradition in black educational criticism. More pointedly, "mis-education" is a decolonial theory intimately aligned with the thinking of many other black decolonial writers.

Along with Woodson, such black intellectuals as the Jamaican scholar Sylvia Wynter (b. 1928), the Martiniquan poet and political figure Aimé Césaire (b. 1913), and the Kenyan writer Ngũgĩ wa Thiong'o (b. 1938) interrogated how education was mobilized as a technology of antiblack control in service of white colonial interests and imperialist expansion. All of these scholars placed an eye toward denigrating cultural ideas about Africa and African descendant people as central to black subjugation and the physical exploitation of black people. *Mis-education* anticipates the thinking of these scholars across the African diaspora. And while Wynter is the only one of these three scholars to explicitly engage Woodson's ideas in her work, there is, nonetheless, a sharp resonance across their analyses. Collectively, these scholars developed a grammar for black education beyond borders. A way of looking at and theorizing about education that extended from a distinctly black position in an antiblack world.

The history of race and slavery in the United States made for a distinct experience of antiblack subjugation. Yet there are many parallels between
black American experiences and those of blacks on the Continent and across
the diaspora, where colonialism took explicit form. Black suffering in schools
might be thought of as part of the bottom line to antiblackness that has cut
across a diversity of experiences. We might understand distortions of black
life in the canons of knowledge and formal structures of schooling as a gen-
eralizable feature, which should also be held alongside antiessentialist cau-
tions that push us to think about difference and divergences, as well as change,
in Afro-diasporic experiences.

Since the late 1960s Black Studies scholars have offered "internal colonialism" to conceptualize the domination of blacks in the United States and
its relationship to that of other racially marginalized groups living under colonial rule.[49] In a similar fashion, Woodson drew a comparison between the
historical oppression of black Americans and the white exploitation of natives on the African continent. He was a forerunner to scholars who interpreted black suffering in education as a global practice of white coloniality
and empire.[50] Antiblack schooling has been integral to the superexploitation
of African descendant people' in the modern world and its political-economic
ordering.

On Wynter and Woodson

Sylvia Wynter, a prominent thinker in the field of Black Studies, has deeply
engaged Woodson as a social theorist. She has thought alongside Woodson's
theory of mis-education to call attention to the exorcism of black people from
Western epistemological constructions of the human.[51] In particular, she
highlighted Woodson's indictment of cultural suppression within the
American Curriculum. There has been "systemic cognitive distortions with
respect to North America, as well as the human past and present," such that
the history and narratives that form the substance of knowledge are couched
in a relation where African descendant people have been constructed as props
to an idealized white human subjectivity. Like Wynter, Woodson raised questions about dominant comprehensions of the human or, put differently,
black people's relationship to an epistemological ranking of human potentiality—who was understood to have the capacities for achieving the highest

forms of human civilization. The Negro was "pictured as a human being of the lower order," Woodson observed, "unable to subject his passion to reason, and therefore useful only when made the hewer of wood and the drawer of water for others."[52] Both scholars were concerned with how these cognitive distortions functioned at the level of the white-European imaginary and, by extension, the canons of knowledge it produced, which formed the curricular foundation of schooling.[53]

Contextualizing her perspective on these cognitive distortions, Wynter asserted, "Black Americans are the only population group of the post-1492 Americas who had been legitimately owned, i.e. enslaved, over several centuries." Their "owned and enslaved status" determined and articulated their position as the furthest from "Man" / human / whiteness in the logic used to classify human groups and their representation in curricula. This "classificatory logic" served to ensure the "stable replication of the invariant relation of dominance / subordination," the denigration of blackness and black people for the propping up of whiteness and white people as well as justifying their accumulation and exertion of power over others.[54]

Woodson asserted, "The Negro is as human as the other members of the family of mankind"; for proof we need only to look to "the domestication of animals, the discovery of iron, the development of stringed instruments, an advancement in fine art, and the inauguration of trial by jury to his credit[;] the Negro stands just as high as others in contributing to the progress of the world." Despite these achievements, however, the white curricula insisted otherwise. "The oppressor . . . raises his voice to the contrary," wrote Woodson. "He teaches the Negro that he has no worth-while past."[55] Black people were excluded from narratives of human culture and civilization. This was a studious exclusion that justified the domination of black people by defining them as a subgenre of the human species. Wynter recognized Woodson as having named these distortions and set out to construct a new story of human history, to rewrite the epistemological order.

Black people became "narratively condemned" through the dominant white curricular imagination, argued Wynter.[56] Distortions in curricula were consequential for black life in the material world. Symbolic condemnation and physical persecution were coconstitutive. The material and the cultural are always interlinked in this way. Official curricula perpetuated miseducation and, in turn, sustained white colonial rule as "an autopoetic or self organizing living system," observed Wynter.[57] Both scholars argued that the hierarchical nature of racial groups in curricula inscribed them into the political-economic order along the lines of these relations of power and domination. Across time and space—Wynter having arrived to the United States in 1974, after a long career as a scholar and artist between Europe and the Caribbean, and Woodson having died in 1950—these scholars called attention to how ideas of human rank are encoded at the level of ideas and reproduced in a material world structured through ideas. Such epistemology acted as a calculus of human social activity. Antiblack ideas in the symbolic order functioned as a social competence, structuring human behavior—physical interactions at the micro level, value association at the psychic level, and decisions about the allocation of resources. Thus, Woodson's mission to transform knowledge was an essential political mission, Wynter professed; because "this rewriting of knowledge is *the* issue and *the* imperative." "Any attempt to dismantle those social hierarchies," Wynter concluded, "must dismantle the 'acts of communication' that motivate and demotivate specific behaviors and replicate status hierarchies and role allocations."[58]

Wynter and Woodson both named how the material and the symbolic interact. Addressing the structural and psychic realities of black suffering in an antiblack world required the rewriting of the epistemological order. Education and technologies of schooling have always been at the heart of the crisis.

"Thingification": On Violence and the Cultural Politics of White Supremacy

The repression of African and black cultural expression in education was inextricably linked to discursive and physical violence experienced by black people. By conditioning black students to "admire the Hebrew, the Greek, the Latin and the Teuton," explained Woodson, while at the same time denying the existence of black diasporic achievement, educators "lead the Negro to detest the man of African blood—to hate himself." He continued: "To handicap a student by teaching him that his black face is a curse and that his struggle to change his condition is hopeless is the worst sort of lynching."[59] Again, antiblack violence expressed in the physical realm held a symbiotic relationship to the distortions of black life and culture in colonial curricula.

The lynched black body and the narrative condemnation of the same were mutually constituted.

"The philosophy and ethics resulting from our educational system," Woodson argued, was the same philosophy and ethics that "have justified slavery, peonage, segregation, and lynching." Based on the epistemological order, "the oppressor has the right to exploit, to handicap, and to kill the oppressed." Woodson's naming and critique of the cultural politics of white supremacy can be traced across Afro-diasporic criticism in education.

In charting the weapons of colonialism, the Kenyan writer Ngũgĩ wa Thiong'o explained that the biggest was the "cultural bomb." Curricula became an effective medium for the expression of colonial ideas, and these curricula were an integral part of the colonial praxis of violence. Its effect is "to annihilate a people's belief in their names, in their languages . . . in their heritage of struggle, in their unity, in their capacities, and ultimately in themselves. It makes them see their past as one wasteland of nonachievement and it makes them want to distance themselves from that wasteland."[60] Thiong'o asserted that the violence against black bodies and the violent ideas in colonial curricula were two sides of the same coin. "The night of the sword and the bullet was followed by the morning of the chalk and the blackboard. The physical violence of the battlefield was followed by the psychological violence of the classroom."[61] This critique was shared by Thiong'o and Woodson (as well as Wynter)—recall Woodson's assertion that lynching was an expression of the classroom, an affirmation of the system of ideas and values inherited through curricula.

Moving from a critique of cultural denial to a proposition for action, Woodson advocated for black schools to "abandon a large portion of the traditional courses which have been retained throughout the years because they are supposedly cultural." By traditional cultural courses Woodson referred to curricula in social studies and the humanities. Schools should "offer instead training in things which are also cultural and at the same time have a bearing on the life of the people thus taught."[62]

Woodson's perspective on black cultural denial was influenced by ongoing discussions on black culture among social scientists and writers extending from the Progressive Era through the interwar period.[63] Some scholars debated whether there was anything distinctly African about black American culture. Woodson observed that such scholars as E. Franklin Frazier were "misled by the contention of Robert E. Park," of the University of Chicago, who "fearlessly upheld the mischievous, unsupported statement that the American Negro retained little which he brought from Africa except his tropical temperament."[64] While the black sociologist E. Franklin Frazier argued that black people retained no culture from their African past, because it was strangled out through the process of enslavement, others such as Melville Herskovits, a Jewish anthropologist, argued that black Americans and others throughout the diaspora retained certain Africanisms that were distinguishable.[65] Woodson largely supported the claims made by Herskovits and critiqued those of Frazier as conservative and self-loathing. "Negroes themselves accept as a compliment the theory of a complete break with Africa," Woodson wrote, "for above all things they do not care to be known as resembling in any way those 'terrible Africans'."[66]

Distortions of black culture and representations of Africa as "the heart of darkness" have been integral to black oppression across the experiences of chattel slavery, colonialism, and their afterlives.[67] The notion of "Africa" and "blackness" were both forged in the white Western consciousness together. As such, one always invokes the other, which is to say "each consecrates the other's value." And while not all Africans are black, the flesh invoked in the Western imagination when Africa is conjured is that of a dark-skinned "black body," "the Negro."[68] The denigration of Africa, and therefore black people and culture, has been central to the process of antiblack domination in the modern world, positioning black people as the liminal category in modern conceptions of the human species—the link between animal and man.

If culture is in fact an "ordinary" aspect of all human society, then to insist that a people have no culture is to fundamentally misrecognize their humanity, to assert that they are not human, or at minimum are a degraded form of the human species.[69] This has been a central antagonism in educational contexts globally among colonized people, and particularly so for black people in the modern world. George Hegel's wholesale exclusion of Africa in his canonical text, *The Philosophy of History*, is a representative example. African people lacked history and culture, and ultimately souls, by Hegel's assessment of the human experience. The Negro "exhibits the natural man in his completely wild and untamed state. We must lay aside all thought of reverence and morality—all that we call feeling—if we would rightly comprehend him; there is nothing harmonious with humanity to be found in this type of character." As such, Africa "is no historical part of the World: it has no movement or development to exhibit." Hegel concluded, "What we properly understand by Africa, is the Unhistorical, Undeveloped Spirit, still involved in the conditions of mere nature, and which had to be presented here only as on the threshold of the World's history."[70] Hegel's philosophical offerings about human history and experience influenced generations of Western philosophical and historical thought, and they continue to haunt black life in the known world.[71] Following Hegel's lead, a "reasonable" conclusion would suggest that black people's absence of culture meant that their only hope was to adopt the ways of life and living offered by white men, who were the model of human civilization and had a proven capacity for rational thought.[72] Imitation, by this measure, offered the only meaningful option for black people.

Black Teachers' Educational Criticism as a Diasporic Practice

Like Woodson, Aimé Césaire had also been thoroughly initiated into the Western canons of knowledge, having matriculated through the most elite institutions of learning in the Francophone world. Césaire was also a schoolteacher, having taught Frantz Fanon—one of the most important political theorists on blackness and coloniality—at the Lycée Schoelcher between the late 1930s and early 1940s. This was a secondary school in Martinique that Césaire graduated from before traveling to France and eventually studying at the Sorbonne. When asked what he studied at the Lycée Schoelcher, Césaire explained that his studies all centered on "Latin, Greek and French literature." He then shared that he studied the same things during his education in France. And finally, Césaire offered, "But that is not all. I went back to Martinique and I taught at the Victor Schoelcher School, and I taught Latin, Greek and French literature."[73]

Césaire's thorough initiation into the Western symbolic order, his alienation within this system of knowledge, and his time teaching all informed his critiques of the larger colonial system and particularly how its antiblack violence was animated by the symbolic order. Césaire argued that the denigration of black cultural life sutured the dialectical relationship between the colonizer and the colonized. Through a conceptualization of what he termed "thingification," Césaire observed in 1955, "The colonizer, who in order to ease his conscience gets into the habit of seeing the other man as an animal, accustoms himself to treating him like an animal."[74] By Césaire's reasoning, the disfiguring of black history and culture is a critical step in the process of colonial rule and, thus, imperial expansion. Thingification maintained a narrative of black inhumanity through cognitive distortions, which structured consciousness, and thereby made racial domination justified and moral. This process of narrative condemnation served the interests of the colonial project, even if it did not initiate it. Thingification (Césaire)—like mis-education (Woodson), narrative condemnation (Wynter), and the cultural bomb (Thiong'o)—was a result of protocols of knowledge and study constructed by human beings that justified and maintained structures of domination. These distortions in knowledge were myth and reality, to the extent that they always had real material and psychic implications.

Expanding on the relationship between coloniality and education, Césaire continued: "For wherever there are colonizers and colonized face to face, I see . . . in a *parody* of education, the hasty manufacture of a few thousand subordinate functionaries, 'boys,' artisans, clerks, and interpreters necessary for the smooth operation of business."[75] Similar to Woodson's critique of "meaningless imitation" in black schools, Césaire asserts that colonial schooling was a parody of white ideas about education. The instruction aimed to divert the oppressed from thinking critically about their experiences of surveillance, control, and labor exploitation or their relationship to the masses with whom their subjugation was linked.

Césaire's "artisans, clerks, and interpreters" are akin to the black educated elite Woodson criticized as mis-educated, those who have been estranged from the black working class and poor. These educated blacks became managers within the very system that subjugated them. They are taught deference and adherence. "When you control a man's thinking you do not have to worry about his actions," wrote Woodson. "You do not have to tell him not to stand here or go yonder. He will find his 'proper place' and will stay in it." Describing this phenomenon in metaphorical terms, Woodson offered, "You do not need to send him to the back door. He will go without being told. In fact, if there is no back door, he will cut one for his special benefit. His education makes it necessary."[76] Wynter commented on this assertion made by Woodson, that curriculum structures the social order as a sort of pedagogy of the imperialist state. "Woodson has gone totally outside the concept that this is 'natural.'

He is saying, 'No. The function of the curriculum is to structure what we call 'consciousness,' and therefore certain behaviors and attitudes."[77] Black students' view of their oppression was compromised and obstructed by a curriculum set up to structure compliance and admiration for the project of white imperial expansion and domination.

In advocating for a transformation in curricula, Woodson worked toward a shift in black consciousness and how black learners were to understand their own subjectivities in a world that was white supremacist and antiblack; the cultivation of an educational program that made rigorous sight a primary objective. Woodson offered a lesson for how to struggle as a people, asserting that the first step began at the level of ideas, the system of representation. One had to see the world and their place within it with a rigorous sight in order to be prompted to action—action that was outside of (and that contested) the known world, careful not to recreate the same structures of domination that produced one's current suffering.

Any educational program in service to black freedom dreams needed to have, at its core, a social analysis of the world and new language that demystified how ideas in the American Curriculum—or colonial curricula—worked to sustain one's subjection. Absent this, black education ran the risk of developing black students to become "blind to the Negro"—estranged from their own subjectivities and trapped in racial myths that passed as a fixed social order. They would be perpetually restrained from imagining new ways for how to be in and toward the world.

Woodson, Wynter, Thiong'o, and Césaire all point to the centrality of black cultural denial in educational models created to serve white colonial commandment. Their theorizations of antiblackness, coloniality, and education resonate with first-person accounts by other educators in the diaspora across time. Adelaide Casley-Hayford of the Gold Coast opened the first African-owned and African-run school in Freetown in 1923, where she merged feminist politics with cultural nationalism. Casley-Hayford argued that the colonial education offered to native Africans "taught us to despise ourselves." The immediate need of young African children, she argued, was "an education which would instill into us a love of country, a pride of race, and enthusiasm for the black man's capabilities, and a genuine admiration for Africa's wonderful art work." Bernard Coard, born and educated in Grenada, attended college in the United States and later became a schoolteacher in London. He, too, observed black oppression to be animated by and endemic to Western education. In 1971 he wrote *How the West Indian Child Is Made Educationally Sub-Normal in the British School System*. Coard argued, among other things, that a "cultural bias" proliferated in the schools, where white educators assumed black children were inferior simply because of their race and forms of cultural expression. These cultural biases led to West Indian children being disproportionately labeled under the established classificatory designation of "educationally sub-normal." Responding to this assault on black cultural identity, Coard and many other community activists pushed for the creation of "black supplementary schools" to instill pride and dignity in students by teaching them about their own history and cultural legacy, a heritage that was denigrated by British teachers and curricula. Again, black cultural denial in Western education has been a consistent feature of black subjugation in the modern world. There is a long tradition of black educators and intellectuals who named and critiqued this reality, while also developing subversive educational models to challenge it.[78]

Engaging in a critique of imposed educational protocols established by white authorities and systems of power have been part and parcel of black people's ongoing struggle. There is a deep resonance across their diverse experiences. Black educational criticism generated language to name and analyze the cultural politics of white supremacy and its relationship to antiblack violence. It has been a practice of diaspora. Its fugitive spirit, a resource in political struggle beyond any single national context.[79]

Black Educational Criticism as Theory in Its Own Right

Woodson's critique of mimicry and his quest for new ways of imagining an educational ethics for black students suggests that he, like many black American teachers—and educators in the African Diaspora—labored to produce ideas that accounted for their experiences of domination. While black education scholars' theoretical ideas have certainly been influenced by and engaged with mainstream white discourse on education, the fundamental ideas shaping the politics of their educational thought and how they engaged the American School emerged from outside the mainstream educational sphere. This is to say, the educational criticism of black educators must be treated on its own terms.

Writing to the audience of the *Chicago Defender* in 1932, Woodson asserted, "The Negro should carry out a program of his own. . . . We must consider his past and approach him through his environment. If these happen to be different from those of others, the method of attack must be different."[80] Black American students needed to be educated *as* black American students, making the experiences of black life legible in the ideological content and aims of their education. The American School was "worked out in conformity to the needs of those who have enslaved and oppressed" and then presented as a blanket system for all students.[81] This disjuncture was irreconcilable for Woodson. A new set of concerns had to be accounted for when thinking about what education should and could mean in the life of black people, and there was likely to be a variation of needs, even intraracially.[82]

Understanding teaching as a fundamentally political act, Woodson argued that education for black children must have a clear indictment of the political system that sanctioned their subjugation. "I would *deliberately* teach the Negro child the falsity of the doctrines which have prevented clear thinking," declared Woodson. The violence black people experienced at the level of ideas and in the physical world demanded the urgency of such a didactic approach at times.[83] In this same vein, the circumstances of black life demanded a different metric for assessing achievement:

> In thus estimating the results obtained from the so-called education of the Negro the author does not go to the census figures to show the progress of the race. It may be of no importance to the race to be able to boast today of many times as many "educated" members as it had in 1865. If they are of the wrong kind the increase in numbers will be a disadvantage rather than an advantage. The only question which concerns us here is whether these "educated" persons are actually equipped to face the ordeal before them or unconsciously contribute to their own undoing by perpetuating the regime of the oppressor.[84]

Rejecting ideas of meritocracy and individual achievement, Woodson placed a high value on a sort of racial uplift and anticolonial aptitude. Less concerned with quantifying the number of newly graduated doctors and lawyers that could be credited to the race, Woodson challenged conventional meanings of black educational success, turning a normative orientation to achievement on its head. This might be thought of as an early critique of an obsessive discourse surrounding the idea of an academic achievement gap between black and white students.[85] The deeper mission of black education transcended such utilitarian perspectives.

Some scholars have read Woodson's contributions to educational theory and practice through the Progressive Education Movement and various factions of late nineteenth- and early twentieth-century development in the social sciences (e.g., cultural pluralism and the cultural gifts movement).[86] These assessments are useful for understanding Woodson in conversation with his contemporaries in the mainstream educational sphere. Yet Woodson was largely alienated from these intellectual groups when he published *Miseducation* in the 1930s. This raises a caution for reading Woodson through these dominant frames. While there is certainly overlap between Woodson's educational model and the Progressive Education Movement, the core aspects of his writing on black education fall outside its parameters.

While many progressive educators pushed for contextual learning, encouraged social transformation and anti-indoctrination, and stressed communal values, the ideas shaping this movement offered no critical social analysis of whiteness or antiblackness, of power and domination. The crux of Woodson's philosophy, on the other hand, offered an explicit critique of antiblackness and, at certain times, relied on a banking-style model of education that put it at odds with key components of progressive education. This is not to suggest Woodson did not also emphasize critical thinking but that his primary concern was educational content and the messages in curricula, before pedagogy in its procedural sense.

The idea of contextual learning assumes that students have the resources around and within them to engage in a critical learning process. This does not fully align with Woodson's offerings. If we understand the contextual nature of black students lives as shaped by racial myths, as Woodson did, it follows that this context posed limitations for any truly democratic learning process. Given this, Woodson worked to instill a new inventory of learning resources and ideas on which students could rely, both to supplement cultural knowledge students already had and to help them recognize the racial myths embedded in American society. The content of the curriculum materials he developed intentionally destabilized students' contexts.

At times, Woodson advocated for a didactic form of pedagogy, where he sought to offer unconventional narratives about black life and a system of ethics that encouraged students to resist the social structures that oppressed them. In teaching students about people like Phillis Wheatley and Nat Turner or explicitly writing about the manipulation of black education by white philanthropists, Woodson offered teachers and students an explicit social analysis of race and power to help develop a politically relevant educational program. This was a critique that needed to be handed to students, and early on.

Furthermore, while progressive educators advocated for communal models of learning, there is no evidence to suggest that Woodson was influenced by this contingency of scholars and teachers. Communal values in education were not newly introduced to Woodson or other black teachers through the Progressive Education Movement. Practices of "communal literacy" were part and parcel of black educational life during the nineteenth century, where literate enslaved people read aloud to others in their community, allowing for a collective engagement in the learning process and permitting illiterate blacks to engage with the written word.[87] This communal pedagogy was integral to black educational heritage since slavery. The early iterations of communal education were cultivated out of political necessity and introduced early on in Woodson's life.

Woodson explicitly critiqued mainstream educational theories for their inability to offer purposeful interventions for black students. Recounting a conversation with one black teacher in 1932, Woodson concluded that this teacher was "well informed on all the educational theories developed from the time of Socrates down to the day of Dewey," yet he had no clear understanding about what was needed for black students.[88] Woodson critiqued mainstream theories of progressive education in his reference to John Dewey (the leading progressive education thinker), arguing that these theories were not grounded in the lives of black people and were insufficient as a resource for interpreting their experiences. This assertion is particularly striking given that Woodson was once a student of John Dewey during the summer of 1902 at the University of Chicago.[89] Woodson's critique of the limitations of white educational theories informs my decision not to read his theoretical perspective—as well as the broader genre of black educational criticism—through the lens of progressive education or primarily through Progressive Era social science scholarship.

While open-ended questions and interrogation of students' context have often been association with critical pedagogy, this does not fully encapsulate the pedagogical model advocated by Woodson. In fact, there have been many cases of black educational thinkers advocating for a retreat from open-ended, question-based forms of learning, advocating instead for more didactic instruction out of political necessity—and most often a hybrid of the two. In these instances, black teachers rejected full reliance on abstract notions of learning-by-doing and individualized processes of experimentation. Writing about this phenomenon, one historian observed, "A focus on self-discovery and self-expression among the voiceless was replaced by a desire to articulate a critique of society to the oppressed."[90] The black independent school movement informed by black nationalist ideology in the late 1960s and early 1970s would later offer one of the most vivid illustrations of this thread in black pedagogy, and it was strongly represented in black teachers' pedagogy all along.[91]

Reading black American experiences into mainstream American epochs often obscures black realities, and this certainly applies to black intellectual history, of which I understand the history of black pedagogy to be an integral part. While the Progressive Era more broadly is remembered to be a period of robust technological advancement and sociopolitical progress in the United States, there is significant overlap between this era and what the black American historian Rayford W. Logan named "the nadir of American race relations."[92] This contrast is reflected in the imagery that proliferates in public memory of black people being lynched from bridges and streetlights. The visual narrative encapsulates the technological progress often associated with the Progressive Era, yet it also marks the ubiquitous violence and social terror that shaped black life. This disjuncture similarly applies to the Progressive Education Movement, which in many ways negated the violent experiences of black people in relationship to the American School. The ideas developed by black people about the role education played in their lives was both a part of and apart from the larger discourse surrounding American education.

Black educational criticism was theory in its own right and should therefore be studied based on the unique conditions under which black educators were living and striving. As the philosopher and Black Studies scholar Lewis

Gordon has argued, "Blackness also requires liberation in the world of ideas."[93] To suggest that black people only offer experiences to be interpreted by and through white theories obscures the fact that black people have been generating interpretive resources all along. Blackness has not only been a site of experience. It has also been a site for intellectual inquiry and incisive analysis of the human condition.

In that dominant conceptions of education continued to exclude and confine black life to the shadows of the American School, prominent black educators and scholars went outside the realm of official knowledge to theorize about black school life and to imagine new possibilities.[94] Black educational criticism reflected a persistent intellectual demand of fugitive pedagogy—the need for new language and ideational resources to name and challenge the function of antiblackness within the American School. Generating new theoretical ideas about education reflected a necessary vigilance of a hostile learning context.

4

The Fugitive Slave as a Folk Hero in Black Curricular Imaginations: Constructing New Scripts of Knowledge

In this approaching era the Negro is going to write school text books for himself. He is going to adorn them with pictures of his own thoughtful men and virtuous woman, with likenesses of his own bright boys and pretty girls. The Negro youth of the land are going to be taught to catch inspiration and hope from the virtue, goodness and intellectual endeavors of their own race.

—RICHARD ROBERT WRIGHT, "The Possibilities of the Negro Teacher" (1894)

Negroes must know the history of the Negro race in America, and this they will seldom get in white institutions. Their children ought to study textbooks like Brawley's "Short History," the first edition of Woodson's "Negro in Our History." . . . They ought to study intelligently and from their own point of view, the slave trade, slavery, emancipation, Reconstruction and present economic development.

—W. E. B. DU BOIS, "Does the Negro Need Separate Schools" (1935)

The curricular imaginations of black Americans have always tarried in fugitive spirit. They demanded new scripts of knowledge out of political and intellectual necessity. Enslaved people asserted that there must be another Bible in the Bible of their masters, an ambivalence which led them to create invisible institutions of black religion and their own analyses of biblical stories. Black people exchanged fragmented information and rumors of slave uprisings in the Atlantic world as models for black freedom and thus instigated acts of rebellion.[1] Susan Paul, a black abolitionist and teacher in Boston, formed a choir of her pupils in the 1830s. They rendered songs condemning slavery and actively imagined a world without it. She turned her classroom into a singing school for justice.[2] "The choice of [songs], like the literature Negroes selected for the curricula of their schools," one historian has written, "spoke metaphorically of a fight in earthly spaces."[3] Black teachers, like Charlotte Forten Grimke, insisted that the freedchildren "should know what one of their own color had done for his race." She proclaimed that black people were historical and political subjects and supplemented the curriculum with smatterings of black life and history, including the story of Toussaint L'Ouverture and Haiti.[4] Black people's insistence on social and political life amid the imposing threat of black social death demanded new scripts of knowledge or, at minimum, a writing and living in between the lines. Their narrative frames critiqued their surrounding context in an antiblack world, while providing learning resources for imagining a new social order.

The first textbooks written by black Americans were authored by fugitive slaves. James W. C. Pennington's *A Text Book on the Origins and History of the Colored People* (1841) inaugurated this tradition, a formalized practice of black people striving to rewrite the epistemological order, challenging the antiblack foundations of the known world. Having observed that "we suffer from the want of a collection of facts so arranged as to present a just view of our historical origin," Pennington assembled a black counternarrative rooted in biblical genealogy and the history of ancient Ethiopia and Egypt. His was a refusal of the master narrative, like the one posed by Noah Webster, architect of the United States' national orthography, who in 1843 explained that as for "the woolly haired Africans, who constitute the principal part of the inhabitants of Africa, there is no history and there can be none."[5] Pennington's fugitive piece was not mere repetition of white Western means of constructing and assembling knowledge in the form of a textbook. It was repetition with polemic intent—appropriating the technology of the textbook as an authoritative form and turning it on its head. Ushered in by an industrial revolution, the nineteenth century witnessed the proliferation of print culture, and black Americans used these new widely available resources to nurse their liberatory dreams.[6] Like newspapers, journals, and various other forms of black print culture, textbooks became tools not only of the master but also of the fugitive slave.

It should come as no surprise that slaves who absconded played an integral role in establishing this intellectual tradition. There is a resonance between Pennington's textbook and the freedom narratives of escaped slaves like Frederick Douglass and Harriet Jacobs. One might also recall how "in

1829 George Moses Horton hoped to buy his freedom with money made from sales of his book of poems, *Hope of Liberty*," in North Carolina. Fugitive spirit was embedded in black literary practices.[7] The fugitive slave William Wells Brown also wrote a textbook in 1863.[8] Black people set out to know the world and themselves on new terms, in anticipation of and as a means of bringing about slavery's demise. Once Emancipation arrived this intellectual tradition continued, as the condemnation of black life persisted in narrative and material forms. There continued to be a need for new scripts of knowledge.

After the Civil War black teachers carried this tradition forward. And in their textbooks, they commemorated the lives of fugitive slaves, black insurrectionists, and enslaved people's fugitive literary practices in epic fashion. What follows is an exploration of this latter theme in the curricular imaginations of black educators and then an analysis of key themes in textbooks published in the late nineteenth and early twentieth centuries. Establishing a new ceremony of knowledge emerged as a cornerstone in the art of black teaching. A new world demanded transformed ways of knowing.

The Fugitive Slave as a Folk Hero in Black Education

The theory of *fugitive pedagogy* indexes the recurring figure of the fugitive slave as a folk hero in the writings and recollections of black teachers and students.[9] The absconded slave, akin to the literate slave—because they were often one and the same—emerged as an archetype who symbolized black people's political relationship to the modern world and its technologies of schooling. As a cultural symbol, this folk hero represented ideas and values shared by black educators, which also had implications for embodied form in black school life; how teachers and students expressed these values in practical ways.

Narratives of fugitive slaves took on typical characteristics of the folk hero genre. Individual narratives of escape and rebellion represented "the feat," where black flight from enslavement represented a deed that exceeded ordinary human capacities. The fugitive slave's continued and collective acts of escape, and in some cases their efforts to lead others to freedom, represented a more expansive "quest." The quest represented "a prolonged endeavor toward a high goal, usually involving a series of feats, contests, and tests, before final attainment." In that the folk hero themselves became metonymic of the grand quest, it follows that the archetype of the fugitive slave functioned as a symbol for the pursuit of black freedom. This ultimate quest transcended any individual act or feat, though it put them all into perspective.[10]

Black schools inherited this folk hero through the oral traditions of those who lived during slavery, when a black countercurriculum had already begun to form. The historian Charles H. Wesley referred to this intellectual phenomenon from the nineteenth century as the emergence of a "new heroic tradition," whereby black fugitives and rebels who were deemed monsters or erased in the white national memory became elevated as heroes in black curricular imaginations. "Slavery . . . produced heroic figures who have long occupied an important place in Negro thought," the historian Lawrence Levine explained. "The concept of Negro History was not invented by modern educators. Black men and women dwelt upon their past and filled their lore with stories of slaves who, regardless of their condition, retained a sense of dignity and group pride." This knowledge was passed on to those who had never seen the days of slavery, and the stories continued to hold meaning. Despite temporal distance, Levine continued, many black Americans "may be said to have lived 'pretty close to slavery' in that they kept slave memories and traditions alive in their stories, their anecdotes, their reminiscences." The stories of fugitive slaves held a more distant meaning after Emancipation, yet their political relevance remained prominent.[11]

The fugitive slave became inscribed in the collective memory of black Americans. The nineteenth-century historian George Washington Williams observed the omission of figures like Nat Turner in traditional school books and the dominant American public memory, yet Turner's story persisted. While "no stone marks the resting-place of this martyr to freedom . . . he has a prouder and more durable monument than ever erected of stone or brass," Williams proclaimed. "*The image of Nat Turner is carved on the fleshly tablets of four million hearts. His history has been kept from the Colored people at the South, but the women have handed the tradition to their children, and the 'Prophet Nat' is still marching on.*"[12] Turner had no proper burial, and the American national culture dishonored him, yet his story was held close and commemorated in the lives of black people, carved in the hearts of black children and passed on by those that came before them.

Black teachers played an important role in passing on this inheritance, beyond oral traditions. The fugitive slave—in myth and fact—functioned as a curricular object, emerging as a concrete focus of study. Accompanying this symbol was the demand for fugitive modes of study. In 1890, black Americans in St. Louis renamed a school after Jean-Jacques Dessalines, the slave insurrectionist turned governor-general of Haiti, after petitioning the white school board to rename their institutions after blacks who had achieved great things. Another school was named for Toussaint L'Ouverture. Black community leaders offered a defanged explanation for their selections, thus concealing their true motivations. In the school board records, Dessalines is simply listed as "a soldier." Local whites mocked this choice of name in the newspaper, noting that black people would likely mispronounce the names of these foreign military figures.[13]

Every textbook written by black schoolteachers between the late nineteenth century and Woodson's first textbook in 1922 included expansive coverage of maroons, fugitive slaves, and slave insurrections.[14] The principal Edward Johnson of North Carolina asserted that Nat Turner "was, undoubtedly, a wonderful character," in his 1890 textbook, where he outlined details about Turner's life and the insurrection he led. Leila Pendleton, a schoolteacher in Washington, DC, noted to her student readers that Turner was "known to the Negroes for miles and miles around as that of a leader and prophet." His mother taught him that he was destined to be "a 'Moses' for his people." Like his predecessors, John Cromwell, a school principal and member of the American Negro Academy, emphasized black people's reverence for Turner in his 1914 textbook. Cromwell also highlighted that "fifty-five white men were killed but not a single Negro was slain during the attack."[15] Black teachers presented the story of Turner running away and leading an insurrection as part of a protracted narrative of resistance and slave uprisings stretching back before the American Revolution. Fugitivity manifested as a through line in black America's social and political history. The characters in these narratives were leaders to whom students could look for inspiration and purpose.

Woodson's first textbook featured narratives of fugitive slaves as well as an extensive array of images: portraits of fugitive slaves and scenes of black people's struggle for freedom in motion. Ellen Craft appears dressed in men's clothing, disguised as her master. This performance of cross-dressing being a key strategy in her escape plan. "The Dash for Liberty" depicted an enslaved man on the run. "Harriet Tubman" is rendered with her shotgun, the barrel gripped tightly in her hand, the stock of the gun resting on the ground, its length nearly the height of her entire frame. "The Negro Calls a Halt" portrays an enslaved man stabbing his white master and white women witnessing this act of retribution in shock. "The Pursuit of the Slave" illustrates a runaway hiding in a tree and a slave patroller pursing him on horse, accompanied by a dog.[16]

Teachers developed supplementary units of study in places like Chicago, Houston, and New Orleans during the 1930s and 1940s that elevated narratives of fugitivity. At times teachers gave more extensive coverage to the story of L'Ouverture and Haiti than any other, even as their units were supposed to focus on the role black people in US history.[17] In 1934 Du Bois presented a lecture at an event organized by the New Orleans Teachers Association. His talk focused on the fugitive slave's impact on the abolitionist movement and how their political efforts precipitated the period of Reconstruction. References to fugitive spirit even appear in the crevices of the archive; an inscription, scribbled in the margins of Madeline Stratton Morris's lecture notes, read: "slaves—steal away to learn." This Chicago educator inserted the origin story of black education in her talk to teachers, insisting that they remember the long struggle they were a part of. The slaves stealing away to learn framed the political stakes of their vocation.[18]

Fugitive spirit (which the fugitive slave symbolized in the flesh) appeared in particular scenarios of students learning and black cultural expression. Third-grade students in North Carolina and Virginia exchanged letters as pen pals in 1935 to share what they learned about "the Negro." They emphasized how Frederick Douglass secretly learned to read and write "from white boys on the streets, and from signs on the wharves." Elementary students in Birmingham learned about enslaved people's use of slave spirituals to convey secret messages, sometimes about physical escape. Songs that were seemingly "innocent amusements"—to borrow from the cultural historian Saidiya Hartman—were in fact coerced performances within the realm of the plantation economy, and simultaneously turned on their heads. The lyrics were flipped as a wink in song. Slaves sang one thing while feeling and meaning another. The students laughed at textbooks that presented the slaves' songs as evidence of their happiness. Off-script lessons from their teachers explained how these songs sometimes communicated hidden messages about escape.[19]

The figure of the fugitive slave indexed the plot embedded within black education, a liberatory fantasy that cut across time and space. This fantasy was

ELLEN CRAFT, a fugitive disguised
as her master

THE NEGRO CALLS A HALT

THE PURSUIT

Fugitive slave
images. Reproduced
from Carter G.
Woodson, *The Negro
in Our History*
(Washington, DC:
Associated
Publishers, 1922),
pp. 35, 72, 92, 113,
115, 149.

HARRIETT TUBMAN

TOUSSAINT L'OUVERTURE

THE DASH FOR LIBERTY

not respectable in the eyes of white school authorities and therefore not spoken of in the open. This tension has implications for how we understand the relationship between curricular content and embodied practice (see Chapters 5 and 6). The dispositions taken by black teachers and students mimicked the intended political function of their education. It mirrored the political form of the folk hero—forced to live within the confinement of an antiblack world even as they constantly pursued a new reality. What education consisted of or what it aimed to accomplish—its metacurricular intent—had implications for how it was performed and enacted. This looks like a substitute librarian in Cleveland, Ohio, secretly disposing of children's literature with racist content when her white supervisor was out of sight in the summer of 1946. "I pitched [them] in the wastepaper basket and went on to the next branch," she recalled while laughing; she then continued, "I cleaned out lots of branches." She also worked to organize Negro History Week celebrations through local libraries as a member of the ASNLH.[20] The struggle over educational content and ideas also manifested in physical acts of practice. In the broadest of terms, the fugitive work of black educators was about advancing their political intent and educational objectives, while masking them to the extent that they were at odds with the established norms of the American School. This balancing act constantly shifted according to time and place. It was never a willing deference but a means of survival and struggle.

The Absence of Black (Fugitive) Life in the American Curriculum

By including the fugitive slave, and black life more generally, in their textbooks, black teachers rebelled against established schools of thought in the American Curriculum. The significance of their curriculum might be appreciated by analyzing what they included and that which they negated. This book opened with Tessie McGee secretly teaching her students from Woodson's textbook at the Webster Parish Training School in Louisiana in the early 1930s. The content of Woodson's book stood in stark contrast to the approved, antiblack curriculum from which McGee was otherwise required to teach. Two history textbooks were adopted by the state of Louisiana for high school: *Modern Times and the Living Past* by Henry Elson and *An American History* by Nathaniel Wright Stephenson.[21] These textbooks covered world history and US history, respectively. All references to Africa and black people portrayed them as objects in white people's journey to expand democracy and civilization or relegated them to footnotes.

In the preface to *Modern Times,* Elson makes clear that students must have a foundation in history to gain "knowledge of the great march of human events." As such, the framing of this world history textbook makes clear its intention to expose students to the important events of human history. "I have given large space to the social and industrial life of the people," Elson continued, "especially in the accounts of ancient Greece and Rome and of the great nations of modern Europe." These historical narratives, he makes clear, compose the "great story of the development of human civilization."[22] In direct terms, Elson explicated that Europeans led all the important events in human history. These stories composed the apex of human history, or "the great march of *human* events." His first chapter outlined the "Four Races of Man," which included the "Caucasian, Negro, Mongolian, and American Indian"—the white, black, yellow, and red race. Using this comparative frame, he asserted, "Not only are almost all the civilized nations of to-day of the white race, but throughout all the historic ages this race has taken the lead and has been foremost in the world's progress."[23] Given their superior contributions to the march of human civilization, "Almost *the entire book* will be devoted to the doings of the Caucasian race," or more specifically, "at least nine tenth of the book must be given to an account of the Indo-European branch of the race, as the Indo-Europeans have dominated the world for the past 2500 years."[24] Based on this mandated curriculum, Tessie McGee and her students were "narratively condemned." Their predecessors were outside the important events of human history based on the "official knowledge" of schools.[25] They were of no human concern.

Stephenson's US history textbook, *An American History,* charted the political development of the United States, with only a marginal discussion of black people, Native Americans, or racial chattel slavery. When slavery was mentioned, it was done so in the most benign and dispassionate tone, and absent any discussion of violence and labor exploitation. "In the houses of the rich might generally be found negro slaves. The Southern colonies with their mild climate and country life were well suited to negro labor," offered Stephenson.[26] The southern plantation was characterized by its "hospitable mansion, its retinue of slaves, its broad tract of surrounding land."[27] That

"hospitable" is used to describe the plantation home obscures any perspective of those who were enslaved on its land and signals the exclusion of black
youth—who were the progenies of slaves—from seeing themselves in the historical narrative. This is more than black people being excluded from US
history. Black teachers and students—as readers—and their antecedents are
rendered ahistorical or, at most, idle props to the historical development of
the nation. The enslaved and their descendants are merely backdrop. They
are inanimate context.

Stephenson only discussed the resistance to slavery through the lens of
white abolitionists, such as John Brown. No mention is made of slave insurrections or fugitive slaves. Black Civil War soldiers were relegated to a literal
footnote about the Fifty-Fourth Massachusetts Regiment.[28] Brown, the white
radical abolitionist, was "reckless" and an "enthusiast" who wanted to "compel
the immediate abolition of slavery." Despite Brown's call for the slaves to rise
up and join him, however, *"The negroes did not rise; and instead there was a
rising of the whites."*[29] The desire for black emancipation was wholly defined
and articulated through the frame of misguided white paternalism. Black
Americans had no desire for emancipation. They played no role in the abolition of slavery. Stephenson introduced the Ku Klux Klan as a "secret society"
formed by southern whites to protect themselves against their "despots," or
political tyrants in the South after the Civil War. Stephenson observed that
some southern whites employed violent tactics as they became more desperate
to carve out political power for themselves during Reconstruction. However,
many of the violent acts reported in the North as acts by the Klan were in
fact done by "crafty imitators" of the Klan, that is to say, by people who were
not actual Klan members.[30] Elson's balancing act of the pen rhetorically neu-
tralizes the historical record of the excessive violence that defined the Klan's
terrorism of blacks during and after Reconstruction.

Tessie McGee's fugitive instructional practice was a refusal of the narrative condemnation of black life facilitated by Louisiana's official curriculum.
At the heart of her pedagogy was an insistence that there was a different way
of knowing the world. The approved school texts defined McGee and her students as outside of human history or, at best, a regressive form of humanity
that only had historical value in relationship to white dominance. The heritage that gave meaning and form to black teaching placed intellectual demands on McGee; and they were manifested by the textbook buried in her

lap. The writing of the textbook by Woodson *and* McGee's covert use of it represented the heritage of fugitive pedagogy.

Adopted textbooks varied by states, but the white supremacist ideas shaping them were shared across regional, state, and school lines. In 1931 Woodson publicly indicted the American Curriculum, which continued to "underrate the Negro." At least five consistent and egregious assessments about black life and history regularly appeared in official school curricula:

1. That Negro music and other contributions to culture in America were copied from the white man for the Negro has no background worthwhile and is mentally inferior to other races.
2. That slavery was a benevolent institution: the masters were not guilty of concubinage with their Negro women; slaves were not hard worked or cruelly beaten; children were not sold from their parents; and wives were not separated by the traffic.
3. That the Negroes were freed by interference of meddlers, for as slaves they were satisfied and in freedom have had difficulty in doing for themselves what their kind masters did for them.
4. That the abolitionists like Garrison and Phillips were emotional falsifiers; John Brown was an insane horse thief; and Lincoln, Sumner, and Stevens were sorry politicians.
5. That the Negroes ruined the South during Reconstruction and because they failed ingloriously, it is inadvisable to extend them the rights of suffrage and office-holding, and they should be segregated for the preservation of civilization.[31]

The historian Lawrence Reddick drew similar conclusions in his 1934 study, "Racial Attitudes in American History Textbooks of the South," published in the *Journal of Negro History*.[32] Having long observed this, black teachers worked to construct a new worldview and, therefore, a new system of knowledge.

Black Teachers' Textbooks as a Vindicationist Project

Woodson was a veteran educator when he published *The Negro in Our History* in 1922, though he was no longer in the classroom. But he was not the first black schoolteacher to publish a textbook.[33] Edward A. Johnson's *A School History of the Negro Race in America: From 1619–1890 with a Short Introduction as to the Origin of the Race* (1890) is likely the first of this kind—a textbook written by a black American schoolteacher with the explicit intention of transforming the classroom experience of black students.[34] Leila Amos Pendleton, a public school teacher in Washington, DC, also modeled this pedagogical tradition with the publication of her textbook, *A Narrative of the Negro* (1912).[35] Johnson's and Pendleton's texts were targeted toward a primary school audience; and while Woodson's textbook was written for a high school or college age audience, it was widely used by teachers across grade levels (even if only as a reference textbook) until his *Negro Makers of History* was published in 1928. Woodson published *Negro Makers of History* for a wider range of student readers, from junior high through early high school years. This chapter only engages Woodson's first textbook; however, he wrote seven in total. These textbooks were adapted to the needs of students at various grade levels and covered both black American and African diasporic history. Woodson was by far the most prolific educator in this tradition.[36]

Taken together these textbooks represent a distinct intellectual tradition within the larger realm of black educational criticism. In particular, they reflect the pervasiveness of *race vindicationism* within the educational life world of black people and how this ideology motivated teachers to rethink learning content. While not interchangeable with fugitive pedagogy, race vindicationism formed a critical part of how it manifested in the curricular imaginations of black educators. Black American intellectual history makes clear that vindicating the race through counterreadings of knowledge and representation became enshrined as an intellectual tradition in the first half of the nineteenth century.[37] Vindicationism was a militant rhetorical practice. Scholars challenged dominant white sociological and historical story lines that portrayed blacks as irrational, subhuman, and outside of history by writing texts with unorthodox portrayals of black men and women in the United States and the African Diaspora. "It was an effort to reclaim the honor of Black humanity through an intraracial dialogue on Black achievement," thus distinguishing itself from moral suasion, which had a more immediate focus on convincing whites of black people's respectability.[38] Writing through a vindicationist lens, black educators were *descriptive* of black life and history from their perspective as an oppressed people. Their textbooks were explicitly *corrective* of narratives that distorted black humanity through either erasure or misrepresentation. And all of these works had a *prescriptive* element. These schoolteachers sought to mobilize historical achievements of Afro-diasporic peoples in service of and as models for larger political goals of racial advancement.[39]

Edward A. Johnson (1860–1944)

Edward A. Johnson has largely been remembered for his long career as a lawyer and politician in New York, where he died in 1944. However, prior to this he was an educator. Johnson was born enslaved in Raleigh, North Carolina, on November 23, 1860. A free black woman provided his early education, and he eventually attended Washington High School in Raleigh before heading to Atlanta University. It was in Atlanta that he began his career as an educator and eventually became the principal at Mitchell Street School in 1883. After returning to his native city in 1885, Johnson became the principal of the Washington High School and published his textbook. Johnson's background as an educator of black students motivated him to write *A School History of the Negro Race in America* in 1890. Many black schools in North Carolina and Virginia used his textbook. Woodson himself recognized the significance of Johnson's textbook, observing that, "although brief and elementary, this book had a wide circulation and did much good in inculcating an appreciation of the Negro."[40]

A *School History* is written in narrative form, and its thirty-five chapters cover topics related to "the origins" of the race, the establishment of slavery in the New World, black resistance to racialized oppression, black participation in the various wars, and their strides toward political, social, and economic justice. Many of the themes explored in the text are largely supported by biographical information on historical figures. Johnson wrote *A School History* for "the many thousand colored teachers in our country." Based on his experience as a teacher, Johnson was sympathetic to the fact that black educators and students only had access to white curricula, which distorted black life and achievement. He indicted the curricular structure of the American School. He framed the book through his personal experience: "During my experience of eleven years as a teacher, I have often felt that the children of the race ought to study some work that would give them a little information on the many brave deeds and noble characters of their own race." Johnson continued, "I have often observed the sin of omission and commission on the part of white authors, most of whom seem to have written exclusively for white children, and studiously left out the many creditable deeds of the Negro. . . . It must, indeed, be a stimulus to any people to be able to refer to their ancestors as distinguished in deeds of valor, and peculiarly so to the colored people." Johnson critiqued the American Curriculum and offered his textbook to vindicate the history and achievements of black people, that the youth might see "their ancestors," and by extension themselves, "as distinguished in deeds of valor."[41]

Leila Amos Pendleton (1860–1938)

Leila Amos Pendleton was born and educated in Washington, DC, where she also worked as a public school teacher. Pendleton's work extended beyond the classroom, and she was by all means a race woman.[42] She served in numerous positions in women's social and civic organizations, as the founder of the Alpha Charity Club of Anacostia and the Social Purity Club of Washington, DC. In 1912 the publishing house of Robert Lewis Pendleton, whom she married in 1893, published her textbook, A Narrative of the Negro.[43] Pendleton and Woodson were acquainted with one another, both having been teachers in DC's public schools. In 1916 Pendleton wrote to Woodson after the first issue of the Journal of Negro History, expressing her "supreme satisfaction" with both the journal and the ASNLH. In this same letter she enclosed a check, becoming one of the earliest life members of Woodson's Association.[44]

Pendleton's 217-page textbook spans black history from ancient African civilizations through the period of enslavement in the United States and then the early twentieth century. She even explores international black experiences by interrogating colonialism in Africa. A Narrative of the Negro regularly appeared on the recommended reading list in The Crisis magazine over the span of ten years.[45] Pendleton also contributed short stories and poems to The Crisis. One in particular was a poem detesting the lynching of black men and honoring the memory of those who were killed at the hands of white mob violence.[46] Similar to Johnson, Pendleton made her political sentiments explicit in the framing of her textbook. In the first chapter, she addressed student readers with the following appeal: "There are some of us who feel that, pitifully small though it be, we have given the very best and done the very most it is possible for us to give and to do for the race, and we are looking to you, dear children, to perform the things which we, in our youth had hoped and planned. We beg that you will not fail us."[47] Pendleton sought to inspire students through the historical narratives of black achievement and culture to fight for social transformation.

Woodson Inheriting and Expanding the Vindicationist Tradition

Woodson built on the groundwork laid by black educators who published textbooks before him. Yet his commitment to vindicationism was more discreet than Johnson and Pendleton, likely due to his formal academic training as a historian. As historian Francille Rusan Wilson has observed of early black social scientists, Woodson was part of a cadre of early twentieth-century "segregated scholars" who used their research to uplift black people socially and to challenge scientific racism. These scholars had to balance the tension between their insistence on objectivity with their lived realities as oppressed people.[48] This was a difficult task, because their investment in the work was always intellectual and deeply personal. Nonetheless, vinidicationism inevitably comes through in Woodson's tone and analysis. According to Lorenzo Greene, Woodson believed that "history was a device to make the Negro proud of his origin . . . to give his people a cultural foundation on which to stand, to stimulate them to strive for a better future and ultimately to gain for the Negro equality of citizenship." But Woodson was not just concerned with presenting the facts, observed Greene; he had to "disseminate them in such a way, both by the oral and written words, so that they might win popular acceptance." Greene once suggested to Woodson that his tone in *The Negro in Our History* came across as that of a preacher. Responding to Greene's critique, Woodson simply replied, "My aim is to get my message across to the people."[49]

Alain Locke, the aesthete and philosopher known as the dean of the Harlem Renaissance, expressed great appreciation for Woodson's textbook in 1928, after its fourth edition was released. He also explained what he saw as clear distinctions between Woodson's textbook and those that came before it. "Before the publication of this book," assessed Locke, "all of the attempts to offset the biased attitudes and correct the omissions of school history with regard to the Negro had been either unauthoritative or too polemical to be soundly instructive." Woodson's textbook was so exhaustively researched he could just let the facts speak for themselves, Locke expressed. *The Negro in Our History* was more "authoritative" than the previous works and thus laid the foundation for more "interpretive" work in the future. Locke saw Woodson's textbook as transformative scholarship—it belonged "to that select class of books that have brought about a revolution of mind."[50]

While the earlier texts by Johnson and Pendleton are transparent in their political intentions, Woodson makes an obvious attempt to remain "objective" (though this is relative, because for many white readers Woodson's text was extremely incendiary). Furthermore, the content in his book is much more expansive and rigorously researched. This is a result of Woodson's academic training and access to a wider availability of scholarship on African history and sources. Another distinction in Woodson's textbook, when compared to those that precede it, is that he had a much more nuanced understanding of race and class, which complicated essentialist interpretations of black experiences, even as he asserted that there were commonalities between black people in the diaspora.

Themes in Black Teachers' Textbooks

Race vindicationism manifested in multiple forms across these three textbooks, but the following recurrent themes were particularly pronounced: explicit engagement with the master narrative, self-determination, diasporic citations, resilience, black rationality, resistance, and African Americans' entitlement to US citizenship. While these themes can be analyzed separately, it is important to note that they were often presented in relationship to one another. For example, there were many instances where passages engaged both self-determination and resistance or citizenship and black rationality. Through the historical narratives in these textbooks, which covered the aforementioned themes and more, Johnson, Pendleton, and Woodson engaged in a rhetorical practice of describing the conditions of black life from their marginalized positionality. They were also correcting distortions that proliferated in dominant curricula and prescribing models of black being that students could look to as they collectively worked toward the shared goals of black freedom. As such, the art of black teaching included the work of rewriting the epistemological order.

A Corrective Project: Explicit Critiques of the Master Narrative. Black educational thinkers had an established history of resisting the dominant narratives of mainstream education.[51] These educators made clear their intent to correct distorted notions of black life that circulated as fact. They were critical spectators of hegemonic historical narratives—*looking back* at misrepresentations shaped by the white gaze—while developing a shadow curriculum from the margins of the American School.

The master narrative was named in explicit terms across these texts, and particularly as it related to discussions of the African continent. Pendleton observed that Africa was often excluded from the history of the world. "Yet we learn from their story how important a part Africa played in the ancient times," she wrote, after discussing the history of a number of ancient African civilizations (e.g., Egypt and Ethiopia).[52] Taking a similar vindicationist approach, Johnson challenged the idea that the black past was only a history of barbarism. He asserted, "The native African had then, and he has now, much respect for what we call law and justice. This fact is substantiated by the numerous large tribes existing, individuals of which grow to be very old, a thing that could not happen were there the wholesale brutalism which we are sometimes told exists."[53] Johnson's references to narratives that "we are sometimes told" was surely referencing the controlling narratives of Africa as "the heart of darkness," which proliferated in Eurocentric epistemology.[54]

A similar disposition manifested in Woodson's writing toward the master narrative in his firm revisionist perspective on the period of Reconstruction. The portrayal of black Americans during the period of Reconstruction in the South was a major source of controversy in American history as evidenced by the contrasting portrayals between the 1915 film *The Birth of a Nation* and Du Bois's *Black Reconstruction* (1935), as well as the backhanded reference to black politicians as "despots" in the textbook Tessie McGee was expected to teach from in Louisiana.[55] Consistent with the popular American narrative that Reconstruction was a failure as a result of poorly qualified black politicians, mainstream textbooks (especially those in the South) vilified blacks as incapable of leadership. Harold O. Rugg, who was considered to be a progressive white historian, published a textbook in 1931, entitled *A History of American Government and Culture*, where he commented that emancipated blacks were like "bewildered children" as they attempted to engage in politics—thus mocking their status as citizens as well as their intellectual capabilities.[56] He further uses a narrative of poorly qualified black politicians as a means of balancing the story of the Ku Klux Klan: "The force used by the Klan was sometimes brutal and wrong, but so were the things the carpetbaggers were doing. *The latter were often corrupt, and their Negro tools were, with a few exceptions, illiterate and incapable of governing.*" He continued, "Thus the white planters, deprived of other means of protection, attempted through secret organization to 'fight fire with fire.'"[57]

Explicitly engaging these racist narratives about black leadership, Woodson argued, "The charge that all Negro officers were illiterates, ignorant of the science of government, cannot be sustained. Some of them had undergone considerable training and had experienced sufficient mental development to be able to discharge their duties with honor." Woodson explained that these claims of black intellectual inferiority were a smoke screen. "Whether or not the Negro was capable, whether he was honest, however, had little to do with the southern white man's attitude toward the Negro office holders.... *The Negro was unacceptable merely because he was black,* because he had not enjoyed the distinction of wringing his bread from the sweat of another's brow."[58]

Black textbooks challenged flattened narratives about black life in the American Curriculum. Narratives that painted black life as simplistic and uncultured supported a larger notion of black subhumanness. Johnson, Pendleton, and Woodson employed biography, historical narratives, illustrations, and, occasionally, statistical data to vindicate the black race as important contributors to a larger legacy of human civilization and as a people with a dynamic history. Woodson charged that "few people" realized "the extent to which the free Negro figured in the population of this country prior to the Civil War."[59] He included a chart documenting the number of free blacks during the antebellum years. "These free Negroes," Woodson continued, "were not all on the same plane.... There were freedmen in possession of a considerable amount of property, others who formed a lower class of mechanics and artisans, and finally those living with difficulty above pecuniary embarrassment."[60] Like all people and all cultures, black life was dynamic and defied narrow story lines. Well aware of the exclusion or flattened portrayals of black life in the dominant narrative, these educators responded with corrective histories that offered more expansive forms of representation.

"Proof of the Negro's Ability to Govern Himself": Self-Determination. The theme of *self-determination* emerged across the textbooks as an expression of race vindicationism. Couched in this theme was black teachers' refusal of historical narratives that portrayed black people as unable to govern their own lives. The historian V. P. Franklin argued that black self-determination has been a cultural value within black Americans' core racial consciousness, one that held a dialectical relationship to white supremacy. Ultimately, self-determination translated to "black control over black life," and black people have pursued this ideal through strategic forms of resistance, of which education was a central part.[61] Textbooks published by black schoolteachers presented many examples of black people exerting self-determination.

In *A School History,* Johnson offered students the narrative of Bount's Fort as a heroic example of black people's desire to control their lives. He described how "Negro refugees from Georgia fled into the everglades of Florida as a hiding-place during the war of the Revolution. In these swamps they remained for forty years successfully baffling all attempts to re-enslave them." Describing the legacy of this fugitive spirit, Johnson wrote, "Many of those who planned the escape at first were now dead, and their children had grown up to hate the lash and love liberty."[62] Bount's Fort presented a historical case of black people refusing to accept their structural position as slaves within the American social order. By fleeing to the everglades, these men and women sought to exert autonomy over their lives. Echoing Franklin's contention that self-determination was a cultural value at the core of black racial consciousness, Johnson emphasized that these former slaves taught their children "that to die in the swamps with liberty was better than to feast as a bondman and a slave."[63]

The history of black maroonage was widely represented in Woodson's and Pendleton's textbooks. Woodson, for instance, depicted Palmares in Brazil as a vivid illustration of self-determination in African diasporic history, despite ongoing attempts to suppress it. "The greatest enterprise of the

Maroons," Woodson explained, was "the little Negro Republic in Brazil, called Palmares." "Because of the bad treatment of the Portuguese slaves, many of those imported from Guinea escaped to the forests, where they established villages called quilombos. . . . At one time it was reported to have a population of twenty thousand, with ten thousand fighting men." Woodson then explained the ongoing threats and sophisticated governing structure of this maroon society. "Palmares, the name also of the capital of the republic, was surrounded by wooden walls made of the tree trunks and entered by huge gates provided with facilities for wide surveillance. . . . Palmares developed into a sort of nation, uniting the desirable features of the republican and monarchial form of government, presided over by a chief executive called the Zombe, who ruled with absolute authority during his life."[64] While Woodson's textbooks were meant to inspire students living during Jim Crow segregation and disenfranchisement, he offered transnational historical narratives as inspiration for imagining new models of black being and sociality. Embedded in this descriptive story of grand maroonage is the prescriptive theme of black self-determination.

In *A Narrative of the Negro*, Leila Pendleton presented Mound Bayou in Mississippi as evidence of black people's ability to be self-determined and capable of developing communities with sophisticated economic and social organization. She used this example to indict the master narrative that portrayed black people as ill equipped for leadership. "In 1888 a handful of colored people under the leadership of Mr. Isaiah T. Montgomery, settled in the Yazoo Delta, Mississippi, and beginning to clear and cultivate the ground, started what has become known as the town of Mound Bayou." Pendleton continued, "A Negro town, in the heart of the South, where the mayor, the council, and all the citizens are colored. *Mound Bayou and similar settlements offer proof of the Negro's ability to govern himself.*"[65] White supremacist ideology deemed black people to be a race outside of rational thinking and moral grounding. Black people were, therefore, in need of direction and rule by a more capable class of people. This oppressive ideology of white paternalism formed the subtext to which Pendleton was responding. Based on the American Curriculum, the white race built the greatest civilizations, possessed superior moral and intellectual fiber, and were entitled, obligated even, to rule over the Negro race. Refusing this pervasive ideology, Johnson, Pendleton, and Woodson offered historical treatments of black people's ability to be self-determined. Their sketches both filled in historical absences and dismissed stereotypical representations that suggested black people were unfit to govern their lives and incapable of prudent leadership.

Diasporic Citations. Johnson, Pendleton, and Woodson were all teachers in US public schools and working to educate black American youth, yet the narratives they constructed to vindicate the race were transnational in scope. They presented diasporic citations of black life and achievements to inspire and construct new possibilities for student identities. This framing of black historical discourse, beyond the nation-state, had the potential to forge an "outernational imaginary"—a process that opened up the possibility for students to see the historical achievements and oppression of black people in the African Diaspora as interrelated and, more than this, as a shared foundation for inspiration and study.[66] Distorted narratives of black American deviance and inferiority were always already linked to global narratives of antiblackness. Therefore, black teachers' resistance to the American School had long been informed by a diasporic consciousness.[67] That all of these textbooks open with narratives about Africa and that these schoolteachers engage historical narratives from the Caribbean and South America are evidence of this.

Diasporic citations offered students a more expansive curricular imagination that transcended the boundaries of their immediate Jim Crow realities. This required a new historical inventory. The Brazilian maroon society of Palmares was one of many examples of black achievement taken up. While "educational diasporic practice" is evident in all three of these educators' textbooks, Woodson significantly expanded on this tradition in the textbooks he published after *The Negro in Our History*. In 1928 he released an additional illustrated textbook for elementary school students, entitled *African Myths and Proverbs*. Woodson professed that black people had a rich culture prior to enslavement and that it was critical for black American children to understand this as part of their heritage. This textbook was advertised as "a collection of interesting African Folk Tales adapted to the capacity of children of the second and third grades."[68] The objective of this book was consistent with Woodson's efforts to challenge the narrative that blacks were a people without culture. During this time Woodson also supported the work of such scholars as Lorenzo Turner, Zora Neale Hurston, and Melville Herskovitz, who contended that enslaved blacks and their descendants retained aspects of African cultures in the Americas.[69]

Woodson further reinforced his position on black culture and diasporic identity in a chapter entitled "Negro Art Appreciated," in *Negro Makers of History,* also published in 1928. "The customary fashion of looking upon the Negro as an inferior and treating him as a sort of *half-human animal,*" Woodson argued, "has prevented the public from understanding his possibilities and achievement." Enslaved Africans were forced to suppress "the promptings of their own native religious instinct and [cease] to give free exercise to their imagination." He went on to caution readers that "all that the Negro accomplished in Africa was not lost." African retentions had informed black American culture. "It tended to revive in the slave on the American plantation. It appeared in the tales, proverbs, and riddles of the plantation Negroes. The tribal chants of Africa paved the way for the spirituals, the religious expression of the slave."[70]

In *Negro Makers of History* and *African Myths and Proverbs,* Woodson offered West African folklore as a sophisticated cultural legacy that can be traced through the development of black culture in the West.[71] Picking up from this line of thinking, he later wrote *The African Background Outlined: or Handbook for the Study of the Negro* (1936) and *African Heroes and Heroines* (1939). In that distorted notions about black life in the United States were always routed through, and in relationship with, narrative condemnation of Africa and the African Diaspora, black educators assembled diasporic citations as an integral part of vindicating the race. This diasporic impulse featured prominently in their curricular imaginations.

Resilience as a Descriptive Characteristic of Black Life. Refusing a deficit narrative of blackness, these schoolteachers constructed narratives of resilience and protracted struggle. Black people persevered despite subjugation. Black teachers' textbooks presented extraordinary examples of black people accomplishing things and overcoming challenges that seemed insurmountable. By showcasing the resilience of black people globally, these teachers assured students of what they could achieve despite the odds set against them in their Jim Crow realities. They disrupted the single story of black failure represented in the official curricula, a script that presented

Woodson's *African Heroes and Heroines* (Washington, DC: Associated Publishers, 1939); dust jacket created by Lois Mailou Jones, artist and professor at Howard University. Used with the permission of the Association for the Study of African American Life and History, www.asalh.org.

Africa as outside of history and black Americans as perpetually failing and unworthy of mention, of no human concern.

According to Johnson, while the Negro was stolen from his home of origin and forced into "strait circumstances as slaves in America," they refused these violent conditions and continued to dream and struggle for a new reality. "Every sort of hindrance has been thrown in his way, but he is overcoming them all." Speaking specifically to the Jim Crow laws and black codes of the late nineteenth century, Johnson wrote, "By the rigid laws of custom, he has continuously lost golden opportunities to forge his fortune; yet he has prospered in spite of this, and it bespeaks for him a superior manhood." Johnson constructed a narrative of black people's insistence on social life despite the perpetual threat of social death; resilience and strong will were described as characteristic of their race.[72]

Pendleton's portrayal of the Haitian Revolution and Woodson's discussion of enslaved men and women learning to read and write in secrecy further echoes this theme of resilience. Writing of Haiti, Pendleton explained, "On this island Europeans built the first city and erected the first Christian church in the New World; here Negro slaves struck the first blow for freedom and here was founded the first Negro Republic."[73] The repetition of "the first" in this passage helps to characterize the story of Haiti as a heroic tale. In presenting Haiti as the first successful slave insurrection, on the land where European contact with the New World was first established, Pendleton positioned this story as a challenge to notions of white European supremacy.

The story line of slaves rebelling and establishing their own republic offered a vindicating narrative, but Pendleton's presentation of this historical event also emphasizes its extraordinary nature. A 1912 review of Pendleton's textbook, by the DC teacher Jessie Fauset in *The Crisis* magazine, points to the author's portrayal of black resilience. Fauset observed, "When one thinks of the fearful odds in slavery times against the black man who dared to try to lift his head, and then remembers that these people dared—there is nothing finer in all history. And these people are ours, not the borrowed types of a hostile race whose members hold us persistently aloof."[74]

Consistent with Johnson and Pendleton, Woodson presented the narrative of black resilience through the stories of men and women learning to read and write despite major barriers set against them. In a section of his textbook titled "Stealing Learning," Woodson wrote, "How some of these slaves learned in spite of opposition makes a beautiful story. Knowing the value of learning as a means of escape and having longing for it, too, because it was forbidden, many slaves continued their education under adverse circumstances."[75] While black life was lived under white domination, black people always insisted on a way of being in the world that was set on escaping the terms of their subjection. Collectively, these teachers demonstrated a commitment to supplanting the dominant narrative of black failure with one that described extreme oppression matched by a dogged struggle to construct new realities of black life. Their stories were corrective of deficit narratives, supplanting these ideas with descriptions of resilience and ongoing struggle—grand accomplishments achieved in spite of. In doing so, students were offered these learning resources as models for black aspiration and ways of being in the world that defied its existing arrangements.

A "Living, Breathing, Convincing Argument" of Black Reason. The problem of black reason, or the constructed idea of black irrationality, has been intimately tied to the maintenance of white supremacy.[76] Furthermore, the eugenics movement in the United States starting in the 1880s, which was deeply embedded in the Progressive Era, gained notable traction during the years these educators published their textbooks. Scholars have documented how antiblack ideas emanating from the pseudoscientific research of this era directly influenced white educational leaders, particularly those that developed curricula.[77] It should come as no surprise that Johnson, Pendleton, and Woodson offered examples of black intellectual achievement as a corrective to widespread assertions that they were intellectually inferior.

Biographies of notable figures were presented as evidence of black intellectual achievement. The narratives of Phillis Wheatley and Benjamin Banneker were iconic examples used across all three texts. To underscore black Americans' intelligence and contributions to this country in one year alone, Pendleton explained, "In 1770, the year in which Phillis Wheatley's poems were first published and Benjamin Banneker was making his clock, the Negro race gave to the cause of American freedom the first martyr—Crispus Attucks."[78] Johnson reflected on Frederick Douglass, another historical figure used across the texts, as "a conspicuous representative of the talents and capabilities possessed by the colored race."[79] In this way, they offered the biographies and extraordinary achievements of black Americans, such as Douglass, Banneker, Wheatley, as *a living, breathing, convincing argument* against the claim that the Negro's intellectual capacities fit him only for slavery."[80]

Beyond biography, Woodson also offered scientific inventions and the cultural productions of the race as vindicating evidence of their intellectual abilities and capacity for sound reason. This is surely the case with his treatment of African proverbs in a chapter entitled "The Negro in Africa." Woodson observed that "In *art and architecture* they had advanced far beyond the primitive stage, *in literature* their achievements attained the rank of the world's best classics in the *Tarik e Soudan,* and *in religion and morals* most of them kept abreast with the times. . . . The African mind exhibited during these years evidences of a philosophy not to be despised." Woodson then cites a litany of African proverbs that index universal values of human goodness: "The African realized that 'the lack of knowledge is darker than night,' that 'an ignorant man is a slave,' and that . . . the African taught the youth that 'there is no medicine for hate' and that 'he who bears malice is a heathen; he who injures another brings injury to himself.'" These proverbs, Woodson insisted, "exhibit more than ordinary mental development."[81] Once again relying on diasporic citations to serve as a corrective of the perceived deficiencies of black people, Woodson offered his student-readers an opportunity to explore a historical narrative of intellectual achievements that simultaneously challenged the myth of Africa as the heart of darkness and the absence of human spirit.

Black Resistance as Ongoing versus Sporadic. The portrayal of slavery in US textbooks rested on imagery of black people as happy slaves who were better off working for their white masters because they came from a savage homeland.[82] After analyzing depictions of black people during slavery in textbooks adopted by southern schools, Lawrence Reddick concluded in 1934 that "the picture of slavery which the average pupil in these sixteen States receives approximates that of docile Negroes with strong backs imported from Africa. . . . The life of the slave was simple and coarse but was not hard, for the Negroes were good natured and sang songs during and after their work."[83] We might recall, for instance, the casual references to enslaved people in the textbooks that informed the curriculum from which Tessie

McGee was expected to teach—the southern climate being "well suited to Negro Labor," the "hospitable mansion" of the plantation, "its retinue of slaves, its broad tract of surrounding land."[84]

Johnson, Pendleton, and Woodson were corrective of the narrow portrayal of black life during slavery within dominant curricula. Taking up these elisions and misrepresentations, their textbooks were descriptive of a steady legacy of black resistance. Students encountered black rebellion as a through line in their history since enslavement. This is evidenced in all of the teachers' treatments of the Haitian Revolution and by depictions of maroonage, slave insurrections, fugitive slaves, and the Underground Railroad.

When referencing black life in the early eighteenth century, Johnson and Woodson both covered the New York riot of 1712. Johnson wrote, "The Riot of 1712 shows the feeling between the master and servant at the time. The Negro population being excluded from schools, not allowed to own land, even when free, and forbidden to 'strike a Christian or a Jew' in self-defense, and their testimony excluded from the courts, arose in arms and with the torch; houses were burned, and many whites killed, before the militia suppressed them."[85] In a chapter of *The Negro in Our History* titled "Slavery in Its Mild Form," Woodson offered a section on "Early Negro Insurrections" where he documents a consistent thread of revolts by blacks throughout the eighteenth century.

They portrayed slave insurrectionists as courageous heroes who were justified in their actions. Nat Turner "devoted himself to the study of the scriptures and the condition of his people," according to Johnson. He was a hero that "struck for freedom." Even in death, Turner is displayed as an honorable man and unmoved by fear. There is even a gesture toward the supernatural to describe the fugitive slave. "The day of [his] execution, strange to say, as Nat had prophesied, was one of stormy and gloomy aspect, with terrible thunder, rain and lightning." He continued describing Turner in heroic fashion: "Nat kept up his courage to the last, and his neck in the noose, not a muscle quivered or a groan was uttered. He was, undoubtedly, a wonderful character."[86]

All of these schoolteachers discussed Turner's 1831 insurrection in Virginia extensively in their textbooks, which stood in stark contrast to the absence of this historical event in white curricula. When Turner was mentioned in mainstream textbooks, it was often in relation to the white abolitionist

William Lloyd Garrison.[87] When black resistance was acknowledged, it was understood as instigated by white abolitionists. In Turner's case, Garrison was portrayed to have "incited the desire for freedom in the minds of him and his fellow insurgents."[88] These authors also underscore how rebellions and slave resistance were organized communal efforts. Take for example Johnson's presentation of the maroon societies off the coastal plain region of Virginia: "The Dismal Swamp colony continued from generation to generation, defying and outwitting the slave-owners right in the midst of one of the strongest slave-holding communities in the South."[89]

Similar to Johnson's portrayal of Nat Turner, Pendleton represented Toussaint L'Ouverture, leader of the Haitian Revolution, in a heroic tradition— by her assessment, L'Ouverture was "a true patriot."[90] Further relying on diasporic citations, Pendleton recalled the Surinamese maroon communities in the eighteenth century who rebelled against their Dutch oppressors: "In 1773 troops were brought over from Holland but were unable to subdue the Negros, who added to their dauntless courage a perfect knowledge of the country, and finally the colonists gave up the contest." She then concluded on a note of self-determination: "The Maroons formed an independent republic with laws and customs of their own."[91] These national and diasporic narratives of resistance all gestured toward the inherent project of black freedom—a teleological ordering that was global in scope and one that had immediate relevance for students' Jim Crow realities.

Building on the tradition presented by Johnson and Pendleton, Woodson read slave insurrections in the diaspora as intertwined. Woodson argued, "Negroes endeavored to secure relief by refreshing the tree of liberty with the blood of their oppressors. The chief source of these uprisings came from refugees brought to this country from Santo Domingo in 1793 and from certain free Negroes encouraged to extend a helping hand to their enslaved brethren."[92] Thus, Woodson anticipated contemporary scholarship that has analyzed the influence of Haitian refugees on slave rebellions in the United States.

Black educators were unapologetic in their presentations of violent slave uprisings, having developed alternative frames of interpretation and analyses as compared to mainstream white scholarship.[93] This tradition of race vindicationism, what Charles Wesley referred to as a "heroic tradition," shaped the ideological terrain among black schoolteachers.

Tales of resistance were far from sparse in black curricular imaginations. These teachers represented it as a consistent thread in black life. Furthermore, resistance was not isolated to black people in one place or region. They cited examples of rebellion in the northern and southern regions of the United States, and it was represented as a diasporic phenomenon. In this way, subversion was articulated as a meaningful part of black existence, in the face of ongoing experiences of violent domination. This lesson was prescriptive. Given the violent domination of black people, their insistence on black social and political life often required fugitive acts. More than this, black teachers' curricular scripts were motivated by a shared understanding that any purposeful education likely required a strategic disruption of imposed schooling norms. In these historical narratives, it was physical resistance; in the context of black education, it meant subverting the official knowledge of schooling with the subaltern histories of black people.

Black America's Entitlement to Full Citizenship. These textbooks emerged as black people wrestled not only with the vestiges of slavery but also the immediate backlash to the Reconstruction period. The Compromise of 1877 ushered in the period in black American history known as "the Nadir," which was characterized by extreme poverty, chronic racial violence, and the plundering of recently gained citizenship rights.[94] While the Fifteenth Amendment allowed black men to engage in the political landscape of the South during the period of Reconstruction, the establishment of Black Codes and the removal of federal troops from the South overturned this progress. The political agency gained after Emancipation was lost, and black Americans engaged in a battle to reclaim it for decades to come. A determination to reclaim black suffrage was a central theme in these textbooks. These teachers shared the proclamation that black Americans had a valid claim to citizenship and were entitled to equal rights. They employed historical recounts of black patriotism, especially during wartime, as well as the contributions of black labor as the driving force of the United States' wealth to assert their entitlement to freedom and citizenship. These narratives corrected a dominant historiography, which positioned black Americans as outside the development of the nation or merely idle props in the story.

"It was the honest and faithful toil of the Negro that turned the richness of Georgia's soil into English gold," argued Johnson; it "built cities and created large estates, gilded mansions furnished with gold and silver plates."[95] Elsewhere he noted, "They were not to feed, clothe, and protect themselves in a government whose treasury they had enriched with two centuries and a half of unrequited labor, and a country whose laws they must obey but could not read."[96] In Johnson's historical treatment, black captive labor had been indispensable to American economic development. Yet their degraded form of citizenship resulted from racist legislative practices that excluded them from the American body politic. He observed the irony that blacks were expected to abide by written law, even as their would-be literacy was forbidden and criminalized.

The role of black people in the various US wars was evidence of their proven loyalty and patriotism to the United States' creed of liberty, Crispus Attucks being the first marker of this legacy. In the words of Johnson, "Though a runaway slave, [Attucks's] patriotism was so deep that he . . . sacrificed his life *first* on the altar of American Liberty."[97] Pendleton also presented Attucks as the "first martyr" of American freedom.[98]

All three of these textbooks gave extensive attention to black soldiers in the US wars, which challenged the complete omission of black American soldiers in mainstream US textbooks. Lawrence Reddick's 1930s analysis of textbooks concluded that students "will find no references to American Negroes as soldiers or sailors; if he reads the actual accounts of the wars and battles as presented, he will be extremely fortunate if his search should be rewarded with one sentence."[99]

One sentence was, in fact, the case for the textbook Tessie McGee was expected to teach from. And that one sentence was relegated to a footnote. Critiquing and correcting the popular omission of black soldiers, Johnson, Pendleton, and Woodson's textbooks are replete with images and profiles of notable black soldiers and the stories of major battles in which black Americans played central roles. Pendleton assessed, "Nearly two hundred thousand Negro soldiers, including a number of officers, fought during the Civil War; they took part in scores of battles and always distinguished themselves for bravery." She goes on to present a "resume of the American Negro as a warrior," where she begins with Attucks and lists major accounts of black soldiers from the American Revolution throughout the Civil War.[100]

Woodson was consistent with his predecessors on the topic of black America's entitlement to equal citizenship. The rebuttals by free blacks to the

American Colonization Society and other attempts to have them immigrate to colonies outside of the United States, such as Liberia or Haiti, was evidence of black patriotism and the story of the long black struggle for equal citizenship. "They claimed this country as their native land because their ancestors were the first successful cultivators of its soil," explained Woodson. "They felt themselves entitled to participation in the blessing of the soil which their blood and sweat had moistened. Moreover, they were determined never to separate themselves from the slave population of this country as they were brothers by ties of consanguinity, of suffering and of wrongs."[101]

Historical narratives about black labor and patriotic sacrifice on the part of black soldiers were used to challenge the restrictions on black Americans' (particularly black men's) ability to exercise their rights, as guaranteed by the Fifteenth Amendment. Johnson spelled out this perspective with unrelenting clarity, writing: "Let us now study some of the efforts of the Negroes in helping to achieve this citizenship [acquired after the Civil War], after which we shall see how well they deserved to be citizens."[102]

Black educators imparted to students that their citizenship and entitlement to complete freedom was bought and paid for by those who came before them. In the context of Jim Crow, where black disenfranchisement was a rule and not the exception, these narratives provided an incisive social analysis for black students to take up and analyze their political realities. These lessons gave students the language and the historical context to refuse the myths shaping the world around them.

Conclusion

Vindicating the race constituted a central element of fugitive pedagogy, comprising literary efforts that countered antiblack distortions and erasure in official knowledge. This intellectual practice maintained important distinctions from the politics of respectability, while closely related to it. Evelyn Brooks Higginbotham theorized "the politics of respectability" to describe the social politics of working-class black women in the National Baptist Convention and their use of conventional standards of womanhood to represent the race as deserving of respect and equal treatment.[103] Black women employed the politics of respectability as a strategy for social reform, but it also extended to the larger racial group. By behaving and comporting themselves along socially established lines of respectability and virtue, black people could prove to the white world that the race had integrity and deserved equal treatment. Embedded in this discourse, to be clear, was also a critique of the white world, an assertion that respectable black women were morally superior to those who oppressed them. While this challenged scientific notions of racial difference and black inferiority, it at times took the form of social mechanisms that reproduced intraracial class politics.[104]

Race vindicationism, as represented by these textbooks, spoke to fundamental assertions about black humanity and dealt less with ideas of racial propriety. Socializing black students to develop racial pride and a critical historical consciousness of their racialized experiences was the central objective. While the politics of respectability served as "bridge discourse" to the external white world, race vindicationism, as it manifested in these textbooks, was an intraracial process, even as both challenged distorted representations of black people. Race vindicationism took stock of black people's history and culture for their own understandings. It pursued a way of knowing the world that accounted for the beauty and terror of black people's lives, a subjugated people bearing submerged knowledge.

Fugitive pedagogy demanded thinking and imagining beyond Western canons of knowledge, thus leading black Americans to develop an *under*canon that shadowed and critiqued the master narrative. There was a political clarity to black teachers' textbooks; critical analyses of antiblackness and curricular distortions were made transparent and were deeply embedded in their curricular content. What's more, the black textbook was itself a literary genre inaugurated by runaway slaves. As represented by Johnson, Pendleton, and Woodson, black curricular imaginations of the post-Emancipation era were informed by a fugitive literary culture with antebellum roots.

5

Fugitive Pedagogy as a Professional Standard: Woodson's "Abroad Mentorship" of Black Teachers

It is certain that boards of education generally cannot be relied upon to furnish satisfactory educational programs for the Negro.

—ALBERT N. D. BROOKS, educator in DC public schools (1945)

The development of black education is embedded in a long history of fugitive planning. For African American teachers, educating black students was about more than developing ordinary academic skill sets. It was fundamentally about challenging and transcending antiblack sentiments that structured the known world. While excelling in various content areas might have been the starting place for some teachers, a primary learning objective for black schoolteachers as a professional class was to help students understand the urgent demand to make the world anew. This distinction must be appreciated when considering the art of black teaching. This was their starting place; this political clarity was a shared understanding and the foundation of their work.

Tracing the collaboration between Woodson and black teachers reveals that fugitive pedagogy was a professional standard among this class of educators. At times they did this secretly. On other occasions they did it through collective strategies organized through black teachers' associations. In this way, Woodson's curricular interventions breathed new life into the fugitive pedagogy of black teachers, particularly during the 1920s through 1940s.

Woodson as an Abroad Mentor

While Woodson never met most black teachers, he surely influenced them through the ASNLH, and especially Negro History Week and the *Negro History Bulletin*. Through these overlapping channels, Woodson developed an intimate relationship with educators across the country by providing curricular alternatives that invited new pedagogical practices for teaching black students to assume their role within a larger plot for black freedom. These alternative pathways were a means to circumvent the stronghold that dominant white educational theories and reform leaders had on traditional pathways of black schooling and teacher training. Through speeches rendered at black teachers' meetings, course offerings through teacher training summer schools, and publications by the ASNLH, Woodson provided educators with timely supplemental training and resources. These interventions transformed the way many black teachers approached their work and created an invigorated learning experience for black students, despite their Jim Crow realities.

Woodson was an *abroad mentor* for black teachers as a professional group. I offer this term as a riff on the memory of "abroad marriages" among enslaved people. These marriages comprised a husband that was owned by one master and a wife and children who were owned by another—they lived on different plantations. Abroad marriages were a common practice during slavery, accounting for approximately 27.5 percent of unions by enslaved people in the antebellum South; yet they were increasingly policed as slave owners worked to minimize outside influences on the temperament of their "property," particularly amid the threat of revolt.[1] Distance engendered a determination to create unique ways to maintain contact and offer love and support. Abroad mentorship underscores geographic and institutional distance, while at the same time acknowledging the closeness of the relationship between Woodson and black educators. The historian Vanessa Siddle Walker has noted that elite black scholars were connected to communities "through their influence on beliefs and practices in local communities rather than their presence." Like many black intellectuals, Woodson used every platform and medium to communicate his vision (e.g., the black press and African American community institutions). The power of black scholars' ideas carried weight across distance in shaping the minds of black people concerned with matters of the race. One West Virginia State student writing to Woodson in the 1930s echoes this point in the opening of his letter: "You do not know me," wrote the student, "but I have met you many times through your books."[2]

Abroad mentorship is also informed by the sociohistorical context of black social strategies for collective uplift and the "politics of racial destiny."[3] Given the infringement of racial domination on black life, unique social and ecological dynamics formed within black communities that shaped the organizational structure and function of black institutions (e.g., family, churches, and social and fraternal organizations) as well as African American identity politics. For instance, fictive kinship in slavery and in freedom is but one example of how black people adapted to meet their immediate social and material needs.[4]

Through their personal and professional networks, black teachers crafted what they believed to be the appropriate methods to meet the needs of their students. They not only borrowed from their professional training in normal schools and colleges, which privileged white educational theories and visions, but these teachers also looked to black intellectuals for critical perspectives as they worked out their own pedagogical vision. They blended the "best practices from schools of education and the best thinking of the black intellectual elite on issues related to black advancement."[5] The ideas of black intellectuals traveled through the social infrastructure of black communities and interacted with and "helped craft an educational agenda for black schools that was designed to lift a people up into full democratic citizenship."[6] These institutional networks were a critical part of fugitive pedagogy, a complex system of communication exchange that challenged traditional pathways of knowledge circulation.

Woodson's abroad mentorship of black teachers—their partnership—was forged at the margins of the American School, outside of its intended web of relations. These unconventional arrangements were a manifestation of fugitive pedagogy in that we see black educators stretching themselves to work around and against the imposed protocols of the American School. Building from this historical social arrangement—and relations of power under white domination—abroad mentorship characterizes how black intellectuals (like Woodson) engaged teachers through pathways beyond educational spheres controlled by white officials and philanthropists. They offered guidance that infused teachers' pedagogy with politics and ideas emanating from the black counterpublic sphere. As an abroad mentor, Woodson translated his educational vision to others equally committed to racial progress but who may have lacked a critical awareness of how white supremacy functioned through curricula or who otherwise had no educational resources to counter it. Woodson remotely mentored black teachers as a professional class through educational institutions he built and by strategically partnering with black teacher associations.

In tracing these institutional and personal ties, we find that educators' efforts to resist antiblack antagonisms within the American School were not isolated events but were instead an organized ideological struggle against the cultural politics of white supremacy that functioned through the curricula and protocols of the larger structure. They came to understand how oppression operated in both blatant and insidious ways through curriculum—there were sometimes blatant misrepresentations of black life and other times absences that were both studious and ornate. This all worked toward the same end: the condemnation of black life.

Black Teachers and the Building of Their Professional World (c. 1861–1920s)

Black teachers resisted efforts to manipulate or stifle their development and took on an active role in shaping their professional realities. They created opportunities for their professional growth early on. The Ohio Colored Teachers' Association convened their first annual meeting in December 1861, where they noted that for at least ten years prior "colored teachers have been actively engaging in preparing themselves for the responsible duties of the schoolroom." From the beginning they were gravely aware that provisions for black schools were far less than white schools and black educators were "teaching for less wages than laborers are employed for." But these circumstances, the educators explained, were "attributable in part to matters beyond our control." Despite these conditions, black educators gathered and expressed their commitment to one another and their race: "We are willing to live upon the fare of the humblest," they explained, "if by so doing we can accomplish the object of our desire, namely, the education and elevation of our race."[7] Of no direct relationship to the Ohio gathering, though certainly resonant in spirit, another beginning commenced in the professional story of black teachers the following year. A former slave by the name of Clement Robinson founded Beulah Normal and Theological School in Virginia in 1862, making it the first black normal school in the southern region.[8] In short, black people developed social strategies to cope with the racial hostility experienced under white supremacist domination—education and the development of their own teachers emerged as a central part of black spiritual striving.

As Michele Mitchell writes, "It was with emancipation that freed people faced formidable pressures to make a way for themselves, and it was with emancipation that race activists devised an array of strategies built around and upon notions of collective destiny."[9] Black Americans continuously exercised their ability to form nontraditional relationships and survival strategies, at times to meet basic needs of survival and, beyond this, to work toward racial progress. Education factored principally in this wide array of strategies and sociopolitical experimentation.

But black efforts were often at odds with those of whites who provided heavy-handed support in the earliest days of black education's institutional development. This was principally white missionaries after the Civil War, but white corporate philanthropists in the North and white southern moderates gained near complete control over the institutional development of black education, including teacher training, by the First World War.[10] An ongoing struggle for ideological hegemony over the minds and work of black teachers persisted in the post-Emancipation era through Jim Crow.

"Let us make the teachers and we will make the people": General Samuel Armstrong made this declaration in 1877, having founded the iconic Hampton Institute in 1868. This emphasis on "making" teachers was the cornerstone of his industrial education vision for blacks. Armstrong emerged as an ideological figurehead of the "white architects of black education" during the Reconstruction era when he honed the Hampton model of industrial education.[11] His vision of black education focused on training efficient workers, therefore offering a bridge for northern industrialists and white southern moderates to reach common ground on the Negro problem. Armstrong's statement foreshadowed how the suppression and manipulation of black teacher training would be an intentional strategy to perpetuate white supremacy during the era of Jim Crow.[12] From the early 1900s into the 1930s, northern industrialists worked to exploit the high demand for black teachers as an effort to expand their campaign for industrial and practical education.[13] For instance, they conceived of county training schools as an alternative to public high schools. The goal was to train blacks to develop domestic, agricultural, and manual labor skills while preparing some to be teachers in the common schools, where they would inculcate these values in the minds of their pupils. A campaign to expand county training schools across the South officially began in 1911 through the John F. Slater fund.[14]

In reality, the majority of white southerners took no interest in the development of black education, let alone secondary schools. By their assessment, the roles carved out for blacks in the social order did not require such extensive education. In some cases, black teachers with advanced education and professional training were discriminated against in hiring practices by white educational officials.[15] W. E. B. Du Bois and his students at Atlanta University observed this phenomenon early on in 1911 when they documented that "wages for black teachers were lower and in some cases poorly trained teachers were preferred to better ones."[16] Due to these competing ideologies, the majority of southern cities with a population of at least 20,000 in 1915 had zero black high schools, yet all of them (totaling fifty-five) had from one to five white high schools. The number of black secondary schools grew at a snail's pace until the early 1930s.[17] Thus, access to higher education, even at the secondary school level, was a major impediment to black teacher development along with the ideological orientation of teacher training opportunities supported by white funders and educational leaders.

The question of how black teachers should be trained, and to what levels, was something teachers themselves strategized around despite white attempts to undermine and control their efforts. The National Association of Teachers in Colored Schools (NATCS) placed a strong emphasis on professional development from its founding in 1904 because of the few opportunities available to black teachers for preservice training.[18] Woodson was also vigilant of these particular questions, having been exposed to the colored teachers' association in West Virginia early in his own development. But his influence in these professional organizations, ideologically speaking, took hold during the mature years of the Association for the Study of Negro Life and History, beginning in the late 1920s.

Woodson's mission became deeply integrated into the institutional agenda of black teachers' associations. This influence was not only a result of his guest appearances but also his personal relationships with many of the organization's presidents, such as Mary McLeod Bethune (1924), William Robinson of North Carolina (1927), and H. Councill Trenholm (1931–1933). Woodson valued black teachers' associations for their collaborative politics. The national and state teachers' associations also offered a reliable network and organizational structure to institutionalize his educational program across the country, outside of traditional teacher training pathways and the public schools he had previously worked in. In these spaces, his role as an abroad mentor had the broadest reach.

The infusing of black life and culture into schools cannot be attributed to a top-down approach, however. Black teachers actively worked to model the educational vision forged through their collaboration with Woodson on a local level. This was done even in the absence of concerted efforts by the state teachers' associations. Black teachers were not simply using Woodson's books as references. They worked to transform the curricular infrastructure of their schools and at times their districts in an organized fashion. Woodson sought them out because they had the power to influence the lives of black youth on a day-to-day basis. They were drawn to Woodson because his curricular interventions helped redefine what a purposeful education could look and feel like in their classrooms.

It was often the work of individual and small pockets of black educators that created the rifts in the learning culture of schools on the local level. As early as 1915 black educators organized around Woodson's research. Roscoe Bruce, the assistant superintendent of colored schools in DC, referenced Woodson's *The Education of the Negro Prior to 1861* to build a case for incorporating black history in schools.[19] Teachers were active agents in this educational campaign to reimagine the curricular foundations of black schooling. It was articulated as an ethical obligation of their professional group. This work of reimagining black education was a shared endeavor. Their partnerships with Woodson was not a procedural mandate; it was a professional obligation they took on because it aligned with the highest aims of their work—cultivating a new human vision of education, one that was affixed to black dreams of freedom. This vision required a counterreading of hegemonic knowledge and the social relations structuring black life.

In a manner that was both cautious and rebellious, Julia Davis made attempts to influence the training of black teachers in St. Louis in 1927. Davis was a fifth-grade instructor of music, language, and reading. She wrote Woodson and requested that he personally reach out to Mr. Boggs, the supervisor of social science education for the St. Louis Board of Education. Davis informed Woodson that she had given Boggs a copy of Kelly Miller's *An Estimate of Carter G. Woodson and His Work* and suggested that Woodson follow up with him directly. Boggs, she urged, "is the man who can and will help us put over *our program*."[20]

The hushed tone of Davis's letter is easily detectable, revealing her strategy to draw Woodson into her local tactics to influence the program for training teachers. In his position as supervisor, Boggs taught night school courses for teachers. Davis encouraged Woodson to reach out to him before he solidified the curriculum for the next round of classes. The tone of Davis's letter amplifies a sense of urgency and yet discretion, and it is a tone that characterizes many of the communications between Woodson and black educators. It was her hope that Woodson's national prominence and academic pedigree might carry more weight than her local influence. Furthermore, she did not want to come across as too pushy with the local white school board.

In 1928 black educators in North Carolina made a similar case. William Robinson, the supervisor of Negro high schools and a past president of the NATCS, wrote to the state Department of Education with a recommendation for textbooks to be adopted for the high school curriculum. This list featured Woodson's *The Negro in Our History* as the textbook for high school seniors. Robinson declared that there was "a general desire amongst Negro school people of the state that there be courses in *Negro Life and History*." The parity of language taken up by black teachers and Woodson's organization, the Association for the Study of Negro Life and History, underscores the intellectual connection between them. Robinson made it clear that his efforts were not only to reimagine history curricula. He pushed for parallel readings on black life to be incorporated in "both History and English courses." Black teachers were working to "foster a wholesome and justifiable racial self-respect based upon facts that every Negro child has a right to know." In a sly tone, Robinson encouraged white schools to adopt texts that attended to the life and achievements of black people as well. However, he made it clear that "our real object is to reach our own Negro boys and girls."[21]

Nannie Helen Burroughs was a teacher and school founder that Woodson admired; arguably she represented the archetype of what he considered to be an effective educator of black students. The National Training School for Women and Girls, which Burroughs founded in 1909 in Washington, DC, blended both practical and classical education for young black women and had a strong commitment to black life and culture. Burroughs's school is listed as one of the earliest institutions to have adopted *The Negro in Our History* as a textbook in the 1920s.[22] Woodson vouched for both her pedagogy and the institution she developed by supporting his niece to attend the school.[23] Burroughs and Woodson both dedicated their lives to the cause of black education and to sustaining the autonomous black institutions they founded. Their shared sacrifice for the cause of black education led to an enduring friendship. Lorenzo Greene would later note that Burroughs was one of only two people he had ever heard refer to Woodson by his first name—Bethune being the second.[24]

More than passive practitioners, black schoolteachers were partners in the educational campaign that Woodson institutionalized. Their intellectual and embodied subversion was a direct extension of the transgressive politics and life world that long defined black educational heritage. Still working within the confinement of Jim Crow, black teachers were continuously thinking and doing, straining against its constraints. Woodson's abroad mentorship fortified their efforts, supporting them from outside of traditional pathways of teacher training. But even as black teachers were strategic in how they struggled against the ideological stronghold of white educational leaders and opposition, they were always consciously aware of potential backlash in the form of firing, defunding, and physical harm. Teachers like Julia Davis, William Robinson, and Nannie Helen Burroughs were cautious because they knew that their efforts could be met with extralegal violence. A few years earlier, in 1925, black teachers in Oklahoma learned that the infusion of black life and history in schools could invite aggression from hostile white school leaders who had direct ties to the Ku Klux Klan.

Violence and the Surveillance of Black School Life

The schoolboard in Muskogee, Oklahoma, discovered Woodson's *The Negro in Our History* being used at the Negro Manual and Training High School in 1925. White educational leaders were outraged. After examining the book's content, they expressed "horror and surprise that such a work should have crept into *our* Negro schools." Woodson's depiction of a mixed-race jury in Washington, DC, was particularly offensive to them, as were his criticisms of the US government for its treatment of black soldiers. The school board was disgusted by Woodson's "frank" discussion about the infatuation some white southern men had with "beautiful negro girls." They also believed the tone of the textbook to be militant and critiqued Woodson's treatment of the race riot in Washington, DC, in 1919, writing that he "comment[ed] boastingly upon the fact that in the second day of the fighting negroes killed more white people than the whites killed negroes."[25]

White outrage led to action in Muskogee. Both administrative and curricular changes were set in place at "*their* Negro school." The training school's principal, Thomas W. Grissom, was forced to resign. Muskogee's educational officials confiscated the school's set of *The Negro in Our History*, and teachers were forbidden from using it any further. Black educators were aware that punishment for this kind of offense could have been much more severe. Violence and terror were central to the ways in which black people were conscripted into the sociality of the American School, and it shaped black educators' professional reality. Muskogee was no different.

The press coverage of this textbook scandal took place alongside a larger discussion about the Ku Klux Klan's stronghold on the Muskogee school board. To address public concerns, white educational leaders decided they would take a neutral stance as it pertained to the Klan. Nothing should be "instilled in the schools that is either klan or antiklan," they announced. But the school board refused to denounce or critique Klan activities.[26]

White mob violence and Klan activity peaked during these early interwar years. In 1921 the thriving black town of Tulsa, Oklahoma, was burned down during a race riot. This recent event weighed heavily on the minds of African Americans in Muskogee, who were just some fifty miles away. Two months after the textbook banning was reported, in August 1925, sixty thousand Klan members marched in Washington, DC, on the National Mall. Thus, the Klan's influence on local school affairs meant that black teachers in Muskogee were always on notice about their vulnerability. Their local realities were tethered to an expansive history of so-called uppity Negro educators being physically whipped or having their homes bombed. At times white aggression was aimed at the black schoolhouse itself: angry whites shot into school yards while students and their teacher played; schoolhouses mysteriously burned down in the middle of the night. Memories and stories of such violence were engrained in the consciousness of black educators.[27]

African American teachers were deeply aware of antiblack exclusion and confinement in the American School, and the pervasiveness of these technologies of control continued to engender fugitive pedagogy among their professional group. The dialectic formed between these mechanisms of control and black educators' fugitive desires required that they form subaltern professional institutions and communities, where they sustained a black under-commons that always existed within the American School. All the while, they were hyperaware of their vulnerability to Jim Crow authority and the various manifestations of this oppressive apparatus. As fugitive pedagogues their existence was always liminal, always in flux—deploying practices of escape yet always within or in relation to an oppressive, hegemonic school structure that was a microcosm of the broader social order.

Woodson institutionalized his educational philosophy to ensure it had a resounding impact beyond isolated events, and these educational materials became pedagogical resources in critiquing the violent realities of Jim Crow. The learning resources were a source of empowerment for students as well as the teachers who brought them into the classroom. They helped shape a new aesthetic that restyled classroom life. Classrooms featured a new historical inventory of the world—pictures of black historical figures, lesson plans that directly engaged the history of slavery, systemic oppression, and yet black achievement and resistance. These themes were lucidly outlined in the lessons taught by the teachers. They represented an epistemic rupture with the American Curriculum teachers were expected to wholly rely on by white school leaders.

Negro History Week (1926–1931)

Woodson's most far-reaching impact on black education manifested in 1926 through Negro History Week, an event that built on a similar week-long celebration Woodson began through his fraternity Omega Psi Phi in 1921.[28] Negro History Week was conceived of as an effort to publicize the work of the ASNLH across the nation and to help generate a larger investment in the organization from community members. More pointedly, the goal was to "dramatize the achievements of the race sufficiently to induce educational authorities to incorporate into the curricula courses in Negro life and history."[29] In its first year, Woodson circulated pamphlets around the country encouraging communities and institutions to participate in the celebration. Responding to Woodson's call, "the State departments of education of Delaware, North Carolina, and West Virginia, and the city systems of Baltimore and the District of Columbia sent out to their teachers special appeals for cooperation in this important celebration. Principals of private schools and presidents of colleges and universities likewise carried the appeal directly to their coworkers."[30]

From its inception, Woodson located the significance of Negro History Week in its function to counter the violence (physical and symbolic) that shaped black life. This commemorative week promoted a counterideology for educating black students that had political implications beyond those which met the eye. In promotional materials for Negro History Week, Woodson constantly reminded his audience of the many ways in which black Americans were denied citizenship and recognition as human beings, thus underscoring the relationship between knowledge and the condemnation of black life. Negro history in schools was a necessary epistemic shift to challenge the violent misrecognitions of black humanity, a process that took form at the ideological *and* material level. During the inaugural year of Negro History Week, Woodson introduced the event in the following terms through the *Journal of Negro History:* "A Negro is passed on the street and is shoved off in the mud; he complains or strikes back and is lynched as a desperado who attacked a gentleman. . . . And what if he is handicapped, segregated, or lynched? According to our education and practice, if you kill one of the group, the world goes on just as well or better; for the Negro is nothing, has never been anything, and never will be anything but a menace to civilization."[31] Woodson used this scenario of a black civilian encounter with racial hostility as a means of demonstrating the disdain for black life deeply embedded in the national culture. The violence circumscribing black life was ideologically motivated. Antiblack violence was intimately tied to the logics perpetuated in the American School and its curriculum.

The goal for Negro History Week, like Woodson's larger educational project, was to vindicate black humanity by rewriting the epistemological order in a way that negated antiblackness. It was about bringing into being new scripts of knowledge for black students to learn from, scripts with new visions of the world and black people's role within it. Negro History Week required shifting from a curriculum that gave "thorough instruction that the Negro has never contributed anything to the progress of mankind" to one that paid homage to black people's contributions to the modern world and that acknowledged their experiences with oppression under the hand of white supremacy.[32] This week-long event invited teachers to articulate reimagined learning objectives, and Woodson offered plenty of resources for engaging this work.

While black teachers' associations encouraged Negro History Week celebrations, they were not a mandated practice. Educators organized among
themselves in their local contexts and made Negro History Week a part of
the cultural milieu of black educational life. This successful campaign was a
result of teachers' grassroots organizing. It is important to appreciate the
additional labor being taken up by African American educators and communities to implement Negro History Week. Their efforts to introduce the
celebrations in black communities were part of a much broader set of politics to challenge antiblackness in schools. Even if Negro History Week's content did not immediately have an impact on white people's perceptions of black
folks, it instilled in African Americans a stronger sense of historical consciousness about their identities and the structural challenges they faced. It both af-
firmed the frustration and rage about the world around them and provided
intellectual resources for challenging it.

These celebrations reveal the close coordination and exchange between
Woodson and black teachers as a professional body. He distributed instructional material with suggestions on how best to observe the occasion, and
teachers wrote back documenting how they answered the call. In 1927 Julia
Davis of St. Louis shared the program held by the fifth-grade classes in the
Simmons School Auditorium. Some of the acts included student performances of Frederick Douglass and Madame C. J. Walker, performances of
the Fisk Jubilee Singers' spirituals, and a talk on citizenship rendered by the
school principal.[33]

But books and learning materials that included the narratives and experiences of black people were not the only things in low supply. Woodson regularly observed that the majority of teachers in schools were not trained to
teach about black life. In 1929 he asked, "Who will teach Negro History when
it is made a part of the curriculum?" Negro History Week, Woodson explained, exposed how little teachers themselves knew about the history and
cultural achievements of black people. To address this, he shared examples
where black educators worked to secure supplemental training to help them
effectively teach and study black life in critical ways.

In North Carolina, for example, black educators found a way to convince
the state education department to offer credit toward teacher certification for
work they did in studying Negro history. "Other groups of teachers and
branches of the Association . . . designate someone as an instructor and pay

the required fees for him to take a course in the Home Study Department of the Association." Through the Home Study Department, participants submitted assignments by mail, which were returned with corrections and feedback. After completing a course through the ASNLH, this person could then be empowered to teach others locally.[34] Woodson also planted these seeds of ideas in person, before the national convenings of black educators. In 1929 the NATCS advertised that from July 30 through August 2 a number of "prominent educators" were "to address teachers at the national meeting" in Jackson, Mississippi. Carter G. Woodson was among those prominent speakers.[35] The following year, in 1930, Woodson delivered a speech before the NATCS again at Tuskegee. He urged teachers to hold themselves and their colleagues accountable for ensuring that "Negro children study Negro history in the schools."[36] The teaching of black life and history could not be by happenstance and sporadic; it was worthy of coordinated and intentional action.

Negro History Week also helped carry the mission of the ASNLH to the larger community, beyond the confines of school classrooms. In 1930, Alice Harris, the supervisor of the Colored Playground and Recreational Association, wrote to Woodson to inform him of the successful Negro History Week held in the city of Richmond, Virginia, which culminated with a pageant in which eight hundred people were in attendance. The week's activities were a collaborative effort between her association, Omega Psi Phi fraternity, the Phyllis Wheatley YWCA, and other community organizations. Harris noted that Professor Rayford W. Logan of Virginia Union—Woodson's former M Street High School student—organized ten-minute speeches to be given by his students at churches across the city on various themes in Negro history.[37]

Speaking directly to the rift Negro History Week created in the learning culture of black schools, Woodson offered, "The celebration has become one of the important objectives of the school year." And this impact rippled throughout black communities, whose community social activities often centered on the local school calendars. By his account, "No other single thing [had] done so much to dramatize the achievements of persons of African blood," and Negro History Week extended the learning process beyond the classroom by inviting in the entire community to bear witness.[38] In most cases, Negro History Week celebrations were a collaborative process between schools, local colleges, community groups, and churches.

Some educators used the momentum surrounding Negro History Week as leverage to nudge school officials to adopt new textbooks and educational resources. Woodson frequently identified cases where "interest was capitalized in the right way," where black teachers wielded Negro History Week most effectively and encouraged teachers in other places to follow suit. In 1931 he described how some teachers made an effort "to discontinue the use of books which teach bias and race hate." He continued: "Boards of education were asked to adopt textbooks on the Negro for appropriate courses of study. Books and pictures of Negroes were purchased for schools and libraries. Documents of value were collected and sent to the Association for the Study of Negro Life and History . . . where they will be preserved under fire proof protection." Woodson publicly highlighted these strategies to show teachers and other educational officials how they could use Negro History Week strategically to maximize its impact. As he articulated, the long-term goal was "the reconstruction of the curricula without the loss of any of the essentials." Mathematics, the natural sciences, and practical languages should continue; however, there needed to be a "radical reconstruction" regarding courses in the social sciences and humanities.[39]

Woodson's materials were used to enhance classroom instruction and teachers took on primary roles in the production of educational materials through the ASNLH and its ancillary publications. The research and educational literature produced through the ASNLH were first and foremost "communicated to the teacher groups and to many individual members, some of whom were among the authors and illustrators of the books; and most of whom, in turn, used those which were appropriate in their classes, clubs, churches, and fraternal organizations." In this way, Woodson cultivated a "direct and positive link" to black teachers.[40]

Thelma Perry—a longtime member of the American Teachers Association (originally the NATCS) as well as the Oklahoma and North Carolina black teachers' associations—underscored the influence of Woodson's scholarship on black teachers.[41] Woodson called "for a new perspective" as it pertained to educating children in schools, one that demanded an intentional "shift away from acceptance of black people as inferior, even sub-human by so-called scholars." According to Perry, Woodson worked to "develop overall a sense of racial identity and pride in black people." "It was his role to spread Negro History throughout the schools and colleges of the U.S., especially the black schools." Perry analyzed that Woodson was working to transform the minds of black children. "He hoped to reach [them] directly and, of course, through the teachers."[42]

Teacher Training and *The Mis-education of the Negro* (1933)

Teacher training became a central concern for Woodson as the work of the ASNLH matured. And, to be sure, there were other black educators who voiced concerns on this topic.[43] As Woodson outlined in *The Mis-education of the Negro*, however, his metrics for good teaching were not beholden to degree attainment and certification standards. Woodson was primarily concerned with the ideological orientation of black teachers, meaning the kinds of shared systems of beliefs and values they were initiated into via their training and its influence on their approach to instruction. By his assessment, a central part of black teachers' vocation was to cultivate a deep awareness of and committed resistance to the cultural politics of white supremacy in their students. To do this, teachers had to develop students' awareness about black history and the history of racism in a way that endowed them with a positive self-image and the capacity to think critically on these matters. To accomplish this, teachers themselves needed to value the kind of knowledge this history represented. In Woodson's eyes, this was the heart of the problem: teachers lacked the appropriate valuation or virtuous orientation toward black life and history, precisely because of their own formal education and training. That being said, it is important to describe rhetorical elements in Woodson's expressed beliefs about teacher training because it is easy to misread the intention of his critiques or dismiss them as hypercritical of black educators.

Woodson believed in black teachers. He critiqued them as a group out of a desire for more systematic strategies to confront the inner workings of the violent system into which they were conscripted. The issue was not just about access to secondary education, teacher training, and certification. Antiblackness operated at the most basic levels of schooling—ideology, curriculum, and the system of representation that was at the foundation of the American School. Matters of institutional exclusion or segregation or school funding—while extremely important—did not address this metaphysical antagonism at the core of black life.

The training received by black teachers failed to prepare them to address the cultural politics of white supremacy enacted through dominant schooling. Woodson argued that "Negro educators of today may have more sympathy and interest in the race than the whites now exploiting Negro institutions as educators, but the former have no more vision than their competitors. *Taught from books of the same bias,* trained by Caucasians of the same prejudices or by Negroes of enslaved minds, one generation of Negro teachers after another have served for no higher purpose than to do what they are told to do."[44] Taking Woodson's words at face value can be misleading. They can seem contradictory. How are black teachers the problem and simultaneously active partners in the process to uproot antiblackness in school? There is a sleight of hand at play here, which requires a rhetorical explanation.

While hyperbolic in his critique of black educators, Woodson's rhetorical fashioning was not inconsistent with trends in black intellectual thought.[45] At first glance, it appears that Woodson berated the very group of people who constituted his greatest supporters. (One might recall here how Malcolm X, for instance, often scolded black people as fools, addicts, and slaves to the white man before suggesting that they might engage in practices of piety and self-transformation that would help them achieve dignity or self-respect.) Through this particular form of political representation of "the Negro teacher with no higher purpose," a collective "we" is formed, that being black educators who actively chose to operate outside the interests of white educational authority.[46] The "Negro educators of today" represented in Woodson's scenario were the ideal political actors based on the dominant ideology of the (white) American School. He anticipated how many educators fell into the traps of compliance, noting that at times "he has committed some of these errors himself."[47]

Woodson's experience as an educator allowed him to speak from a place of self-narration, where he put his prior self in the same category subjected to his critique ("the Negro teacher with no higher purpose"). Here Woodson is doing something similar to religion conversion discourse, whereby a speaker/initiate appeals to an audience by saying, in essence, "I, like you, was once lost, but now am found." I was once parroting these white lies—I was even worse, given how deeply immersed into the system I was (a graduate of the University of Chicago, Harvard, etc.)—but now I am free, or vocationally sound, and you can be too. Woodson made it a point to express that it took him twenty years to recover after his PhD from Harvard.[48]

In crafting an archetype of the American School's ideal black educator, Woodson politically represented the kind of training and black teacher subjectivity to be refused and negated. Embedded in this rhetorical move was the assertion that the preferred educators were those who sought a higher purpose, those who committed to doing more than "what they are told to do" by white school authorities.

Woodson rhetorically constructed the apolitical black educator—which was part fact and fiction, to be clear—as a means to articulate a refined political subjectivity for what it meant to be a black educator, one who is studiously suspicious and antagonistic toward the dominant schooling apparatus of the state. For these reasons, black teachers could read *Mis-education* or sit in the audience during Woodson's speeches and nod in agreement. Their identities were formed over and against the picture painted of the abstract "Negro educators of today" (likely not the enlightened ones in the auditorium or reading his books).

Woodson highlighted that "Negro History was not required of our teachers when they were in school, and they cannot be blamed for knowing less of this than of other things."[49] While sympathetic to this fact, Woodson critiqued teachers' lack of attention to the history and culture of black people in schools. His critiques about black educators, which were at once a critique of black teacher training, manifested in written and spoken form, in newspaper columns and *Mis-education,* as well as speeches rendered at churches and black teacher convenings. The rhetorical task before Woodson when articulating these critiques about teacher training and practice was to get black educators to recognize and describe their education in the impoverished terms of "mis-education," to then distance themselves from it and become ashamed enough (for lack of a better phrase) to engage in self-correction. This was to be in service of a self-transformation in line with their deepest vocational commitments, a realignment of the virtue of the black teacher. Woodson was appealing to commitments black teachers imagined themselves to have already possessed. This is not something he handed to them. His desire was to show them how they had fallen short, "how we missed the mark" as he put it. They might then reform themselves and their institutions in light of these collective shortcomings. Critique here was a necessary form of love and accountability, a critique of that which one values and seeks to make better.

Woodson stressed the importance of black teachers' associations as a space for teachers to engage with new ideas, emerging research about black life, and political demands of the day. He understood these meetings as a necessary alternative to the mainstream white teachers' association. Talking to one black educator who preferred to attend the white professional meeting, Woodson responded as follows:

> Good enough. . . . You should attend the National Education Association [NEA]. You may get some help from it, but how often have you or other Negroes been invited to address that body? How often have they discussed problems of special bearing upon the work which you are doing? . . . If you cannot get some help also from the National Association of Teachers in Colored Schools, which is organized to render you special service in your particular task you cannot be seriously interested in the enlightenment of Negroes and you should be eliminated from their teaching corps.[50]

This teachers' lack of engagement with black teachers' associations, as far as Woodson was concerned, indicated a lack of professional integrity, someone with no vocation for the art of black teaching. While the NEA might have allowed this black teacher to attend its meetings, the interests of black teachers were not represented on the organization's agenda in any substantive way. Therefore, attending the national white meeting could not serve as a replacement for engaging the NATCS, an organization wholly committed to improving the experiences of African American teachers and prioritizing the needs of black students. After attending the NATCS meeting of 1932 in Montgomery, Alabama, Woodson commented, "It was one of the most profitable meetings which he had ever attended." He proclaimed that any teacher in a school with black students needed to be a part of this professional organization. The teachers at this meeting were "awakening more rapidly than the other schools to realize that the Negro in the ghetto must be developed from within and under his own leadership."[51]

As an abroad mentor, Woodson encouraged teachers to develop a more critical and informed perspective on the history of their race. This was essential for teachers to be effective instructors of black students, in addition to mastering knowledge in their content areas. While black life and culture was not centered in traditional teacher training pathways, black teachers encountered these ideas through their own professional channels and through Woodson's ASNLH. As Woodson put it, the training received by both teachers and students conditioned them to become "blind to the Negro."[52] Therefore, black teachers had to actively work against this intentional underdevelopment of their group. His mission was to meet these needs in their veiled professional world.

Black Teachers as "Scholars of the Practice"

Beyond their encounters with his ideas at teachers' association meetings, black teachers took up Woodson's curricular interventions and put them to use in a variety of ways. His curricular materials—textbooks, the *Negro History Bulletin,* and various supplemental learning content—aided teachers in challenging the American Curriculum in the private spaces of their classrooms, which were nodes of the black counterpublic sphere—restricted spaces, (mostly) beyond the surveillance of white authorities. There, black teachers engaged their students without the mask of compliance they were forced to wear otherwise. Let us return to a rare and vivid account of such fugitive pedagogy: the anecdote of Tessie McGee with which this book opens. This scenario from McGee's classroom offers a peek backstage, or access to part of the hidden transcript of black teachers' work in their schools, which their public performance of deference concealed.[53] Woodson's textbooks were appropriated by black teachers like McGee to contest white supremacy in the hallowed sites of their classrooms, where they cultivated the freedom dreams of future race leaders and worked to push black children to their highest potential.

At the same time, the fugitive demands of black education required teachers to perform bold acts of defiance. Otherwise, they were forced to collude with a studiously structured program of mis-education. If black teachers were to teach against the grain of dominant curricula, to humanize black students and inspire them to push for social transformation, it would have to be deeply camouflaged.[54] The concealment of Woodson's textbook in McGee's lap, underneath the desk, was a clear marker of her fugitive pedagogy. She wore the mask of compliance even as she strained against the constraints of her Jim Crow classroom.

McGee was likely not the only teacher in Webster Parish to use Woodson's textbook, given the close association of the school's faculty. Most of the school's teachers, which totaled less than ten, boarded at the home of J. L. Jones, the school's principal and a former presidential candidate for the Louisiana Colored Teachers' Association.[55] The close interlocking of these teachers' professional and home lives—given that they lived in a teachery—invites us to imagine how they may have shared instructional materials and planned their lessons with one another. Knowing that well-rehearsed performances of obedience were part and parcel of black teachers' art of resistance, it is safe to infer that the action taken by McGee to secretly use Woodson's textbook was not an isolated incident. The well-established channels of communication through black teachers' associations were places where this political ethos of being "double agents" was cultivated and modeled.[56]

Fugitive pedagogy also took place beyond the classroom. For example, Willis Nathaniel Huggins taught at Bushwick High School in Brooklyn and was the only black teacher of history in the New York public schools, where he began working in 1924.[57] Huggins became the first black PhD from Fordham University in 1932, taught Sunday courses on black history through the Negro History Club, and also opened a bookstore in Harlem. It was through these capacities that the renowned scholar John Henrik Clark came to refer to Huggins as "a master-teacher."[58] Huggins served in the capacities of president and instructor of the ASNLH's New York City branch and in 1933 organized the First Annual Dinner of the Negro History Club, which included the participation of such Black Renaissance giants as Arturo Schomburg, Jessie Fauset, and Paul Robeson. And in 1937 Woodson recognized Huggins for the powerful lectures he gave around the city during Negro History Week.[59]

The West Virginia State Teachers Association actively "encouraged membership in the NAACP" and similarly "endorsed the work of the Association for the Study of Negro Life and History."[60] Dr. Luther P. Jackson, a historian and committed colleague of Woodson's, made sure that the state program of the Virginia State Teachers Association incorporated Negro History Week celebrations across their schools as well.[61] Furthermore, in 1934 Jackson organized a fund-raising campaign among black teachers and proudly boasted that more than three hundred teachers and hundreds of students donated money to the efforts of the ASNLH in his state.[62]

By 1935 Woodson would come to name Negro History Week "the most popular effort ever made by the Association."[63] The historian Lawrence Riddick shared that Negro History Week was a "mass education program." Woodson's largest influence on the public came through this initiative. "The response to it from young and old, educated and uneducated, pleased him to no end."[64] Woodson himself declared that even if people were not familiar with the ASNLH or his career as the founder, they "nevertheless heard of and felt the impulse of Negro History Week."[65] To be clear, Negro History Week was not created as the one time throughout the year when students should learn about black history and culture. Woodson constantly reminded the public of this. In fact, he declared that it was the "duty of all teachers," no matter their subject, to incorporate the life and history of black people into their curricula throughout the school year.[66]

The success of Negro History Week relied on the efforts of black teachers' associations, its wide coverage in the black press, and the work of individual educators who spread the cause in their local communities. One such figure was H. Councill Trenholm, a graduate of Morehouse College, a very influential leader of the Alabama State Teachers Association (ASTA), and an ASNLH board member.[67] Through his leadership in the ASTA, Trenholm conducted a study by circulating questionnaires "among black educators throughout Alabama to determine to what extent black students and the black community were being taught about the contributions of black people."[68] He went on to develop a two-year Negro History Project that began in 1936. This included "distributing Negro History Project study kits to black teachers throughout Alabama. As a result, black schools began to hold annual Negro History Week programs, initiate essay and oratorical contests devoted to Negro themes, and feature Negro life and history themes in school plays and bulletin boards. Black educators also made efforts to secure books by and about black people for their classrooms and libraries."[69]

The ASTA published and distributed a handbook about the uses of Negro life and history in schools at its Fifty-Fourth Annual Convention in Birmingham, held March 26–28, 1936. The handbook outlined explicit goals of the Negro History Project and included relevant data on the schooling experiences of black students. This project aimed to establish "the presence of Negro history in all public and private schools; the formation of a course of study in black history; the development of creative expressions by Negro scholars leading to essays, books, monographs, and scientific research by and about black people; the development of a more tolerant relationship between the races; an increased awareness and pride among Negro people of their contributions to ancient and modern civilizations."[70] The handbook also covered the history and resources provided by Woodson's ASNLH to this cause. The language employed by the ASTA through this Negro History Project underscores how black teachers operationalized Woodson's educational philosophy through their professional organizations. Woodson delivered the keynote address at this convention. His partnership with the ASTA exemplifies the way he moved through the professional world of black teachers across state lines.

The benefits of this relationship between black teachers and Woodson flowed in both directions, and the ties were mutually sustained. The Association welcomed black teachers as leaders and intellectuals within its ranks, even as they were not formally trained historians or social science researchers—though many black teachers did acquire advanced educational degrees. Black teachers represented a large constituency of the ASNLH's dues-paying members. Speaking to this point, historian John Hope Franklin recalled encountering "large numbers of teachers, of high schools and elementary schools" at his first annual meeting for the ASNLH in 1936, which was held in Petersburg, Virginia; and he noted the active role teachers took in the ASNLH's academic program.[71] The large presence of black teachers at the annual conferences of the ASNLH signals not only their investment in the work of the organization but also their critical role in keeping the organization afloat during the economically challenged years of the 1930s.

Some teachers took the lessons offered through Woodson's ASNLH and its publications to develop outlines for new courses in Negro history as well as other subjects, such as civics. Ira B. Bryant wrote a thirty-page "Study Guide" outline in 1936 for a class on Negro history, which he taught at Phillis Wheatley High School in Houston, Texas. Bryant developed the outline so that other teachers in the local public schools could use it as a resource. There were nine aims for the course:

1. To trace the history of the Negro race from its origin to the present, in order to acquaint the pupil with the glorious heritage of the Negro group.
2. To give the student a comprehensive knowledge of the African culture.
3. To point out the achievement of a race transplanted from the shores of Africa, and thrust in a strange culture, but, in spite of handicaps, has made progress in all the fields of modern civilization.
4. To show clearly to pupils that all of the Negro's friends are not above the Mason-Dixon Line, nor all of his enemies below the Mason-Dixon Line.
5. To point out the loyalty of the Negro race in each American crisis.
6. To acquaint the student with the truly great Negroes who have achieved in spite of handicaps.
7. To acquaint the student with Negro pioneers in the various fields of endeavor.
8. To show the contribution of the Negro to the political, social and economic life of the United States and of the world.
9. To point out to the pupil *how a culture has developed within a culture* in the United States of America.

Woodson's textbooks and the *Journal of Negro History* were listed throughout the proposal as key reading, along with many other books identified for various units within the general course outline.[72] Mirroring Woodson's advice that the study of black life should inform other courses, Bryant also developed a civics unit for high school seniors entitled "Social Problems: A Report on Negro Housing Conditions." Students worked individually and in groups to study various blocks in their neighborhood, looking at details shaping black living conditions in their local community. Bryant believed students needed to apply an analytical eye to the social problems of their communities in order to help address these matters as future leaders.[73] There are other examples of teachers in different cities, from New Orleans to Chicago, who developed similar courses of study. These cases underscore how black educators took on additional labor to work around the constraints of the school systems they were forced to function within. To be effective in the lives of black students, black educators constantly strove to be in and not of Jim Crow schools.[74]

Bethune, Brooks, and the *Negro History Bulletin* (1936–1940)

At the 1936 annual meeting of the ASNLH, Mary McLeod Bethune was elected president after the passing of John Hope, also a longtime educator and prominent member in the National Association of Teachers in Colored Schools.[75] An educator, political figure, and school founder, Bethune was a giant in the world of black teachers. She was also a familiar face to the membership body of the ASNLH, having been the first woman to present a major paper at the 1923 annual meeting.[76] She was a past president of the NATCS (1924) and founder of the Daytona Educational and Industrial Institute. In 1935, as a recently elected member of the ASNLH's executive council, she delivered an address entitled "The Association for the Study of Negro Life and History: Its Contributions to Our Modern Life," at the twentieth annual meeting. She emphasized the importance of "interpreting" the findings produced by trained scholars to the masses. "Already we have an ample supply of investigators," she asserted, "but it appears to me that there is a shortage of readable and responsible interpreters, men and women who can effectively play the role of mediator between the trained investigator and the masses."[77] Bethune's appeal for a greater emphasis on developing "interpreters" surely influenced the focus of the 1936 meeting (convened under the theme "The Teaching of Negro History, Literature, and Art"), where key sessions focused on using academic scholarship to shape the learning experiences of students at the elementary through collegiate level. She would play a critical role in doing so by recommending that Woodson create the *Negro History Bulletin* in 1937.

The *Negro History Bulletin* was created within the first year of Bethune's presidency[78] and became a major resource for black educators to supplement and critique the prescribed educational curricula approved by public school officials. While Woodson would execute this vision, it was at Bethune's request that the ASNLH publish a magazine for teachers and general readers that prompted its development.[79] This publication became a forum for black teachers to exchange ideas on how to make education more relevant to students, a medium to celebrate the work being done in their schools, and an opportunity to share about the progress of their pupils. Furthermore, many of the magazine's articles, stories, lesson plans, and class assignments were written by schoolteachers themselves. As the historian John Hope Franklin would state years later, the *Negro History Bulletin* was perhaps the "most vigorous extension of the work of Dr. Woodson" into the lives of black students. "Teachers were to find in it materials for use in classes in secondary and elementary schools, while students themselves were to discover in its pages stimulating and inspirational materials that would be valuable to their studies."[80]

Woodson intentionally targeted black teachers when he created the publication. He was clear in his objective: "the stimulation of the study of the Negro in the public schools."[81] The language in this publication was to be aligned with a fifth-grade reading level. According to Woodson, this made it accessible to younger students and a general African American audience. Nine issues were released each year, between the months of October and June, which fell in alignment with the school year calendar. In advertising the first year's series to teachers, Woodson informed them that the *Negro History Bulletin* would be a good supplement to the poster printed and circulated by the ASNLH to schools around the country on "Important Events and Dates in Negro History."[82] In partnership with black educators, the Association engaged in a process of ongoing production of curricular materials, and these materials systematically built on one another.

Albert N. D. Brooks was an educator in the Washington, DC, public schools and served on the editorial team for the *Negro History Bulletin* from its inception in 1937. He was an administrator at Shaw Junior High School and eventually served as the editor of the *Negro History Bulletin* after Woodson's death in 1950.[83] Woodson recognized Brooks for the central role he played in recruiting members to the ASNLH and for increasing the circulation of the *Negro History Bulletin* through the newsstands.[84] Brooks's support of Woodson's educational vision stemmed from their shared critique of dominant schooling. According to Brooks, Woodson understood that "history is the basis of the educational philosophy upon which the whole school system rests" and exposed how historical distortions sustained a program of mis-education "over several centuries." He proclaimed that Woodson provided an alternative educational philosophy that supplied black students with "motivation and inspiration" to "rise in spite of all handicaps to his *highest potential*."[85]

"Important Events and Dates in Negro History," poster included in Carter G. Woodson, *The African Background Outlined: Handbook for the Study of the Negro* (Washington, DC: Associated Publishers, 1936). Used with the permission of the Association for the Study of African American Life and History, www.asalh.org.

Brooks concluded that black teachers could not depend on white boards of education to recognize the urgency of their work. "It is certain that boards of education generally cannot be relied upon to furnish satisfactory educational programs for the Negro," he wrote. "Programs of education in the past have not promoted and were not calculated to promote the social efficiency of the Negro." He argued that to achieve meaningful results in their schools, they would have to work around white school boards. Brooks celebrated the sentiments shared by one of his colleges in Alabama, that when white Jim Crow authorities attempted to suppress black teachers' professional and political work, "we will just have to take it underground."[86] The ideas expressed by Brooks reveal the ideological undercurrents of black teachers' fugitive pedagogy: a purposeful education for black students required constant, structured acts of subversion. Brooks encouraged black teachers reading the *Negro History Bulletin* to organize "Negro Planning Committees" in their local communities for school matters and to develop effective local strategies.[87]

Woodson utilized the infrastructure of black teachers' associations to popularize the *Negro History Bulletin*. After its first issue in October 1937, Pearl Schwartz, the chair of the Missouri State Association of Negro Teachers, wrote to Woodson asking for three hundred copies of the publication. She intended to circulate and publicize the magazine at their state meeting the following month. Woodson's friend and protégé Lorenzo Johnson Greene reinforced the promotion of the *Bulletin* at this meeting. He ensured Woodson that it was his "intention to personally present the matter of the *Negro History Bulletin* to this group."

As an abroad mentor, Woodson was intimately situated within the national community of black schoolteachers. However, when he was unable to personally address the congregation at black teachers' meetings, there were close associates and active members of the ASNLH already in these spaces to further the cause.[88] Greene, who was a professor at Lincoln University, had a great deal of access to black teachers in Missouri because he taught summer school courses. In 1938 Greene requested that Woodson send him materials to circulate among the teachers in his summer courses and copies of books that could be purchased from the Associated Publishers, Inc., to stock their schools and class libraries. In return, Woodson requested the mailing addresses of the teachers enrolled in summer schools, and he included them in the outreach campaigns of the ASNLH.[89] Communications between Woodson and Greene underscore the consistency of Woodson's strategies for reaching black teachers across time. He continued to rely on the infrastructure of black teacher networks and the personal relationships he had with key people in black institutions across the country.

The *Bulletin* became Woodson's proudest accomplishment in his efforts to transform the learning culture in black schools after Negro History Week. Together they represented the heart of Woodson's vision to disrupt the stronghold of mainstream, white curricula. Early on, he used the *Bulletin* to explain and clarify the purpose of Negro History Week and cautioned teachers against reducing Negro history to an annual one-week marathon. "Some teachers and their students have misunderstood the celebration of Negro History Week," he explained. "They work up enthusiasm during these few days, stage a popular play, present an orator of the day, or render exercises of a literary order; but they forget the Negro thereafter throughout the year. To proceed in such fashion may do as much harm as good," Woodson argued. "It is a reflection on the record of the race to leave the impression that its history can be thus disposed of in a few days. Negro History Week should be a demonstration of what has been done in the study of the Negro during the year and at the same time a demonstration of greater things to be accomplished."[90] These celebrations were meant to disrupt and ultimately displace the oppressive learning culture that otherwise persisted in schools. Negro History Week was an opportunity to dramatize a new educational vision that was to shape learning year round.

Woodson provided teachers with different activities they could conduct with their students and made recommendations about how to push for more systemic change at the district level through textbook proposals and strategies for lobbying public libraries to purchase books on black life and history. He implored teachers to "throw out of the school all books which thus smear over the truth" and "invite attention to those facts of Negro life and history which have been purposely omitted. . . . In this way propaganda may be uprooted, and truth will secure a hearing in our schools." Black students needed to know "the place [their] race holds in the development of civilization."[91]

While Woodson desired to inspire pride in students, it was even more critical to develop in them "a questioning attitude towards existing conditions and to understand causes . . . of such conditions."[92] More than just offering new narratives, the *Negro History Bulletin* supported students in naming how and why dominant curricula positioned black people as ahistorical and without culture. It aimed to teach students to be aware and critical of their oppression, while gaining an expanded inventory of knowledge about black history and culture. Woodson and the teachers on the editorial board made these goals transparent to all readers—teachers, students, and community members.

Near the end of its first year in publication, Woodson reported that the number of subscribers for the *Negro History Bulletin* surpassed 3,500.[93] It was a multifaceted publication, presenting historical narratives, current events, sample lesson plans, and explicit social analysis. Its themes varied from one month to the next. The first year the publication covered such themes as "the negro in America when he was enslaved," "the free Negro," "the anti-slavery effort," "colonization," and "achievements in freedom."[94] In addition to the feature articles on historical topics, there were also contributions by teachers sharing lesson plans from their classrooms on effective methods for incorporating black life and history into curricula. The section entitled "School News" served to highlight the achievements and developments of black schools across the country that were using the *Bulletin* effectively or that offered special courses on Negro history. "School News" also featured stories about recent developments at particular schools like new buildings or successful Negro History Week pageants. Issues profiled new books for school-age children. These reviews were meant to make teachers and students aware of the scholarship being produced about black life and history and to inform educators about new books to purchase for their school libraries. Pictures and images of historical black figures, teachers, and schools were also incorporated into the *Bulletin* to supplement the magazine's written content.

In the October 1938 publication of the *Negro History Bulletin*, Elise Derricotte, principal of the George Bell School in Washington, DC, questioned: "What type of materials are teachers giving our children? Just the cut-and-dry books furnished by the school systems? Or are they using supplementary materials, magazines, pictures, stories, news, articles and clippings to fill in the vacant places in the lives of these children?"[95] This inquiry raised by Derricotte underscores the void Woodson and the team of black teachers writing for the magazine hoped to fill. It also criticized the quality and content of the books provided by "the school systems" as insufficient and uninspiring.

In this same issue, Lisa A. Duckett, also of Washington, DC, shared a lesson plan she developed with her students to study Negro spirituals after students heard Howard University's Male Glee Club on the radio one night. After providing contextual information on why the songs were sung by the slaves, Duckett read a story entitled "Sunday with Great Grandmother," which gave an account of slavery appropriate for elementary students. She then developed group projects for the students, which included interviews, library research, and developing creative stories and artistic representations of their findings.[96] Duckett's article not only emphasized the *content* of this improvisational lesson but also the *process* of instruction. As such, the *Negro History Bulletin* had implication for curriculum content and pedagogy, for both students and teachers.

Duckett's lesson plans implicated a politicized educational agenda. She prefaced her lesson plan on Negro spirituals with the following statement: "This study . . . will also arouse in them a desire to overcome their own hindrances. These obstacles place new demands upon Negroes. They will be able to surmount these through constant, united effort and cooperative planning in the interest of all."[97] While the language here is coded, it is clear that Duckett is referring to the violent realities of Jim Crow. There was a lived understanding about the antiblack circumstances shaping the world in which both teachers and students lived. They had a shared vulnerability. Duckett's emphasis on a "constant, unified effort" explains why students worked as a group to research information about the period of slavery and the evolving significance of Negro spirituals. A communal work ethic would be necessary for them to overcome the obstacles they were sure to face in the future. The process and content of her lesson carried embedded meaning.

The *Negro History Bulletin* explicitly critiqued the master narratives found in adopted textbooks. Key examples include the reframing of the Civil War narrative, enslavement, the abolitionist movement, and dominant representations of Africa. Mainstream textbooks often represented the abolitionist movement as one led by kindhearted whites, filled with a conviction to fight for the emancipation of enslaved blacks. The *Bulletin* explicitly disrupted such narrative arcs. In the issue on the abolitionist movement in February 1938, Woodson acknowledged white sympathizers, but he also makes it clear that white abolitionists did not incite the desire for freedom in the hearts of black people. "The very mention of Frederick Douglass discloses the important fact that the abolition movement was not a movement by others for the Negro," wrote Woodson, but instead "a movement by the Negro for himself. The

Negroes from the very beginning were the first abolitionists." Woodson re-framed this historical narrative so that black students would understand that "during the days of bondage the slaves ever struggled in some way to be free."[98] This analysis countered representations of enslaved blacks in popular textbooks as docile and content.

Historical narratives were also tied to the contemporary moment. The No-vember 1939 issue covered African American education before the Civil War through twentieth-century Jim Crow. The section entitled "Educating the Negro before the General Emancipation" underscored that prior to the nineteenth century some slaves were allowed to acquire varying degrees of education; however, it detailed that after an increase in slave revolts, laws were implemented that made it illegal to teach blacks to read and write. Another article entitled "Snatching Learning in Forbidden Fields" explored how some enslaved men and women went to extreme lengths to acquire literacy. The issue also discussed the topic of "Education of the Negro Today," whereby progress had been noted regarding access to schools and an increase in the number of college-educated blacks. Woodson's critique of education also came across in this issue in a column entitled "Suggestions for Improvements in the Education of the Negro." In this section readers were offered an abbre-viated version of *Mis-education*.[99] Thus, the expansive narrative of black people's struggle for education was offered for teachers and students to see themselves as part of; the narrative makes clear how fugitive pedagogy was a central component of this legacy, the *Negro History Bulletin* itself being a material artifact of this heritage.

An array of pictures representing the history of black education were also featured in this issue. These included images of black children in school, new school buildings, a photo of a group of principals studying at Fisk Univer-sity, and a commencement processional at Xavier University. These visuals aligned with Woodson's and the editorial staff's desire to create a black learning aesthetic that could inspire students. This aesthetic reflected a dig-nified narrative of black educators and their work, as well as a story of their collective striving. Contributions by black teachers around the country in-creased as the magazine became more popular. By 1940, the circulation of the *Negro History Bulletin* was approximately five thousand and increasing.[100]

Like Negro History Week, the *Negro History Bulletin* became a critical re-source for teachers to exercise their fugitive pedagogy. They engaged these mediums as both thinkers and doers, translating and producing new scripts of knowledge. Black teachers partnered with Woodson to develop a shadow curriculum that critiqued the American School and simultaneously cultivated an affirming learning culture centered on black achievement and resistance. The fugitive pedagogy of black American educators persisted at the margins of the American School, striving to transform the learning experiences of students even as they had to function within an educational structure that was fundamentally antiblack and hostile, often punitive, toward their efforts. African American educators were imaginative in their thinking as *scholars of the practice* who deeply reflected on the art of teaching in the context of antiblack domination.

Fugitive Pedagogy as a Protracted Struggle

By the 1940s access to education improved for black Americans, which included access to preservice training for black teachers. Yet conditions continued to be far from ideal. There continued to be a battle for black teachers to be equally compensated as their white professional peers (prompting the NAACP's teacher salary-equalization litigation campaign), and the condition of black schools, the overwhelming majority of which were one- and two-room rural schools in the South, continued to be underresourced. Furthermore, the movement to provide public transportation for students through the 1930s largely bypassed black schools, so attendance continued to be an issue. Despite the ongoing structural challenges, which have been well documented, black educators continued to be imaginative in their practices and strategic in their efforts to circumvent oppressive educational structures that served as impediments for their work.[101]

Julia Davis was persistent. Resulting from her efforts that began in 1927, a conference was put together between Woodson and Mister Boggs that led to the recommendation and final adoption of Woodson's *Negro Makers of History* in a local traveling library, and in 1940 the first exhibit featuring black life and culture in the St. Louis Public Library was installed. Davis was the first director of the exhibit, and it became an annual event to commemorate Negro History Week, which she led from 1940 to 1951.[102]

Negro History Week continued to expand and took on particular nuance in specific communities. In 1941, Dr. Akiki Nyabongo wrote to Woodson sharing the activities he helped coordinate with his students at the State Teachers College at Montgomery, Alabama, and the local black schools.

Nyabongo highlighted the theme of the program held by a sixth-grade class, which focused on "Our Heritage of African Civilization." Nyabongo, a prince from Uganda, held degrees from Howard, Oxford, and Yale. His interest in offering black youth a more rigorous engagement with the African continent complemented his own scholarship on African cultures and languages.[103] Under his direction and with the assistance of students from the Alabama State Teachers College, these youth performed songs in different languages from West Africa and read papers on "Civilization of West Africa in the Middle Ages" and "African Womanhood." Nyabongo noted to Woodson that "what pleased [him] most was the way these students with little training, were able to render these songs in two African languages."[104] Nyabongo's work elucidates how Negro History Week functioned as an educational program that hinged on the communally bonded nature of black schools. Not only were teachers and students a part of these celebrations, but members of the broader community were also engaged in the program to expand the reach of Negro history. Furthermore, his efforts reflect how many Negro History Week celebrations cultivated a black diasporic consciousness among students and communities.

Woodson continued to partner with educators across the country. Hilda Grayson, for instance, was a South Carolina field agent for the ASNLH. She utilized her leadership role within South Carolina's black teachers' association to advance the work of Negro life and history in schools. In 1941 Grayson attended summer schools across the state, mobilizing black educators to subscribe to Woodson's publications while explaining to them the larger mission of the ASNLH. These summer courses were popular professional development opportunities among black teachers.[105] Woodson described Grayson as a "field representative of the Association." In this capacity, she worked "with the teachers through their conferences, associations, and conventions to demonstrate how the work of the Association may be correlated with what they are doing from day to day. In the performance of this task she has conducted a number of demonstrations with exhibits set up according to suggested themes, with pictures, newspapers, magazines, and books appropriate for school work."[106] Woodson was intentional in elevating key teachers to actively do this work on behalf of the ASNLH. Again, the success of Negro History Week and the circulation of knowledge about black life and culture depended on the "direct and positive link" between Woodson and ordinary teachers in local contexts.

By 1943, Woodson reported that 95 percent of the ASNLH's income came from black people. He publicized this fact with great pride because it was evidence of a communal investment in the work of the Association. "Negro teachers and their students are busy trying to fill the columns of the Bulletin with such materials as will be helpful to them," he explained. Woodson also pointed out how letters written to him from community members often used possessive language to describe the Association's magazine, denoting co-ownership of and a shared investment in the publication. Teachers and students referenced the *Bulletin* as "our magazine," "our periodical," or "our publication," he shared proudly.[107]

The support from black communities across the country was essential for the sustainability of Woodson's educational program. "In order to be independent and untrammeled for the task before them Negro agencies must be financed by the Negroes themselves," Woodson continued to argue. For proof of this necessity, one only had to look at the curricula adopted by the "boards of education to inculcate an appreciation of the past of the United States [that] never mention[s] the Negro except to condemn the race." Black patrons financed the *Negro History Bulletin* and Woodson developed the content of the magazine in collaboration with black educators who volunteered their services. In more ways than one, African American teachers and communities double taxed themselves to meet the needs of their students and to create new educational opportunities amid inequitable distribution of resources within the American School. While already overworked and underpaid, black teachers took on the labor of editing the magazine. They answered Bethune's call for more "translators" of Negro history.[108]

Two decades after his formal exit from the classroom, Woodson had become even more immersed in the professional world of black teachers as a "schoolmaster to his race." Intimately aware of the challenges under which black teachers worked in the American School, he made it his responsibility to meet educators where they were, offering resources from outside of formal school structures to fortify their political relevance in the lives of the students and communities they served.

Over twenty-five hundred delegates of the Georgia Teachers and Education Association (GT&EA) walked up the steps and through the six pillars of

Sisters Chapel at Spelman College to hear Carter G. Woodson's opening address. "Do not hang your heads in shame because your face is black for yours is a great heritage," he said to them. Do not teach students "away from their environment and leave them suspended in the air, but teach them with a more realistic approach." Woodson had uttered these words many times before, but they landed in a particularly powerful way on this Friday evening in April 1942. In plain language, he declared, "The whole educational system as applied to the Negro is wrong." Woodson criticized popular geography books, representations of Africa in school curricula, and cautioned the teachers against "imitating whites."[109] They must approach their work through critical study of black history and culture. Explicit engagement with structural systems that undermined black attempts at freedom and justice needed to be named and addressed head on. This was as basic as any of the fundamentals students were to learn in school. This was their work.

Members of the GT&EA filled the pews inside of the historic redbrick structure of Sisters Chapel beyond capacity. There was a pristine aesthetic to this collegiate sanctuary. Its crisp white walls, wooden pews and stage, and towering pipe organ that served as backdrop all mirrored the beauty and prestige of Spelman College. Black teachers were overflowing from the chapel. Many of them stood on chairs outside, while leaning their weight against the brick structure and glass windows to listen in. This opening meeting lasted until nearly midnight. Despite bodily fatigue, the teachers listened with a slight level of fanfare while basking in the presence of this felt encounter. The materiality of the space and its quaint architecture, however, are of less importance than the atmosphere of purpose and urgency that contoured the bodily experience. It is perhaps this contrast that helps make the point most clearly. Treating this space as a revival tent offers a more resonant imaging, a time and space where formal protocols and etiquette are suspended for more immediately demanding matters. This is to say, while standing on chairs outside and leaning into the windows of Sisters Chapel might have been perceived as unbecoming under ordinary circumstances at Spelman College, in this case, mission trumped etiquette and social comportment.

This was not Woodson's first time addressing a large body of educators; nor was it atypical.[110] Black teachers' association meetings were a critical extension of the black counterpublic sphere, where educators debated and honed their collective national and local agendas. Woodson explicitly identified

Postcard photo of Sisters Chapel at Spelman College. Hip Postcard.

these teachers' associations as vital publics for strategizing about future directions in black education, and it was an effective platform for spreading his vision on Negro life and history. This was a fact he knew quite well, given that his high school principal and cousin was an early member of the black teachers' association in West Virginia, which was founded in 1891.

While Woodson's partnerships with black educators was strongest in southern states, there are many examples of exemplary black educators in northern and midwestern states taking up the work of Negro life and history. Even when few in number, they found strategic ways to challenge the antiblack sentiments propagated by the American School. The additional labor these educators took on to elevate the cause was extraordinary.

Wilhelmina Crosson was one of these teachers who went beyond the classroom in taking up the work of the ASNLH. Crosson taught English and history in Boston, and she made wide appeals to incorporate Negro history in schools. She gave presentations for other educators at the Teachers College of the City of Boston, on how and why they should make the curricular changes advocated by Woodson.[111] As early as its inaugural year, Crosson, with the help of her brother, also coordinated Negro History Week celebrations.[112] Highlighting Crosson's unyielding commitment to the cause, in 1943 Woodson wrote the following: "[She] keeps the people of both races there thinking about the good rather than the evil to the credit of the Negro. She holds up before the young people of the city high ideals of the best in the race and to finance the work of the Association she secures from friends an annual appropriation."[113]

In 1944 Crosson contributed to the organization in an even greater capacity. She served as the local coordinator of the ASNLH annual meeting, which was held in Boston. Woodson had concerns as to whether Boston was a suitable location because of the small number of blacks in the city and its great distance from the majority of ASNLH members, who were heavily populated in the South. Crosson reassured Woodson that she could help him host a successful meeting in Boston. Her connections to teachers and her active role in the Boston chapter of Alpha Kappa Alpha Sorority, Inc., made her well positioned to get the job done. Woodson emphasized that Crosson deserved "honorable mention" for the meeting's success. "Miss Crosson appealed to her friends to rally as a committee to sponsor the meeting. . . . She sought no honor or any other consideration for herself . . . and the citizens, especially the women, rallied to the call." Because of Crosson's effective organizing with the local host committee, "they secured about 200 members whom they have organized as the Boston Branch of the Association."[114]

Despite the many successes, the condemnation of black life in the American School persisted. Curricular fights remained an ongoing battle, as did African Americans' struggle for social transformation more broadly. In the late 1930s the Louisiana Colored Teachers Association "formulated a committee to review the textbooks used in the public schools to assure that unfair statements dealing with black people were not included" and that more expansive representations of black life were featured in curricula.[115] A decade later blacks in this city continued to struggle with the narrative condemnation of black life in school books. In 1947 George Longe, an influential educator in New Orleans and local champion on Negro life and history, informed the school board that a book in the schools described blacks to be "ugly as monkeys and stupid as owls."[116] Black teachers had to maintain their vigilance of the school structures as long as their struggle for freedom and justice continued to be incomplete.

Antiblack domination in the American School engendered two competing scripts of knowledge and standards of practice in black school life. Woodson's mission to popularize black history and culture in schools and the covert manner in which educators partnered with him toward this end is but one thematic (though essential) case in the protracted story of fugitive pedagogy. Beyond the master narrative and imposed protocols, an alternative narrative script and political ideology from below continued to shape the ethical underpinnings of black teachers' work. Their pedagogical vision was a product of their persecution and their insistence on striving for a new world not premised on the condemnation of black life. Their teaching was first and foremost a political act to make the world something it had yet to be.

Conclusion

Tessie McGee's secret use of Woodson's textbook, large-scale Negro History Week productions, and appeals to local boards of education for curriculum changes—these were only some of the varied activities taken up by teachers to expand the educational program that Woodson formalized. Through his close ties to black teachers as a professional class, Woodson emerged as an abroad mentor, empowering them to disrupt the status quo within schools. His influence on black teachers appeared in the variety of ways they took up his education program and materials across time and geographic locations. In partnering with him, black teachers challenged the ideological underpinning of dominant schooling by placing the interiority of black life and struggle, past and present, at the center of their pedagogy.

Fugitive pedagogy often required bending (at times breaking) the rules, establishing new educational ethics. This moral conflict harkens back to the enslaved person "snatching learning in forbidden fields." Without conflating the two sets of experiences, it is important to name the recurring set of political relations formed between black people and the power of white authority within the American School. Tessie McGee, for example, subverted the Eurocentric curriculum that she was expected to teach by engaging in a physical act of defiance: the standard white curriculum on her desk, Woodson's textbook hidden in her lap. She *enacted* subversion; she didn't just teach it in an abstract manner. The counterdiscourse that ran through Woodson's curricula and its appeal to black teachers was reflective of an embodied understanding of the moral and political imperatives of education in black life. African American education, at its highest calling, required a fugitive disposition toward the moral codes of the American School. This was a demand of black spiritual strivings.

Black teachers clung to Woodson's educational model not simply because of his personal accolades but because his philosophy tapped at the core of their consciousness. To be clear, his critique of black schooling was unique, but it did not occur in a vacuum. The writings of black educators before Woodson demonstrate that there was a scattered yet consistent desire for black cultural achievement to be incorporated in schools. What Woodson did, however, was create the institutional structure around this counter-ideology, giving the ideas greater emphasis and impact. His institutions and innovative educational resources fortified the political racial socialization that was often already taking place in the private spaces of black teachers' classrooms. Through his writings, Woodson developed a theoretical language to explain why the teaching of black history and culture was necessary. As he put it, studying black life and history was an essential part of black America's pursuit of freedom and a more fulfilling life post-Emancipation. "The so-called freedom mentioned in the emancipation proclamation and the Thirteenth Amendment merely showed a step in the right direction," argued Woodson. "Very little has been done since that time to emancipate the mind of the Negro by which real freedom may be attained.... On the other hand, however, a systemic program has been worked out and promoted in enslaving the mind of the Negro."[117]

Woodson's abroad mentorship of black teachers and, likewise, their fugitive pedagogy had direct implications for student identities. Routines, rituals, and moral behaviors modeled by black teachers shaped the ecological context for black student development. The cultural content introduced by teachers was just as crucial in shaping students' orientations to school as students' witnessing of black teachers' fugitive disposition toward the American School and white authoritative power. Chapter 6 analyzes students' experiences, looking to classrooms where black teachers incorporated Woodson's textbooks and educational materials with a spirit of dissent. We find black students, like their teachers, confined by the external strictures of antiblackness and yet engaged participants in a dogged pursuit of education as an activity of escape and black subject making.

6

"Doomed to Be Both a Witness and a Participant": The Shared Vulnerability of Black Students and Black Teachers

The teacher's life is a double one. He stands in a certain fear. He tends to be stilted, almost dishonest, veiling himself before those awful eyes. Not the eyes of Almighty God are so straight, so penetrating, so all-seeing as the wonder-swept eyes of youth.

—W. E. B. DU BOIS, *Darkwater* (1920)

Black students were always watching. They bore witness to the rituals and behaviors that shaped their worlds. As is the case in all learning contexts, black education extended beyond what was uttered in lectures or written in homework assignments. Students learned from the value systems that shaped school routines and norms. What was seen, heard, and felt in these encounters all shaped experiences of knowledge transferal and creation; and the actions and deeds of black teachers communicated essential lessons.[1]

Tessie McGee's students were partners in her performance of fugitive pedagogy. They knew that with the turn of a door handle and the flick of McGee's eyes, her spoken narrative would change, leading perhaps to absurd or self-contradictory story lines in the history they were being taught. But they were not to question these shifts, in part because the lesson they were to learn did not change: education, as a freedom-seeking project, required constant subversion of antiblackness. Students discerned that McGee's reading from Woodson's textbook was both a deviation from the required curriculum and that her performance of compliance—reading from the openly displayed outline when someone came into her class—was an act of survival. Disjointed messages were not uncommon in black school life. Black Americans were constantly straddling two worlds. Negotiating the constraints of antiblack control within the American School on one hand, while engaging in the liberatory work of teaching and learning toward a new world order on the other. McGee's actions demonstrated this; so did the active participation of students in her classroom and the many other classrooms like it around the country.

It was Jerry Moore who recounted the scenario of McGee reading passages from Carter G. Woodson's "book on the Negro" instead of the preapproved history outline provided by Louisiana's white board of education. The student bore witness to his teachers' pedagogy of escape, thus leaving behind some record of this act and making possible its recovery. As a small boy, Moore also watched his father organize local farmers in Webster Parish to set aside plots of land to raise cotton and help pay for the very school in which he learned from McGee. Moore "grew up in the classroom," as he put it. Before he was old enough to go to school himself, he sat on a pallet in the corner of his mother's classroom as she instructed her primary school students. He watched her use flash cards and teach students to read and write on the blackboard.[2] He became perceptive of instructional practice at an early age.

Without recalling the specific passage McGee read from Woodson's textbook, Moore's witnessing of this subversive pedagogical tactic gestured toward the political demands of his education. These kinds of ephemeral moments tapped into a critical memory that black students inherited and carried through their educational journeys, inherited knowledge that informed *a way of looking* at black education as deeply political and embedded in a more expansive struggle for freedom and justice.

Student perspectives are largely submerged in the history of black education. Yet they are central to the story. First-person accounts from students allow us to explore their experience of black educational heritage in more ways than just dictated lessons and instruction. They provide textured detail about extralinguistic forms of communication and knowing— phenomenological insight about what shaped their development as black learners, how rituals and routines, cultural symbols, and especially relationships with teachers and peers informed their subjectivities. What follows is a close engagement with what was seen, felt, and experienced by black students in relationship to Woodson's curricular interventions as a means of analyzing their broader experience in the story of fugitive pedagogy.

This chapter asks: If black students were always watching, what did they see in their educational worlds? How did they understand their relationship to black teachers? How did bearing witness to black teachers' fugitive pedagogy, and Woodson's curricular materials in particular, influence the construction of student identities? In responding to these queries, the observer finds that black students were taught to see education in ways that were deeply informed by their alienation within the schooling apparatus of the United States. This shared oppositional gaze had long been nurtured under the tutelage of black teachers.

The Black Student as Witness: Living and Learning in an Antiblack World

Black students' "oppositional gaze" was not an opposition to learning itself but a way of looking that critiqued the practices of antiblack exclusion and confinement in education and that challenged the racist ideas that animated these experiences of of domination. It was a way of looking that documented and destabilized relations of power by cultivating an awareness from black students' marginalized perspectives.[3] This looking back challenged the position of black learners as "substudents"—whereby black people were written into the social contract of the American School or included through distorted ideas that defined blackness as the antithesis of the human subject: the ideal (white) citizen / student.[4]

The visual politics of schooling in the black social world developed its early meanings from the vantage of black pupils on the outside of the schoolhouse. During the early crusades for common schooling, education was a project of citizenship, which became merely a metonym for whiteness.[5] The countless narratives of black learners during slavery who were dramatically denied access to education or who were reprimanded for pursuing it are evidence of this. Martin Delany provides an iconic example. While born legally free, Delany was literally turned away from the schoolhouse he attempted to enter when accompanying a white playmate in Charleston, Virginia. In fact, in 1822 his family fled Charleston after their literacy was discovered and whites in the town began to chatter about the Delany family's offense. Years later, in 1850, Delany was admitted to Harvard to study medicine along with two other black students. Their admissions were terminated after white students protested.[6] Relatedly, Jenny Proctor was born enslaved in Alabama in 1850 and would recall how "none of us was 'lowed *to see a book* or try to learn. Dey say we git smarter den dey was if we learn anything."[7] Proctor employed fugitive tactics to learn to read and write, and Delany pieced together an education over the course of his life. Even for those black Americans who did gain access to education during the antebellum period, various racial provisions restricted it—distinctly reflecting their status as "substudents" in the US social order.

Stories of black learners developed into a critical black memory—a visual narrative comprising individual yet interrelated historical events. These accumulated accounts of black student witness formed a vantage point from the view of the black pupil: first, outside the American schoolhouse; then, inside on contingent and probationary terms. These memories prefigured the oppositional gaze of black students as a historically situated group of learners. The oppositional gaze of black students was made and remade through shared testimonies and personal experiences, and these memories were called on in black students' educational journeys.

Writing about black witnessing, Elizabeth Alexander has argued that black people have been looking and "forging a traumatized collective historical memory." This memory is "reinvoked at contemporary sites of conflict." It is a "practical memory," one that "exists and crucially informs African Americans about the lived realities of how violence and its potential informs our understanding of our individual selves as a larger group."[8] Just as black people developed a way of looking at the world and their place within it, education factored significantly into this repertoire of visual narratives on blackness, power, and the social order. In addition to forging a traumatized collective memory, black people also forged a memory of black fugitive life—moments where black people subverted structures of antiblack control and social technologies of terror. They witnessed black precarity as well as black people straining against their confined realities. Both sides of this phenomenon were critical for black students' interpretations of their educational encounters.

Black students' oppositional gaze developed well before Woodson's educational program in the twentieth century, but their witnessing took on new meaning with the educational materials Woodson produced through the Association for the Study of Negro Life and History. The content of his curriculum materials aligned with how black students were taught to look at black education all along, in that black counterperspectives and analyses were represented in the curriculum materials and images of the Association's educational program. This was a new alignment between content and pedagogy, and it was all revealed before the eyes of black students.

Cultivating a Black Learning Aesthetic

What students did and did not see in their books and on the walls said something about what was valued and worthy of study. In 1927 Woodson observed, "In practically all the schoolhouses of Europe and America there is not a picture on the wall or a book on the shelf to show that a Negro has ever achieved anything."[9] To challenge this erasure of black life, Woodson formalized a *black learning aesthetic* that reflected the souls of black classrooms more than ever before. This was done through his textbooks, Negro History Week, and supplementary curricular materials; even when these materials were not physically present, the ideas that informed them were taken up and used to shape learning experiences. This aesthetic restyled the contextual nature of learning in black schools by representing the underlying politics of fugitive pedagogy with more ideological and visual clarity than ever before. This had enormous implications for the development of black student identities. ASNLH president Mary McLeod Bethune compared the Association's curricular interventions to the statues of "great men" that studded the highways in ancient Rome. She emphasized the developmental significance of placing before the eyes of young people monumental symbols that enshrined important cultural ideas, instilled pride, and cultivated aspiration. Commemorating a more expansive African past and celebrating the stories of fugitive slaves, black artists, and political figures in the African Diaspora were a means toward erecting new curricular monuments. Black youth "gazing upon their faces, might be stimulated to greater achievement and accomplishment," Bethune asserted.[10] This refined learning aesthetic was something black students could look to and see a future in.

Both Woodson's and Bethune's assertions reveal their heightened awareness of the social context of development. They recognized how antiblack logic shaped the ecological landscape of schools, as well as its visual culture and institutional ethos. The literal absence of black life and culture in schools—in the physical images around classrooms, on the walls, and in books—were extensions of the larger obscuring of black humanity. The

absence of curricular monuments informed by the cultural and political realities of black people was an impediment to black aspiration and, at worst,
served to demotivate black students. Woodson partnered with teachers to develop new standards and principles for what classrooms should look and feel
like for black students—hence my use of the word *aesthetic*. They recreated
and reconceptualized artifacts of learning to be used for the students they
taught.[11] Woodson and the teachers he partnered with operated from a belief that transforming the symbolic order of schools was an integral part of
transforming the world in which they lived. Student accounts are replete with
examples of how this came to life in the interior of black schools.

Allen Ballard recalled how in 1930s Philadelphia, "throughout the year, the
halls and classrooms of the school were decorated with pictures of such no-
tables as Harriet Tubman, Frederick Douglass, and Alexander Dumas, and
each of our weekly school assemblies began with the singing of the Negro
National Anthem." He then emphasized how Woodson's educational program enhanced these cultural practices or perhaps brought them into more
explicit focus during Negro History Week. To his teacher, "Nelly Bright,
Negro History Week . . . was something special. It was a time for skits about
the underground railroad, poetry readings of the works of Paul Laurence
Dunbar, art contests for the best Negro History poster, and a special chorus
to sing such spirituals as 'Walk Together Children,' or 'Steal away.'"[12]

If the objective of black education was freedom and transforming the lives
of black people, then, in Woodson's mind, these values should instruct the
visual culture of schools and the ideas shaping students' experiences. The idea
of black freedom posed a visual problem that both blacks and whites began
negotiating—in separate and distinct ways—well before Emancipation. This
politics of representation was routed through, over, and against derogatory
images of Africa and African people, slavery, and caricatures of black path-
ological deviance.[13] The visual culture of classrooms was positioned squarely
within this struggle. Woodson encouraged educators to stage their classrooms
in a manner that positioned it as a key site in the broader struggle for freedom,
which required a new articulation of black racial heritage.

The aesthetics of black learning—visually, ideologically, and affectively—
were to be aligned with the primary social and political objectives of fugitive pedagogy. This aesthetic transformation required teachers and students
to defy the normative protocols of the American School. A black learning aes-

thetic was at once a critique of the national culture as well as the Western epistemological order, in which black life and black people had long been narratively condemned.

A Black Learning Aesthetic as a Resource in Student Identity Formation

Comprising more than just good stories and exciting pictures, this learning aesthetic represented critical ideas about the black condition and stories of people with whom students could racially and politically identify, helping them to understand their subjectivities as black learners. It provided new resources for learning and for shaping their racialized and academic identities. As theorized by Na'ilah Nasir and informed by ecological theories of development, "identity resources" delineates key aspects in the social emergence of students' individuated identities, which is always a contextual phenomenon. Identity resources include tangible artifacts ("material resources"), ideas ("ideational resources"), and people ("relational resources"), all of which shape learning contexts and inform interactional processes as students come into themselves as individual subjects, as they come to know themselves as a learner, and a learner of a particular group(s).[14] Engaging in activities and rituals also shapes the emergence of student identities, what Nasir calls "putting something of oneself into practice" (e.g., saluting the American flag or singing the Negro national anthem). These resources make available *and* foreclose possibilities for how students see themselves and visions about who they can become. This twenty-first-century conceptualization of student development and school contexts provides an analytic resource for understanding the relationship between the learning aesthetic developed by black teachers and its influence on black student development.

The pictures and textbooks Woodson published offered material resources that presented broad and alternative images of black life that defied racist notions of black inferiority (e.g., illustrations of Crispus Attucks and Sojourner Truth or paintings by black artists like James L. Wells and Lois Mailou Jones). The ideas reflected in this content (ideational resources) were powerful—not only stories about the ubiquitous violence of slavery and Jim Crow but also vivid stories of slave revolts, black civic engagement during Reconstruction, and black independent nations in precolonial Africa and the African Diaspora.

Black teachers' fugitive pedagogy combined with this new learning aesthetic enhanced students' learning, culturally and politically.

In 1929 a student at the National Training School for Women and Girls reflected on the newly emerging black learning aesthetic at her school in Washington, DC. In a yearbook entry, she explained, "This school teaches History and Negro History, and the students are tremendously inspired by learning the truth about their own race. We know now that our race has been going on in the building of world civilizations." She outlined specific ways that these ideas were implemented at the National Training School: "Dr. Carter G. Woodson's books are used as the text here and we have a room, a real library—if you please—set apart for the Study of Negro Life and History." As described by this student, not only were alternative representations of blackness central to her school's culture; she emphasized the materiality of this knowledge system via textbooks and "a real library." This black learning aesthetic also had practical implications for students. "If you want to see us in our glory visit us on Appreciation Day, February 22nd, and hear us tell what the Negro has done for the world." She continued, "When it comes to this race history the Training School Girls have the world beat, not including Dr. Woodson. . . . We know our material." In her assertion that "we know our material," this student emphasized how being grounded in a historical consciousness of black heritage became a meaningful part of the academic identities cultivated at her school.

The training school students celebrated Katherine Allen, one of their peers who made a reputation for being outspoken against matters of racial injustice. Inspired by their lessons in Negro history, Allen became a "race agitator." In fact, "Many race agitators have been discovered," the young women explain, and "Miss Allen, a senior is sure to be another Sojourner Truth."[15] They celebrated the young activist in the making. She had been "helped" and "inspired" by their studies of black people's persistent struggle for freedom. As previously noted, the fugitive slave functioned as a folk hero in black curricular imaginations. Even as Truth was an illiterate woman, she asserted herself as a rational subject and a political actor that students might aspire to emulate. Truth is featured in the student yearbook as her own superlative category. These students likely found the story of Truth, as it appeared in Woodson's textbooks, to be inspiring. He described Truth as a fugitive and fierce abolitionist who "acquired miraculous power" through her ability to "stir audiences with her heavy voice, quaint language and homely illustrations." Truth's contributions to the cause of black freedom went beyond the words she uttered; she also "served the Union army as a messenger and spy."[16]

Students across the country would come to associate the study of black history and culture in their schools, and Negro History Week in particular, as a source that sparked their commitment to participating in the black struggle for freedom. Decades later, Carlotta Walls LaNier became a "race agitator" like the students at the National Training School. LaNier emphasized how the black learning aesthetic in her elementary and junior high schools helped inspire her to participate in the desegregation of Arkansas's Central High School in 1957, as one of the Little Rock Nine. "We were standing on shoulders of others," she stated. "We had Negro History Week in the segregated black schools. And I was always proud to read more and hear about what African Americans or Negroes or Coloreds did for this country. . . . I knew I was standing on their shoulders."[17]

Congressman John Lewis (1940–2020) reflected on his youth in Troy, Alabama, in similar ways when describing "the unbelievable teachers" in his schools. "When I was a little child growing up in rural Alabama, a short walk to the cotton fields . . . my teachers would tell us to cut out photographs and pictures of great African Americans for Carter G. Woodson's Negro History Week," Lewis explained. These educators discreetly informed students about the Civil Rights protests and boycotts taking place in cities like Montgomery by encouraging them to read black publications that widely covered these events. The stories, images, and ideas inspired Lewis to imagine ways that he might contribute to black people's struggle for freedom. In 1956, prior to his involvement in the student sit-in movement or the founding of the Student Nonviolent Coordinating Committee, a sixteen-year-old Lewis gathered his siblings and cousins to try to register for library cards at the Troy public library, even as they knew they would be turned away. The stories of Negro History Week started him on a path of "making good trouble" toward social transformation.[18]

For students like LaNier and Lewis, the black learning aesthetic allowed them to situate themselves in a continuum of consciousness. They were taught to aspire to be part of a tradition of black people who disrupted an antiblack social order, a lineage of thinkers and political subjects whose mission centered on transforming a world predicated on black suffering.

"Dr. Woodson assembled an impressive array of pictures and scenes of distinguished Negroes and Negro Life," wrote Thelma Perry, a member of the
American Teachers Association. "They could be procured for modest prices
from the Association headquarters: small pictures for schoolwork, litho-
graphs with suitable margins for framing, and large, nearly life-size photographs for assembly halls and offices."[19] With these materials, teachers and
students could have "the history of the Negro race told with pictures of its
great men and women." Woodson encouraged his audience to "frame them
and decorate your home with them" and, above all else, "hang them on the
walls of your school room."[20] These decorative materials included photos that
could but cut and pasted for schoolwork, "scenes from the life of the Negro,"
and pictures of various black men and women of achievement. The images
were catalogued under such themes as "Negroes Internationally Known,"
"Negro Women of Distinction," "Negroes of Genius," or "Negro Artists."

Dwight O. W. Holmes, president of Morgan State University, stressed that
Woodson's decorative prints were "a minor, but none-the-less important
project . . . instilling in the minds of school children, respect for and familiarity
with successful colored persons." This one intervention helped transform
the learning aesthetics for many schools across the country. These images
could be found "displayed in large urban high schools and in small schools in
towns and rural areas for use at special exercises for pupils in classes in history,
but hung *so that they could constantly be seen.*"[21]

Racial socialization took place in schools and society, whether done explicitly or not. The prevalence of antiblackness in US popular culture and school
content made it necessary to offer purposeful and humanizing perspectives
on blackness to support the healthy development of black student identities.
The learning aesthetic offered through Woodson's program presented resources that supported the development of student identities that were historically grounded, aware of their oppression, and committed to imagining
and building new possibilities for their collective futures. It was enacted discursively through curriculum development, materially through decorative
educational resources produced for classrooms and schools, and affectively
through performances and dramatizations during Negro History Week celebrations and classroom activities. This aesthetic presented new symbols of
being and belonging that were distinct to black students, all of which offered
explicit critiques of the master narrative about black life shaping their Jim
Crow surroundings.

Student Accounts of Woodson's "Atmospheric" Impact

What black students witnessed in school extended well beyond decorations and posters on black history. The black learning aesthetic was entangled with a more expansive visual politics in black education. These visual politics included, for instance, black students noticing the sharp contrasts between their schools and the white schools they passed every day. Allen Ballard described the aesthetics of Negro History Week in 1930s Philadelphia as "an intellectual and emotional anchor in the midst of overt racism, legal segregation, and the attendant myths of white superiority." The aesthetics of Negro History Week supported students as they became consciously aware of their subjugated position in society. It "meant a lot to us as we daily walked by the spanking brand-new white school with its high wire fences on our way to the Hill school three blocks past it."[22]

John Bracey described Woodson's impact as "atmospheric" at his school in Washington, DC, during the 1940s. It was all around him at Lucretia Mott Elementary School. From the singing of the Negro national anthem, to celebrating Negro History Week, to studying from the *Negro History Bulletin*. In deploying the language of "atmospheric," Bracey gestured toward the felt quality of the learning aesthetic Woodson helped to cultivate, especially in DC schools, where Woodson lived.

Students also recognized these aesthetic practices to be distinct from the dominant curriculum and the expectations of white school authorities. Bracey recalled an occasion when the teachers of Mott elementary prepared students to sing "The Star-Spangled Banner" in preparation for white visitors. "But in homeroom every morning—you had to do as part of your culture, you sang the Negro national anthem. . . . We only sang 'The Star Spangled Banner' when white people showed up," Bracey explained. "You had to go to the assembly hall the day before and practice 'The Star Spangled Banner' because nobody knew it."[23] While black educators cultivated their own norms and ideas about what constituted a purposeful education, this did not mean they were not required to appease white educational officials, who held the final authority over the operations of black schools. These educators developed strategic means of acquiescing to the edicts of their higher-ups while simultaneously teaching to transgress. In this scenario, Bracey recalled a moment of students witnessing the subversive pedagogy of black teachers. In fact, the entire school participated in this staged act of dissemblance. In these moments, students came to understand what was valued in their education and what it meant to maneuver through the strictures of Jim Crow. Black teachers wore the mask of compliant educators that deferred to the norms of the American School, even as they subverted it on a daily basis in having their students sing the Negro national anthem.

"Lift Every Voice and Sing" (popularly known as the Negro national anthem), written and composed by James Weldon Johnson and his brother John Rosamond Johnson, became a fundamental element of "black formalism" by the 1920s. As Black Studies scholar Imani Perry notes, black formalism denotes "practices that were primarily internal to the black community, rather than those based upon the white gaze or an aspiration for white acceptance."[24] The song was a cultural text that became integrated into the protocols of black institutional life, ways of structuring events and occasions. Singing this song was a ritual that held embedded meaning related to black people's history of oppression, resistance, and futuristic visions of freedom and justice. It reflected the interiority of the black world—a range of feelings and a distinct political plight. Like most black institutions during this period, Woodson's ASNLH took the song up at its annual meetings, and lesson plans urging teachers to incorporate the song into the learning culture of their schools were also published in the *Negro History Bulletin*. In many instances the song functioned as a sort of daily devotional and, more generally, part of the soundtrack to black educational life.[25]

The anthem became engrained in the mind of students like Bracey, having become part of the atmosphere. "If you said national anthem," explained Bracey, "we stood up and sang 'Lift Every Voice and Sing,' but if there was a white superintendent or somebody . . . 'EVERYBODY REPORT TO THE AUDITORIUM!' We have to practice the national anthem." He explained their bewilderment as students: "Everybody'd say, 'We already know the national anthem.' They'd say, 'No, the white national an . . .' 'Ooooohhh . . . *that* national anthem, okay.'" Bracey and his classmates were then required to participate in the staged performance of compliance. He recalled, "Then you had to go down to, 'Oh say, can you,' (which is a horrible goddam song). When the white person showed up, you sang both of them. You'd open up the program with 'The Star Spangled Banner,' but you close with 'Lift Every Voice and Sing.'" Bracey recalled, "If you had wanted to bet money with me when I was in fourth grade, I would have told you 'Lift Every Voice and Sing' was the

national anthem. White people had some crap they sang, but this is the national anthem."[26] Black teachers prepared students to sing "The Star-Spangled
Banner" when they had white visitors, perhaps to avoid raising any unneces-
sary suspicion. Nonetheless, the daily routines and rituals in black schools informed the way black students came to look at the world and shaped their
learning identities. Singing this song was a ritual where black students put
something of their racialized selves into practice. The same can be said of their
participation in the act of staged compliance when white visitors arrived.

Students learned how their education was both a part of and apart from
the mainstream project of the American School. This was a complex form of
civic education, reflective of the complex identities of black Americans—two
warring ideals: one black, one American, perpetually in tension with one another. The very idea of a "Negro" national anthem signaled their estrangement within the nation and within the American School.[27] More generally,
Bracey's account underscored how students witnessed their teachers navigating the politics of Jim Crow and how students arrived at important understandings about what it meant for them as black people living in the world:
*We sing "The Star Spangled Banner" when white people come to our school,
but on regular days we sing "Lift Every Voice and Sing," the Negro National
Anthem.* Allegorically speaking, black students learned what it meant to
"wear the mask," as Paul Laurence Dunbar wrote. Bearing witness to their
teachers' fugitive pedagogy revealed a moral orientation toward black education that suggested there were multiple layers to its meaning. These meanings were not always explicit, but black students developed their own command of them through accumulated experiences—both in and outside of
schools. They developed an informed gaze that helped them discern what
they were witnessing in these fleeting moments—where their teachers made
decisions to appease white authorities even if their truths were masked for
the time being.

Woodson's impact on the learning aesthetic in black schools not only
showed up in implicit ways, such as formalized cultural practices, but it also
materialized through his textbooks. LaVerne Beard Spurlock offered her recollection of this. Spurlock was born in Richmond, Virginia, in 1930 and became an educator in the city's public schools. She recalled one of her teachers,
"who was just perfect," during her years at Armstrong High School in the
1940s. Joseph Ransom taught a class on Negro history. "It was not required,"

clarified Spurlock, "but everybody took it because we all loved Mr. Ransom."
What she remembered most about the class was its emphasis on pushing students to engage new narratives about black life on the African continent;
Ransom pushed students to think about "how they worked with each other,
and their values."

When reflecting on how she felt as a student in Ransom's class and what
she remembered from his lectures, the eighty-seven-year-old retired educator
suddenly recalled the textbook he used. "*The Story of the Negro Retold*, by
Carter G. Woodson; that was the name of the book. Oh, you're calling on my
memory today," said Spurlock as she smiled, impressed with herself for re-
membering the title of this textbook after what seems like a lifetime ago.
Ransom "strayed from the book quite often," but it was Woodson's textbook
that anchored the class. Spurlock shared, "I'm sure some of the things I've
done as a teacher were some of the *things I saw done by the teachers that taught
me*. . . . Their habits were so established, and . . . they made such a difference
in our lives." She explained how these powerful stories about black life became
a part of her own repertoire for educating students once she herself became a
teacher.[28]

Accounts of student witnessing are critical for extending the historical
transcript of black education, and Spurlock's witnessing is evidence of this.
Black teachers, like Spurlock, were once students themselves, and they represent an important source for exploring how black pedagogical traditions
carried over. There are many cases that elucidate this point—where we see
the cultural and political transmission of black pedagogical practices through
students who became teachers. When responding to a Negro History Week
survey in 1950, E. A. Hightower, a teacher in New York City, shared that she
implemented the program for her students because it positively affected her
own life as a student in Washington, DC, public schools.[29] The story of fugitive pedagogy has long been a story of movement, migration, and flight. James
Weldon Johnson emphasized this in the story of "Lift Every Voice and Sing."
After students sang the song for the first time in 1900, they kept singing it in
the many places they traveled as students and teachers. Johnson explained,
"Some of them became schoolteachers and taught it to their pupils."[30] This
process of pedagogical transmission speaks to the blurred lines between the
subjectivities of black teachers and black students.

Angela Davis was born in Birmingham, Alabama, in 1944. The scholar and activist recalled that Negro History Week was "the highlight of our year." During these commemorative weeks, teachers instructed students to slam shut and "cast aside" the books that "did their best to persuade us that our ancestors were much better off during slavery than they would have been had they remained in Africa . . . and we were allowed then to rely on our own ability to produce knowledge about the conditions surrounding our lives." Davis underscored that black students engaged in a collective critique of the normative white curriculum in their *casting it aside*—linking black learning and the work of teachers with a radical history of black subversive educational practices. More than a captive audience, black students actively participated in the tradition of fugitive pedagogy. Davis understood this "casting aside" as a conscious effort to escape racist narratives imposed through the "discarded history textbooks from the white schools."[31] Through these pedagogical acts, black teachers were enacting subversion, not just teaching it, and students often took part in critiquing and challenging antiblack norms.

Shared Vulnerability and Shared Participation in Black Educational Heritage

Black teachers' and students' intersubjectivity become evident in moments when their relation moves from teacher and pupil to, instead, partners in a tradition of fugitive pedagogy, as the previous scenarios revealed. The educator, writer, and political activist James Weldon Johnson described this *shared vulnerability* between him and his students in a backwoods school in Georgia during the early 1890s: "In an instant's reflection I could realize that they were me, and I was they; that a force stronger than blood made us one."[32] This entangled reality gave meaning to black racial belonging, which had critical implications for experience in black classrooms.

The precarity of black American life in slavery and freedom shaped core aspects of black sociality. What was witnessed in the life of one black person held meaning for what could be in the life of another. Take Frederick Douglass's iconic account of his aunt's violent assault in his slave narrative. He takes care to note that he was "doomed to be both a witness and a participant."[33] Shared vulnerability is central to black witnessing—which is distinct from spectatorship. This was an integral part of black teachers' and students' experiences in the classroom and the world. One might recall here how black schools became targets of white supremacist violence in the nineteenth century and the ways in which black adults and children were hyperaware of their vulnerability to antiblack violence in society.[34] Accounts from Louisiana in the 1940s described how Ku Klux Klansmen "would tie the bodies of lynched black men to the fronts of their cars and drive them through crowds of black children."[35] Coming to know one's people as a race, for black folks, meant coming into an awareness of black people's shared vulnerability—an integral part of black subject formation, in the developmental context of schools and otherwise.

Angela Davis gave language to the shared vulnerability between adults and young people, teachers and students, when recalling the racialized violence in Birmingham during her childhood. "I remember, from the time I was very small, I remember the sounds of bombs exploding across the street, our house shaking," Davis explained. "I remember my father having to have guns at his disposal at all times because of the fact that at any moment . . . we might expect to be attacked." Davis named her mother's relationship, as a teacher, to one of the young girls killed in the bombing of the Sixteenth Street Baptist Church in 1963. "My mother taught one of them in her class," shared Davis. "In fact, when the bombing occurred one of the mothers of one of the young girls called my mother and said, 'Can you take me down to the church to pick up Carol, you know, we heard about the bombing and I don't have my car.' And they went down and what did they find? They found limbs and heads strewn all over the place."[36] While this spectacle of antiblack terror happened after Woodson's death, it nonetheless speaks to the perpetual threat black students, teachers, and communities had to reckon with—in and outside of the classroom. Student recollections of this "traumatized collective memory" that violated the innocence of black childhood were widespread. Given this shared vulnerability between teachers and students, fugitive pedagogy demanded shared participation.

Students have always held an active role in the expansive story of black educational heritage. Frederick Douglass's strategic efforts to maintain his educational advancement even after his master expressed strong disapproval of him learning to read is the most widely known example of this. Douglass traded food with poor white boys in exchange for lessons after his mistress was forbidden to teach him.[37] Similarly, while Jenny Proctor was not "lowed to see a book or try to learn," she nonetheless made strong attempts at literacy anyhow. "We slips around and gits hold of dat Webster's old blue back speller," Proctor recounted, "and we hides it 'til way in de night and den we lights a little pine torch, and studies dat spellin' book."[38] These accounts from the time of slavery provide early markers of the fugitive practices employed by black learners in the making of their own academic subjectivities. As such, they were active participants in the dissident politics of black educational heritage. They offer the earliest models of fugitive pedagogy in the story of black education, often as *self-taught* learners—their insistence on self-possession itself being an act of transgression.

William Holtzclaw's formerly enslaved mother helped him devise schemes in the late nineteenth century to circumvent their landlord's demand that Holtzclaw work in the field and not go to school while growing up in Alabama. She instructed her two sons to take turns hiding on different days when the landlord came to collect them for work—one hid behind pots and pans while the other went into the field to pick cotton. "But when I became too large to be conveniently hidden behind our few small pots," Holtzclaw explained, "I had to take my place on the farm." But he continued to engage in fugitive practices of learning. Holtzclaw continued: "When I was nine years old I began work as a regular field-hand. My mother now devised another plan to keep me in school: I took turns with my brother at the plow and in school; one day I plowed and he went to school, the next day he plowed and I went to school; what he learned on his school day he taught me at night and I did the same for him."[39] Black students' status as learners continued to be contested, and, therefore, a subversive disposition long shaped their identities.

After slavery, black students became included in the American School under quarantined conditions and, therefore, continued to be active participants in fugitive pedagogy. Black teachers actively cultivated this participation, in part because teachers understood their fate to be linked with their students. They were embarking on a collective effort to achieve freedom through educational advancement. They appealed to black students, in a similar fashion as the black teacher and textbook author Leila Amos Pendleton, who explained: "There are some of us who feel that, pitifully small though it be, we have given the very best and done the very most it is possible for us to give and to do for the race, and we are looking to you, dear children, to perform the things which we, in our youth had hoped and planned."[40] At times, black teachers relinquished dominion in favor of a more transparent pedagogy of entanglement, acknowledging that in reality black teachers and students faced the same threats. Pendleton signaled a collective racial project in which both she and her students were engaged and implicated. There was a shared plot between them. The racial kinship between students and teachers functioned as a relational resource in the development of black youth identities.

Student participation was encouraged in Woodson's educational program. The Students Literary and Debating League of Brooklyn hosted a "history bee" during Negro History Week in 1933, bringing together more than two hundred people at the Carleton Avenue YMCA in Brooklyn. High school students from Manhattan, northern New Jersey, and Brooklyn competed to become prized Negro history champions. Students were quizzed on "several hundred questions" ranging from the meaning of the NAACP acronym to Phillis Wheatley's place of birth. Students invited Arturo Schomburg—the famous bibliophile and Black Renaissance scholar—to deliver the keynote speech. Events like the bee allowed students to engage in a practice of race consciousness, where knowledge of black history and culture was celebrated and award worthy.[41] These activities gave meaning to who they were as students who occupied a particular racialized and academic identity. Similar events around the country became fertile grounds for stirring up new ideas about how students could carry their identities as black learners—unapologetically proud, steeped in a heritage of struggle, and members of a community actively working toward the higher truths of justice. The program also included musical and oratorical performances. While black struggle was certainly a central theme of Negro History Week, black students' cultural performances also made space for enjoyment and creative expression.

In 1935, Tamah Richardson and her student-teacher, Annie Rivers, conducted a ten-week unit of study with their third-grade class at the George P. Phenix School in Virginia, on "Progress of the Negro." The ten-week module was sparked by student demand. A student posed the question: "May we study ourselves, too?" Responding to this demand, posed in the form of a question, Richardson and Rivers called a vote among the thirty-seven third graders to assess whether they shared their classmate's desire.

"All hands shot up." Richardson and Rivers put together a course of study inspired by an outline provided by A. D. Wright in a 1934 issue of the *Journal of Negro History.*[42]

These teachers outlined their goals: to "teach the Negro child as much as we can about (1) the background from which he has come, (2) the circumstances of his coming to this country, (3) slavery and emancipation, (4) the story of the accomplishments of *men and women of his race who have risen above handicaps, difficulties, discrimination, prejudice, and even active opposition, to accomplish great things.*" Students engaged in a range of assignments from interviewing community members that were formerly enslaved, writing and mailing letters to black students at other schools about what they learned, inviting black international students from Hampton University to talk about life on the African continent, and writing poems to express comprehension of their lesson.[43]

Richardson and Rivers engaged students as partners in the process of learning something about themselves, a shared critique of the American Curriculum's lack of engagement with their lives as black people. The young students' inquiry to learn something about themselves "too" was an implication that standard objectives for learning did not include opportunities for black self-knowledge. Critiquing the American School became a way for black students to "[put] something of oneself into practice."

An exchange of letters between Mattie Bizzell, a third grader at the J. C. Training School in Smithfield, North Carolina, and Calvin Cooke, at the Phenix School, linked black education to the history of slavery and the black struggle for freedom. In responding to Mattie's request that he share "some of the interesting things [he had] found out about the Negro," Calvin shared the iconic story of Frederick Douglass learning to read and write, the infinitely appearing figure of the fugitive slave, and fugitive literacy, again manifesting as a folk hero in black curricular imaginations. "At the age of eight he was sent to Baltimore where he learned to read from a white woman," Calvin explained. "When the lady's husband stopped her he learned from white boys on the streets, and from signs on the wharves."[44]

Students also interviewed some of the oldest living members of their community. In doing so they encountered Joana Shands, who was their teacher's grandmother. Walter Weaver wrote the following about Shands:

A Living Ex-Slave in Our Community

Mrs. Joana Shands is the oldest living ex-slave in our community. She is nearly one hundred years old. It is very sad, but interesting, as she smiles and talks about her life as a slave.

Her master never sold her, but he took her from her mother at the age of five to give his daughter as a wedding present.

She remembers well her life as a slave weaving, carding, spinning and knitting. She can knot, sew and card now. I have seen her use these carders. She can sew and knit without glasses. She is the mother of six living children, sixteen grandchildren, and one great-, great-grandchild. She is the grandmother of our teacher.[45]

In this unit of study, students were partners in the process of collecting and sharing knowledge about black life and history. Their teachers were intentional to expose them to critical aspects of their heritage largely unacknowledged and distorted in the official curriculum.

The political significance of black education had always been routed through and understood in relationship to the history of slavery. Bill Parker's poem emphasized this point. Parker wrote a poem based on the memory of slavery in his own family, a theme he would also speak on for his school's Negro History Week production:

My Poem for Great-, Great-grandfather
When my great-, great-grandfather was a slave
They'd whip him to death if he didn't behave
They made him carry cotton by the ton,
And even shipped his little son,
They didn't teach him to read or write
Or even let him out of their sight.
Now do you think it was right
To whip poor great-, great-grandfather with all their
Might?[46]

Shared vulnerability triangulated between teachers and students and black American family lineage. Teachers' and students' shared family histories of enslavement were explicitly acknowledged. Students interviewed their teacher's grandmother, who was formerly enslaved, while Parker crafted a poem about his family's memory of slavery. Richardson and Rivers took a similar stance as Woodson, who pushed back against the idea that "the Negro should cease to remember that he was once held a slave, that he has been oppressed, and even that he is a Negro."[47]

Black teachers supported students in developing an oppositional gaze, exposing them to critical narratives about black life and culture and helping them understand its relationship to their own family as well as black people's struggle for education. This is what I have referred to as "rigorous sight" in previous chapters. Through this way of looking and knowing, education was positioned as an extension of a much longer black political history that ultimately had to do with matters of freedom and racial justice.

Some students took on roles of civic responsibility in relation to the work of the ASNLH. They participated in fund-raising efforts for the ASNLH during Negro History Week, the same way many black teachers required students to pay student membership fees to their local NAACP branches. Shared participation was operationalized in black school life as students took on civic responsibilities for the future of the race. Some even required students to bring money to subscribe to the *Negro History Bulletin*. In doing so, students were putting something into practice that had political implication for who they were as a distinct racialized group of learners. There were also junior branches of the ASNLH in schools, where students engaged in sustained, year-round activities associated with black life and history.[48]

In 1942 Woodson communicated with teachers and ASNLH members across the country regarding a national membership drive, of which students were to play a key role. Like he did with many other educators, Woodson wrote to Martha M. Wilson, principal of the J. H. Smythe School in Norfolk, Virginia, encouraging her to invite teachers and students to support the Association. He explained, "The fifteen or twenty thousand dollars that we receive annually for the advancement of this work comes mainly from the poor Negroes themselves who contribute from one penny to a dollar each year." It was Woodson's hope that the faculty and students of her school would join in this shared sacrifice. "Almost every child is willing to give a penny to help his race," Woodson explained, "and teachers, as a rule, do not consider it a sacrifice to give 15 cents, 25 cents, 50 cents, or $1.00 a year for this cause. We sincerely hope that you will join with us in raising the $500.00 or more which we have annually secured from Virginia during the last six years."[49] Luther P. Jackson, president of Virginia State University and ASNLH state chairman for Virginia, helped to facilitate this effort through his influence in the Virginia Teachers Association. In March 1942 he wrote to Woodson, noting fourteen contributions from different schools totaling $140.22 and assuring him that more funds would follow. Jackson made clear that this money did not consist of membership fees, which Porter had also been collecting. "None of this is dollar sustaining membership money," Jackson assured Woodson, "but rather the fifteen, twenty-five, and one cent contributions from teachers and pupils over our State."[50]

John Bracey recalled that students at his elementary and middle school in the 1940s and early 1950s in Washington, DC, were accustomed to routinely bringing money for *Negro History Bulletin* subscriptions, just as they were expected to bring money for milk. This was likely engrained in the school culture at Benjamin Banneker Junior High School because Albert N. D. Brooks was the assistant principal. Brooks was also the editor of the *Negro History Bulletin*. Nevertheless, Bracey was so accustomed to this practice that when he arrived to attend the recently desegregated Roosevelt High School in the mid-1950s, he was shocked to learn that this was not standard of all schools. "I asked them when they were taking the money for the *Negro History Bulletin*," he recalled. "The woman looked at me like I was nuts."[51] The *Negro History Bulletin* had been used as a tool for schoolwork and even a collectible item for some. Bracey emphasized: "You had to do your paper. You got two copies sometimes because if you had your paper, you cut out your pictures. You didn't want to mess it up, so you bought an extra copy so you cut the pictures out."[52]

Black students were partners in the fugitive project of black education all along. This went beyond listening to their teachers stealthily read stories from Woodson's textbooks or standing by in silent consent as their teachers employed subversive pedagogical tactics. They watched the work of their teachers and the politics they embodied. Likewise, black youth were positioned as students inheriting a tradition of protest through education. Just as Woodson's early educational experience taught him that education was about the unfinished project of freedom, this continued to be the case in black educational heritage. Circumstances had certainly changed since the nineteenth century, but the political ends of black education continued to be shaped by an aspiration for freedom—an effort to ameliorate the material and social conditions of black life. Black students were learners in a distinct educational tradition with a distinct political mission and historical memory.

Leaving a Deep Impression: On Rituals and Embodied Learning

A system of counterideology animated the actions of black teachers' pedagogy and the socioemotional learning contexts they created. These ideas were verbally expressed to students by their teachers and community, but they were often communicated through the nature of student-teacher relationships in black schools and the cultural memory black people shared about the political significance of education. Woodson's educational program empowered teachers to make this underlying counterideology explicit through the black learning aesthetic they worked to formalize.

Houston Baker's recollection of Negro History Week at his Kentucky elementary school in the 1940s emphasized the political clarity of his teachers. "In Louisville—at Virginia Avenue Elementary School—we saw the blackboard décor from last year come out again, and we recited the mantra of Negro contributions to America," Baker recalled. Then, his teacher Miss Carter intoned, ""Children . . . you must never be ashamed of being Negroes!"" She instructed them that ""Dr. Woodson wants us to be proud of our history."" These weeks were about more than just empirical data on black achievement, Baker explained. They were not "dedicated exclusively to hard-and-fast contributions and actual songs written by the likes of James Weldon Johnson. No, those weeks were not exclusively pragmatic, honorific, and ceremonial events." A deeper meaning manifested through the atmosphere and rituals of these celebrations that set Negro History Week activities apart from ordinary school assignments and events. "In the vague background of the blackboard décor and off-key singing," Baker insisted, "there was always an implied 'conceptualist' claim upon the imagery of Negro History Week. . . . Great and abiding spiritual concepts that seemed specific to our 'race' formed *a kind of freemasonry in the winks, nods, and quiet 'race resistance' gestures that we met as students*—even from Ms. Carter, as she indicated that Johnson's anthem was not just one of many songs in a list of things we were supposed to know."[53] The inventory of knowledge emphasized during these weeks represented a set of racial politics students were to put into practice in their own lives. Baker likened these experiences to a kind of initiation into the race that came with expectations of what students were to do in the world. They were inducted as neophytes in a continuum of consciousness. This coded message, communicated in the "winks" and "nods," was a felt lessons that Baker and his classmates received through the songs and skits, as well as their teacher's "quiet 'race resistance' gestures."

Dramatizations centering on black history and culture stimulated a sense of racial pride and purpose in students that should not be understated. In 1937 Woodson reflected on the psychic implications of these formalized performances, such as reenactments at historical landmarks like the home of Frederick Douglass and Sojourner Truth. A picture of one of these reenactments was featured in a 1935 Negro History Week circular and another printed as a poster and circulated in later Negro History Week kits. Teachers and students gathered on the grounds of Douglass's home in Anacostia, DC, wearing costumes for reenactments of scenes from Douglass's life.[54] A group of young men are dressed in war uniforms as a black regiment from the Civil War; others can be seen holding signs proclaiming: "Douglass Our Hero." One picture reveals a black woman teacher in the center of the circle reading from a sheet of paper, likely an excerpt from one of Douglass's many historical speeches. "Exercises rendered on these hallowed spots *left a deep impression* which the participants will carry with them throughout the years," Woodson explained. These activities imparted "not a thought as to the imitation of what these forerunners did but a determination to meet life's challenge in responding to the call of duty with that nobleness of soul which actuated these heroes to unselfish service." These events, Woodson hoped, would inspire "a clarification of vision so essential to the preparation of the youth who must serve on tomorrow."[55]

Staged performances of black formalism and rituals during Negro History Week were meant to contour a bodily experience—to "leave an impression." These rituals, as a process of *embodied learning*, marked the black student body in ways that negated antiblack story lines otherwise stamped onto it, and they shaped a shared racial identity among students and teachers.[56] Acts of ritualization critiqued the power relations in the Jim Crow society that surrounded them and engendered new relations of power among those within the interior of black educational heritage.[57] The substance of these experiences

PUPILS OF THE WASHINGTON PUBLIC SCHOOLS
In exercises in honor of Frederick Douglass on the grounds of his home in Anacostia, D. C.

Negro History Week poster (1948) published by Associated Publishers, Inc. Used with the permission of the Association for the Study of African American Life and History, www.asalh.org.

presented a new semantics for interpreting the black student body, both their cause and their color. This was the "conceptualist claim" that Houston Baker spoke of. The meaning of blackness was not to be confined by the things the world said about them. It meant they had a purpose in this world, the

IN HONOR OF FREDERICK DOUGLASS
Washington, D. C., Public Schools

"In Honor of Frederick Douglass," 1935 Negro History Week circular. Used with the permission of the Association for the Study of African American Life and History, www.asalh.org.

same purpose to which the people whose lives they commemorated were committed. These ideas were at the heart of the black learning aesthetic shaping black school rituals and performances.

Students and teachers from Boston's Hyde School and Sherwin School collaborated for Negro History Week in 1948, staging a dramatic presentation of Hildegarde Swift's pictorial book *North Star Shining*. A key scene in their production was "THE NEGRO YEARNS FOR EDUCATION FOR FREEDOM," which opened with a performance of Phillis Wheatley, played by a sixth-grade student totting her quill pen. The finale performance included a narrated processional featuring students in costume of various characters in black history. One sixth-grade girl wore costume attire in the like of Dr. Charlotte

Hawkins Brown—the founder of the Palmer Memorial Institute in North Carolina. Wearing "a smart business suit (Gr. 6 size!) chic hat and veil, and well-filled brief case," this young girl walked down the aisle in character. Her presentation was met with a reassuring smile from Brown (sixty years old) in the audience, who witnessed the miniature version of herself with delight, and surely a bit of humor.[58] The young girl felt both joy and some anxiousness as she paraded in the processional with her peers, paying tribute to the black leaders and historical characters they studied. This was a proleptic ritual, projecting ideas about resistance, race vindication, and purposeful leadership onto the futures of black students: ideals and virtues symbolized by the historical personas students wore in costume.

Angela Davis's recollections of her childhood also extend this idea of students' immersion in a black counterideology through assignments and embodied experience. "The weekend before Negro History Week each year, [Davis] was hard at work—creating [her] poster, calling on the assistance of [her] parents, clipping pictures, writing captions and descriptions." These activities offered "a positive identification with our people and our history," Davis recalled.[59] And there was always a unifying theme from one year to the next: "The theme was always, whether explicitly or implicitly, that of resistance to the status quo of racism." All the historical figures students learned about were understood as having challenged antiblack oppression in some way. "It was the week during which we celebrated many of the firsts," shared Davis, "you know, first black person . . . who broke the barriers of racism. But I remember that it was always assumed that if there could be a first, then there could be a second, and then there would be a third, and so on, and so on, and so on." They celebrated the achievement of historical figures, not simply as exceptional people and individuals but people who did great things with and for their communities. "When individuals were celebrated they were represented as having strong connections to their communities," Davis observed. "They were rising up for themselves, but they were also rising up for their people."[60] Heroic figures held up during Negro History Week functioned as relational resources in the identity development of black learners, historical characters that students should understand as representing some part of themselves.

This black learning aesthetic incubated the continued legacy of resistance that was to come. Davis gestured toward this proleptic dimension, where resistance was projected onto students' futures.[61] Davis recalled a photo she encountered of Harriet Tubman as a student. "And I remember," she stated nostalgically, "I always visualized Harriet Tubman as my grandmother. I thought my grandmother bore this striking resemblance to her and that remains with me to this day." Tubman's picture inspired Davis because of the story that gave it meaning. Her teachers emphasized how "Harriet Tubman helped more slaves to gain their freedom than any other conductor on the Underground Railroad."[62] They celebrated Tubman not just as a historical character but as a folk hero. She was an iconic representation of black achievement and victory over antiblack persecution. She was the ultimate embodiment of the black tradition of struggle that gave meaning to all of their lives—values and ideals worth emulating.

John Bracey recalled that Haiti frequently appeared in his DC schools. During Negro History Week one year, teachers called on students to embody the story of revolt. They performed a reenactment of the Haitian Revolution:

> I always wanted to be Toussaint L'Ouverture. He got to wear the hat and carry the sword and sit in the chair, right? You're on the stage. You got to think elementary school. You're on the stage and you have Toussaint with the big hat and the sword. Then you have Christophe and Dessalines. Then you have the other people. We had to be the soldiers who marched around and changed clothes to trick the French, right? That meant you went offstage and you put on another shirt and you came back. . . .
>
> I wanted to be Toussaint. I thought he was the baddest dude in the world anyway. We were taught that he was the greatest military leader the world had ever seen. Don't worry about all these other people, George Washington, no, no, Toussaint, Toussaint L'Ouverture. Why? Because he freed Haiti. He ended slavery; he defeated all the Europeans that attacked him; he was the baddest dude in the world. We knew that.[63]

The celebration of Haiti at Mott Elementary in the late 1940s and the celebrity status Toussaint carried among Bracey and his peers speak to the centrality of resistance in the black learning aesthetic. It was embedded in the lessons students learned. In this case, student identities were connected to a global history of black resistance.[64]

The celebratory engagement with the history of slave insurrections and fugitive slaves was quite common. The actor, writer, and civil rights activist Ossie Davis felt inspired by the stories of Toussaint L'Ouverture and Nat Turner (among others) during Negro History Week celebrations of his youth in Waycross, Georgia, during the late 1920s and 1930s. "We gloried in these heroes," shared Davis. "Sometimes we would create among ourselves . . . our own version of what Nat did and what we would have did if we would have been ol' Nat and how that would have satisfied us greatly."[65] Nathan Hare, the founding director of the first Black Studies department in the country, recalled the pleasure he derived from the story of Nat Turner as a student in the 1930s and 1940s, especially because they had similar names. It is also worth noting that all of the schools Hare attended—elementary, junior high, and high school—in Oklahoma were named for Toussaint L'Ouverture.[66]

Vernon Jarrett (b. 1918), born and raised in rural Tennessee, recalled his community's ecstatic response to his dramatic reading of an essay on the Haitian Revolution as a junior high student. Jarrett explained, "Now I had heard about Toussaint L'Ouverture during . . . Negro History Week. . . . I didn't know where Haiti was but I was told that he led a slave revolt on the island of Haiti. And they—over the city and the plantations and everything—and he amassed an army. And that the French owned the island. And that Napoleon Bonaparte, Napoleon himself came down to this island to defeat the slaves, ex-slaves and that Toussaint defeated Napoleon." Clarifying that he did not have a full appreciation of all aspects of this historical event as a junior high student, Jarret went on to explain that the punch line of the story made an impression on him: enslaved black people defeated the powerful and wealthy French army. "I didn't know who Napoleon was really. I didn't know where France was hardly on the map," he shared. "But I had heard 'Napoleon-this, Napoleon-that.' He must have been a . . . heavyweight in history, and the brother defeated him?!" This moved him to action: "So (chuckling) I wrote me an essay. I made up half the stuff, but the audience stood up and cheered. I mean they just got carried away." The emotional response from the black audience was so overwhelming that it convinced Jarrett to become a writer. Even as a young student, Jarrett recognized something was significant about a group of self-emancipated slaves defeating an iconic French military leader. More than the military history of some distant island, Haiti's victory held significance—or a conceptual claim—for Jarrett's own reality living in the rural South. The deeper meaning of this historical event was understood in relationship to his own racialized, embodied reality, and it was routed through Jarrett's racial kinship to "the brother" that defeated the French oppressor.[67]

The black student body was itself a site of learning. Through dramatizations, pageants, rituals, and class assignments, students became *bodies in dissent*, to riff on performance studies scholar Daphne Brooks.[68] Davis's recognition of her grandmothers' likeness to the image of Harriet Tubman had key implications for her own raced and gendered body. Perhaps the lessons became most clear when the student body became L'Ouverture, when there was an embodied recognition between Tubman and the students' grandmother. These were lessons that marked the student body in ways that negated their alienation in an antiblack world. Students became fugitive pedagogy enfleshed. In the cases recalled above, students literally enacted narratives of black fugitive life—their putting on different colored clothes as they marched on and off stage to "trick the French" as rebel slaves. This image resonates with Bracey's earlier recollection of students' staged performance of compliance—singing "The Star-Spangled Banner" when white school authorities visited their school, while masking their daily ritual of singing the Negro national anthem. Students immersion in the heritage of black education not only required intellectual acts of subversion; it also required them to physically navigate the constraints of the American School, where school represented a broader world in which they were living and striving.

The fugitive learning of black students was a dress rehearsal. It was preparation and training for "the mission of Negro children."[69] Student participation in the subversive politics of black education during the nineteenth century up and through Woodson's program on "Negro life and history" anticipated and prefigured black students' active involvement in the Civil Rights and Black Power movements on the horizon. As the historian Robert L. Harris explained, black resistance was omnipresent in many of the classrooms in black segregated schools. "Contrary to popular assumptions," black teachers "promoted that resistance in the minds of their students," and it "built up over time and culminated in the modern freedom struggle."[70] Black teachers' pedagogy was like a river, and it moved through the lives of their students. It ebbed and flowed, took unexpected turns, but it always continued in the direction of a new world.

Conclusion: Black Schoolteachers and the Origin Story of Black Studies

I believe in the Negro schoolteachers.... With the proper training they are the finest teachers in the world because they have suffered and endured and nothing human is beneath their sympathy.

—W. E. B. DU BOIS, "The Tragedy of 'Jim Crow'" (1923)

This book has connected the politics of black education in the time of slavery to those of black teachers and students post-Emancipation through Jim Crow; revealed how black educators and their students constantly struggled to subvert the American School's technologies of exclusion and confinement, in both intellectual and physical ways; and traced black teachers' development of alternative protocols of study and new scripts of knowledge in this process, while underscoring how they often did these things in a manner that was only partially visible to the public eye. Building from this history, these final pages seek to clarify the crucial relationship between fugitive pedagogy in these former periods and the curricular object of modern Black Studies. I argue that there was a direct and distinguishable relationship between this work done by black educators and what became Black Studies in the late 1960s. Here, again, Woodson is an emblematic figure. His story as an educator and partnerships with schoolteachers offer the necessary bridge between the two. But first, a final note on the language used to frame the story and arguments of this book.

Educating while Enslaved

Our modern word *pedagogy* derives from an ancient term for a slave who was tasked with teaching. The Greek *paidagōgós*, later Latinized as *paedagogus*, refers to a slave of relatively "high status" (if you will) who escorted children to and from a site of learning.[1] *Paedagogi* were responsible for the moral development of their charges. They carried the children's books, supervised them, and sometimes taught them foundational educational skills. This person—though enslaved—made learning possible. The enslaved also embodied unwritten lessons for the young master: they taught lessons of power to charges who wielded authority over them by virtue of their differentiated social status and bloodlines, and the former's status as property.[2] The perspective of the enslaved yields a different script of knowledge, however, a witness to systems of power that rely on their subjection. This has implications for pedagogy in a universal sense, but it is particularly generative for thinking about pedagogy in our modern world, ushered in by racial chattel slavery.[3]

In that *fugitivus* (Latin) means flying, fugitive, or running away ("esp. a runaway slave")[4] and that *paedagogus* names the slave who makes learning possible, *paedagogus fugitivus*, then—the fugitive pedagogue—might be interpreted as the absconded slave who disrupts the dominant, systemized protocols of knowledge production and transferal, how knowledge is produced and the conditions under which it is taught. In fleeing from their assigned role in the order of things, paedagogi inspire new lessons. Their flight prefigures alternative paths of learning, new systems and ceremonies of knowledge. An education beyond paths that serve as a pass-through initiation for those in power, where the paedagogus is simply a prop in the enlightenment process of young masters, the elite, those of noble blood.

Fugitive pedagogy in its ancient and modern historical meaning generally refers to the enslaved fleeing from the dominant protocols of teaching and learning and the narrative scripts that structure these experiences. Their violent alienation demands their suspicion and refusal. As such, the entire apparatus of schooling is called into question when the enslaved think and plot their own course of action, when their response is flight, when they steal possession of their own life.

Fugitive pedagogy—thinking now of the post-middle passage context, as conceptualized in this book—encapsulates the enslaved and their descendants engaging in the process of thinking the world anew and building an educational protocol with this curricular object at the center. It is grounded in the assertion that those who have been marked as slave / black in the modern world might initiate a new ceremony of knowledge.[5] This is a system of knowledge that began forming just as the impulse for escape awakened, in thought and deed.

Developing alternative scripts of knowledge and physically subverting imposed protocols for learning have long been defining features of black educational heritage, a heritage whose early emergence began in the cells of slave castles and in the hold of slave ships, where plots for escape and new modes of being emerged as a primary object of study: as fugitive pedagogy.[6] As Woodson reminded teachers and students in 1922, education was forbidden among enslaved blacks, yet many of them pursued "learning as a means of escape."[7] And yet the logic and sentiments that animated chattel slavery continued to shape the relationship between processes of schooling and black social and psychic life during the time of Woodson's writing. He observed that after Emancipation there continued to be attempts "to enslave the Negroes' mind inasmuch as the freedom of body had to be conceded."[8] No longer fugitive from the law, black teachers' and students' educational strivings posed a perpetual threat to a world order where notions of humanity and civil society were structured on and by black death and dying—through the narrative and physical condemnation of black life. As such, learning as a means of escape persisted.

Black schoolteachers and their pupils were the progenies of literate slaves. *Black*education meant pedagogy as plot. This assertion is true, only if we understand the genealogy of this social, political, and spiritual project of *black*-education as extending from the desires of black-fugitive-learning-flesh: a means of study not primarily concerned with upholding the pillars of the republic; instead, a plot to make the world something it had yet to be, whereby *black*education would no longer carry traces of an oxymoron—reminiscent of contradictory terms like *slave narratives* or *literate slaves*. What sustained enslaved people and their descendants was fugitive planning, as the historian Robin Kelley reminds us, staking claim in a world that had yet to exist and actively pursuing it.[9] This is what was at stake in black teachers' work.

More often than not, black educators approached teaching from a place of political clarity about their alienation in US society. Their work followed from this posture of criticism; their pedagogy, an extension of a larger political struggle as opposed to mere desires to impart benign subject matter or help students develop expertise in reading, writing, and mathematics. Their vocation demanded more. Teaching was an act of spiritual striving, for oneself and one's people.

"I believe in the Negro schoolteachers," wrote Du Bois. "With the proper training they are the finest teachers in the world because they have suffered and endured and *nothing human is beneath their sympathy*."[10] Observed here is a claim about the structural positionality of black teachers and how it came to bear on teaching and learning, a named relationship between pedagogy and ontology. Black educators possessed a marked capacity to recall the world before the eyes of their students. Their alienation, Du Bois suggested, could be a resource in flight for all students. This, of course, assumes a consensus— that all students benefit from a world not premised on violent binaries of chosen / unchosen, white / nonwhite, or the antiblack partitioning system currently ordering society.

With the proper training black educators possessed the potential to become a new kind of teacher, a teacher with pedagogical insight cultivated from the margins. As Sylvia Wynter wrote, black people's ambivalence in and toward the known world "is at once the root cause of our alienation; and the possibility of our salvation."[11] Those who have been subjugated as props of the world's structures of domination know good and well why the terms of what it means to be human are in need of reimagining. Recognizing this demand, blacks are "called to be a new kind of people," Wynter asserts, "*a witness people*."[12] In the context of schooling, this means exposing the violence that is endemic to the current ordering of knowledge and the social arrangements structured by it, a physical and symbolic violence that black people know all too well. Furthermore, it means demanding the work of imagining and building something different.

Fugitive pedagogy was the work of a witness teacher, a plot not for equality or integration—because even when those terms were deployed, they never fully represented the political desires at the heart of the movement—but for something new entirely: transformed curriculum, a transformed way of defining what it means to be human, a transformed way of knowing. Fugitive pedagogy was grounded by a liberatory scholastic vision, not just of school but also of the world.

The Early Black Studies Movement

The story of black education is a submerged history in the field of African American history in particular and in Black Studies in general. Yet the phenomenon of black education—the violent opposition against it and black people's protracted struggle for it—is the origin story of both. As a final gesture, this book offers an appeal to reconceptualize the relationship between the history of black education—especially the story of black schoolteachers—and the metadiscipline of Black Studies, which formed in the US academy as a result of college student protests beginning in 1968.[13]

That there was a textual universe on which to build modern Black Studies suggests that its content and academic aims extended from a much longer heritage in black American education. The history of fugitive pedagogy makes clear that the formation of Black Studies may have been novel to white universities in the late 1960s; however, its protocols were not infant in form.[14] Established protocols were reclaimed and transplanted into a new context.

A rigid disciplinary lens has been used to frame Woodson as the scholar that popularized black history, obscuring a larger part of the story. Negro History Week and the ASNLH were about more than just "history" as defined by current disciplinary boundaries. While speaking from a Harlem pulpit in 1926, Woodson professed, "The whole course of study in public schools needs to be reconstructed." The entire school curriculum—not just history— "continue[d] to teach white superiority propaganda and brood over the inferiority complex, which they would hound into the conscience of every young Negro child."[15] Black literature and folklore, economics, art, contemporary political issues, and more were all on the table, even as they were often studied in historical context. Woodson and the teachers he partnered with conceived of "Negro history" in broad terms. They operated from a capacious intellectual frame and did so at a time when the boundaries between social science disciplines were much more porous, even in the mainstream academy, and lines between academic research and public advocacy were not well settled.[16]

The early work of Woodson's Association held more in common with what we currently call Black Studies than with the more discipline-oriented field of African American history, even as it was undoubtedly integral to the latter. The need to call what became formalized in the late 1960s Black Studies was a response to academic developments that were yet forming when Woodson created the ASNLH in 1915. What is remembered as "the early black history movement," then, can appropriately be understood as *the early Black Studies movement*. Pero Dagbovie, who coined the term "the early black history movement," originally framed this intellectual phase as "the proto Black

Studies movement." Dagbovie's earlier framing, in my assessment, is more revelatory. He argued that Woodson "helped lay the ideological foundation for the evolution and flowering of the black historical profession as well as the modern Black Studies Movement." Through the ASNLH and its ancillary publications, Woodson "converted an authentically African American scientific academic discipline into a practical tool of self-empowerment and liberation."[17] The literary theorist Hortense Spillers also pointed to black intellectual networks in the early twentieth century as "prototypical Black Studies," asserting that Woodson's ASNLH was the institutional forerunner to the Black Studies of today.[18] Houston Baker, having been an elementary student in Kentucky during the 1940s, where he was immersed in Negro History Week celebrations, and now a senior Black Studies scholar, also argued that, "academically, Black Studies may be seen as an empiricist outgrowth of the Negro history movement."[19]

Dagbovie, Spillers, and Baker all trace the relationship between the insurgent intellectual work by black Americans in the first half of the twentieth century, particularly in black schoolhouses and HBCUs, with the formation of Black Studies in the US academy during the late 1960s. Given this, it should come as no surprise that one of the courses inaugurating the first Black Studies Department, at San Francisco State College, was titled The Mis-Education of the Negro.[20] The theme of this course signaled the reclamation of a literary culture and curricular object from the black past.

(Under)Common Schools: A Long Memory of "Fugitive Planning and Black Study"

My theorization of fugitive pedagogy in this book is indebted to many scholars. Among them is Stefano Harney and Fred Moten. Their conceptualization of "the undercommons" formed by the insurgent intellectual in the university has been important for thinking about fugitivity, education, and black social life. It seems important to expand our understanding of what these scholars refer to as "fugitive planning and black study" in a way that is accountable to the history of black education. The fugitive planning and black study in black schools and colleges were a precursor to any undercommons of black study at white universities, to which Harney and Moten generally reference.[21]

The subversive intellectual "disappears into the underground, the downlow lowdown maroon community of the university," observed Harney and Moten, "in the *undercommons of enlightenment,* where the work gets done, where the work gets subverted, where the revolution is still black, still strong."[22] In expanding the aperture here, I would suggest that the fugitive pedagogy of black scholars in pit schools on the plantation, in black literary societies in the antebellum North, and in the private spaces of black classrooms during Jim Crow, as well as the covert planning of black professors and students at HBCUs, and especially the counterpublics of black teachers' associations, all anticipated the fugitive planning and black study that emerged in the late 1960s.[23]

The undercommons emerged from a black intellectual tradition that took form underneath and in the shadows of America's Common School Movement of the late eighteenth and nineteenth centuries, a movement that achieved prominence alongside the proliferation of antiliteracy laws, which criminalized black education. Black study emerged in *the (under)common schools* formed by black fugitive learners—a people striving even as they were pushed to the nether edge of the American School, in all of its varying iterations. Such is the origin story of black education and, likewise, Black Studies.

Black Teachers, Their Students, and the Beginnings of Black Studies

Long playing the role of bard and counselor, institution builder and community advocate, artist and intellectual, the black teacher had been the most ardent disciple of black study for more than a century. Before demands rang out at San Francisco State and Harvard, at Berkeley and Howard, at Brandeis and Northwestern, and elsewhere beginning in 1968, black teachers wrestled with questions about the relationship between knowledge production and the social, psychic, and material realities of black life. These questions were at the heart of their pedagogy and shaped the socioemotional learning contexts they developed.

African American Studies, Africana Studies, or Black Studies—as it was implanted in higher education after centuries of negation—is a metadiscipline with deep roots in the fugitive pedagogy of literate slaves and, subsequently, black Americans who developed a literary culture set against the order of an antiblack world. Black teachers were an enfleshed manifestation of this tradition. We have the tradition of black study because it passed through them. The relationship between black teachers and black study can be traced to individual writers who produced the literature reclaimed in the US university in the late 1960s through the 1980s. It can also be identified by looking to the roster of scholars who developed the first wave of formalized academic protocols in Black Studies. Among the former we find that many late nineteenth- and early twentieth-century scholars were schoolteachers. Among the latter, one finds that a sizable contingency, if not a majority, of Black Studies scholars and institution builders were former students of black schoolteachers during Jim Crow, many of whom have explicitly referred to their early education as formative to their black studies orientation.

Situating Teachers in the Literary Universe of Black Studies

A Black Studies "canon" might be somewhat of a misnaming; however, there was absolutely a literary universe of black scholarship when the metadiscipline began to take institutional form in the university. Schoolteachers were strongly represented in this black literary universe. Many of the authors and scholars at the center of the early Black Studies movement were teachers who taught in primary and secondary schools. Recall here Jimmy Garrett's class entitled The Mis-education of the Negro, a clear nod to Woodson's 1933 book that was deeply informed by his nearly thirty years as a public school teacher. And among Woodson's contemporaries—scholars who were or had been schoolteachers—we find a who's who of black political and cultural voices of the late nineteenth through early twentieth centuries—Anna Julia Cooper, W. E. B. Du Bois, Richard Robert Wright, Mary Church Terrell, Ida B. Wells-Barnett, Jessie Fauset, Jean Toomer, James Weldon Johnson, Mary McLeod Bethune, and more.

Writing of educators during the Black Renaissance, the historian Daniel Perlstein observed, "On Sugar Hill and elsewhere, hundreds of educators made Harlem home, they were at the center of New Negro intellectual life." Perlstein identifies a wide range of black playwrights, editors, poets, novelists, salon hosts, and a cofounder of the Negro Experimental Theatre who were teachers in Harlem, uncovering their centrality to "much of Renaissance Harlem's intellectual infrastructure." The literary and cultural activities of these educators were often complemented by their political engagement as well. For instance, black schoolteachers did much of the organizing for the 1927 meeting of the Pan-African Congress, which took place in Harlem.[24]

The list of black teachers in the literary universe of Black Studies is expansive. These educators were integral to the development of black study even beyond the physical geography of the Jim Crow South. While few in number in northern and midwestern cities, these educators were part of broader black networks. Madeline Stratton Morris in Chicago, for instance, an active member of Woodson's ASNLH, introduced black history and culture to the Chicago school curriculum in the 1930s.[25] These educators were affiliated with black institutions stretching across regional lines, many having been southern migrants themselves or the children of migrants, and some attended HBCUs.

Many of the scholars readily associated with Black Studies were teachers in or products of the academic and socioemotional learning contexts of black southern schools. Though plagued by the violence and stigma of Jim Crow—and it is important not to lose sight of this—black teachers working in these contexts created a tradition that inspired generations of black thinkers, cultural workers, and political activists. The story of black education—by which I mean the story of fugitive pedagogy—is also the origin story of Black Studies. Schoolteachers were the primary vessels through which this tradition carried across generations.

It is true that the prestigious list of black teachers in the early twentieth century resulted from limited professional opportunities available to black people. However, this explanation is important but insufficient. The political significance black Americans placed on education also played a major role. Black teachers, as thinkers, dreamers, and political actors, understood schools as a site to express and enact political visions for a new reality through pedagogy. Teaching, as Daniel Perlstein rightfully observed, "constituted a way of articulating and fostering new consciousness as befit a new age."[26] Black teachers' practice and the scholarship they produced reflect these beliefs. Their intellectual contributions, while represented in the literary culture they helped establish, were most prominently reflected in their coordinated efforts to expose the developing minds of black students to this tradition in systematic ways. This is to say, the pedagogy of black American educators represents an intellectual tradition beyond written or spoken form. Black students, time and time again, bore witness to this. This heritage was at the center of the black revolution on campus that took hold in 1968.

Institutionalizing Black Studies

A tradition passed between black teachers and their students, especially those who became educators themselves. James Weldon Johnson observed this black study migration narrative when reflecting on the formalization of "Lift Every Voice and Sing" as the Black national anthem. After a choir of five hundred black students sang the song for the first time in 1900, "the school-children of Jacksonville kept singing the song," Johnson explained. "Some of them went off to other schools and kept singing it; some of them became schoolteachers and taught it to their pupils."[27] This story of pedagogical transmission, it seems to me, is a call to rethink many aspects of black cultural and political history.

Black college students demanded that a formalized Black Studies curriculum be recognized in US universities beginning in the late 1960s. In the wake of the Civil Rights movement, amid widespread black disillusionment from the immediate backlash to hard-won victories, old protocols of study were implanted in the US academy. They were implanted at the "nether edge of the university" but archived, nonetheless, into its academic and physical architecture. The historian Martha Biondi observed, "Black students organized protests on nearly two hundred campuses across the United States in 1968 and 1969, and continued to a lesser extent into the early 1970s. This dramatic explosion of militant activism set in motion a period of conflict, crackdown, negotiation, and reform that profoundly transformed college life." Resulting from this, argued the historian Ibram Kendi, "black campus activists forced the racial reconstitution of higher education."[28] I would add that among those responsible for this transplantation of black study were the former students of black educators—and in strong showing.

Black Studies was not simply a result of the critical mass of black students on some campuses for the first time. It had as much to do with these students' newly acquired access to historically white universities and the militant climate shaped by a post–Civil Rights disillusionment as it had to do with a system of knowledge many of these scholars were raised up in, having been taught by black teachers. To be clear, some early proponents of Black Studies were rebelling against near totalizing experiences of mis-education and racist neglect. Huey P. Newton characterized his education in Oakland, California, as irrelevant to his life and experiences. Oakland public schools "nearly killed [his] urge to inquire" and "explore the worlds of literature, science, and history."[29] However, Newton's experiences should not be accepted as the norm. Other political thinkers and intellectuals, like Angela Davis and Hortense Spillers—from Birmingham, Alabama, and Memphis, Tennessee, respectively—characterized their formative educational experiences as having been shaped by the structural neglect characteristic of Jim Crow, certainly, but also learning environments that made available a rich cultural and political tradition. White supremacist curricula were imposed on black schools, but black students also attested to being exposed to educational resources that encouraged them to interrogate and critique power and injustice, as well as the very curriculum imposed on them from white school authorities.

The former students of black educators appear in the first wave of scholars demanding Black Studies and developing formalized Black Studies protocols. This cohort of scholars taught by black teachers—particularly black southern teachers—representing no monolithic ideology, includes the following: Margaret Walker Alexander, Robert L. Allen, Molefi Asante, Houston Baker, Lerone Bennett, John Bracey, John Blassingame, John Henrik Clarke, Angela Davis, Nathan Hare, Evelyn Brooks Higginbotham, bell hooks, Bertha Maxwell-Roddey, Sonia Sanchez, and Hortense Spillers. These scholars, along with many others, championed the cause of Black Studies through their intellectual contributions and as institution builders.[30]

Many black students were prepared to champion the mission of Black Studies having inherited a tradition through the tutelage of black educators. The art of black teaching centered on carrying the plot forward through pedagogical transmission. Having been initiated in the early Black Studies movement, these former students helmed the fugitive planning of Black Studies in the earliest years of its emergence in the US academy.

Teachers have historically been and must be repositioned as central political actors in the project of Black Studies. By "teacher" I am not referring to the black American or Black Studies professor but particularly schoolteachers responsible for attending to the minds of young people and nurturing their aspirations. This is an intentional refusal of contemporary trends where teachers are deprofessionalized in general and where black teachers in particular have been systemically alienated, often being positioned as unintellectual and nonpedagogical knowers.

As this book has shown, there is a long history of black educators approaching their work as what I would call "scholars of the practice." Understanding that fugitive educational acts were part and parcel of the demands placed on them as a distinct group of professionals, black educators recognized themselves as within yet against the American School. The best among them were well studied on the educational structures they were forced to function within, and they immersed themselves in the intellectual currents of black counterpublics to develop strategies for transgressing the American School's imposed limitations. This is the prelude to the undercommons and the insurgent intellectual of the late 1960s. These teachers were not just conduits for the transferal of knowledge; they were knowledge producers in their own right.

Black educators established a pedagogical model worthy of our attention today. Their professional world comprised a porous relationship between scholars in higher education and the K-12 levels. Black schoolteachers, professors, and political figures shared organizational affiliations and developed black education in communion with one another. They debated across ideological differences. They struggled and strategized in pursuit of shared political aims. Whether this rich intellectual climate was partially a product of racial barriers into other professional avenues or intentionally created out of political necessity, the value added is undeniable.

My insistence here is not merely recuperative or a call to remember. It is also prescriptive. There is desperate need for intentional relationships between Black Studies and K-12 educators, especially black teachers, whose alienation in the educational sector has continued to increase since—ironically—the time Black Studies became implanted in US universities. This has coincided with the dismantling of black teachers' associations and massive firings of black educators and administrators.[31] This is an appeal for something we know to be effective and of transformative potential from the historical record. While closing on these lines of argumentation, it is my hope that this ending might also be the beginning of a renewed conversation between the field of Black Studies and black teachers, as well as other practitioners who are committed to working against the physical and epistemological violence black people experience in schools and the world.

Orbiting at the margins of the American School was a black educational heritage, where freedom dreams inherited from the enslaved became enacted in pedagogical form. While the US social order has transitioned into new and distinct racial domains since slavery and Jim Crow, we continue to hear echoes of the past, as this history sits in the classroom beside us. Pernicious sociopolitical relations in society and its schools have endured. As such, there continues to be a need for black teachers to hold influence at the table of black study and the work of fugitive planning, not for the sake of nostalgia but because the social analyses and fugitive protocols made possible by Black Studies are necessary resources in the lives of students well before the collegiate level. The violent assault on black life begins in the classroom for all students, not just the select few who make it to college. Finally, it is important because the structural position of the black teacher in the American School continues to be an important site for analyzing the conditions of black life in the known world. Their experiences, like those of black students, whose vulnerability they share, have historically been markers for key aspects of black reality.

For so long black teachers carried the tradition of black study forward. Along with preachers, they were the dream keepers and the first leaders of freedpeople. Their teaching conjured a world "that has never been yet; and yet must be."[32]

Notes

Preface

1. James Baldwin, *The Fire Next Time* (New York: Vintage, 1963), 69.

2. Henry Louis Gates Jr., "'A Negro Way of Saying,'" *New York Times,* April 21, 1985, sec. Books.

3. Nathaniel Mackey, "Other: From Noun to Verb," *Representations,* no. 39 (1992): 55.

4. Stephen Best and Saidiya Hartman, "Fugitive Justice," *Representations* 92, no. 1 (2005): 1–15; see "Fugitive Dreams," in Saidiya Hartman, *Lose Your Mother: A Journey along the Atlantic Slave Route* (New York: Farrar, Straus and Giroux, 2008), 211–235; Stefano Harney and Fred Moten, *The Undercommons: Fugitive Planning and Black Study* (Wivenhoe, UK: Autonomedia, 2013); Damien M. So-joyner, "Another Life Is Possible: Black Fugitivity and Enclosed Places," *Cultural Anthropology* 32, no. 4 (2017): 514–536; Savannah Shange, *Progressive Dystopia: Abolition, Antiblackness, and Schooling in San Francisco* (Durham, NC: Duke University Press Books, 2019) 62, 68.

5. "He stopped speaking English because there was no future in it." Toni Morrison, *Beloved* (New York: Knopf, 1987), 25.

Introduction

1. Bureau of the Census and Tessie McGee, "Sixteenth Census of the United States, 1940" (Minden, Webster, Louisiana: US Bureau of the Census, 1940), National Archives and Records Administration, Ancestry.com.

2. State Department of Education of Louisiana, "Louisiana High School Standards Manual of Organization and Administration (Section on Social Science Curriculum)," Bulletin (Baton Rouge, LA: State Department of Education of Louisiana, July 1, 1929), Harvard Graduate School of Education, Gutman Library Special Collections.

3. "'Negro Education' and 'The Webster Parish Training School,'" *The Signal-Tribune and Springhill Journal Historical Edition,* December 31, 1934, sec. Parish

School Organization Famous Over USA; on "double taxation," see James Anderson, *The Education of Blacks in the South, 1860–1935* (Chapel Hill: University of North Carolina Press, 1988), 156.

4. Jerry Alexander Moore, Speech at ASALH Founder's Day Event 2009 (Prince George County, 2009), personal collection of Mrs. Barbara Dunn Spencer.

5. Stephen Best and Saidiya Hartman, "Fugitive Justice," *Representations* 92, no. 1 (2005): 1–15.

6. Carter G. Woodson, *The Negro in Our History* (Washington, DC: Associated Publishers, 1922), 108; Thomas L. Webber, *Deep like the Rivers: Education in the Slave Quarter Community, 1831–1865* (New York: Norton, 1978).

7. Heather Williams, *Self-Taught: African American Education in Slavery and Freedom* (Chapel Hill: University of North Carolina Press, 2007), 7–8.

8. James D. Anderson, "James Anderson Lecture on Researching the History of Black Education" for Beacon Press and Simmons College Series on Race, Education, and Democracy (transcript of lecture, March 14, 2007).

9. I share the sentiments of the historian Steven Hahn in his appeal for scholars to "identify [and take seriously] constituent elements of slave politics" as we strive for rigorous understanding of "what happened after slavery." Steven Hahn, *A Nation under Our Feet: Black Political Struggles in the Rural South from Slavery to the Great Migration* (Cambridge, MA: Belknap, 2003), 3.

10. Campbell Frank Scribner, "Surveying the Destruction of African American Schoolhouses in the South, 1864–1876," *The Journal of the Civil War Era* 10, no. 4 (December 2020): 470; W. E. B. Du Bois, The Souls of Black Folk (New York: Barnes & Noble Classics, 2005), 15.

11. "Plot" has a layered meaning: the plot of a novel, a literary form that rises to prominence with the rise of the plantation; a plot of land given to the enslaved to feed themselves as a means of sustaining labor on the plantation; also plots of rebellion and the counterculture of the enslaved. See Sylvia Wynter, "Novel and History, Plot and Plantation," *Savacou*, no. 5 (1971): 99, 101.

12. Glenda Gilmore, *Gender and Jim Crow: Women and the Politics of White Supremacy in North Carolina, 1896–1920* (Chapel Hill: University of North Carolina Press, 1996), 185–186.

13. Vanessa Siddle Walker, *The Lost Education of Horace Tate: Uncovering the Hidden Heroes Who Fought for Justice in Schools* (New York: New Press, 2018).

14. Hayden White, *Tropics of Discourse: Essays in Cultural Criticism* (Baltimore, MD: Johns Hopkins University Press, 1978), see chap. 3, "The Historical Text as Literary Artifact," 83–84, and chap. 4, "Historicism, History, and the Figurative Imagination," 111–117.

15. This designation of "the American School" recognizes the schooling apparatus of the state as comprising a set of heterogeneous institutions informed by dominant racial ideology and social hierarchies. The American School (and "the

American Curriculum")—by way of its capitalization—indexes the hierarchies of power within these structures. My understanding here is situated at the intersection of the following texts: Charles Mills, *The Racial Contract* (Ithaca, NY: Cornell University Press, 1999); Louis Althusser, *Lenin and Philosophy, and Other Essays* (New York: Monthly Review Press, 1972), especially "Ideological State Apparatus and Repressive State Apparatus," 146–159; David Tyack, *The One Best System: A History of American Urban Education* (Cambridge, MA: Harvard University Press, 1974); Carl Kaestle, *Pillars of the Republic: Common Schools and American Society, 1780–1860,* 1st ed. (New York: Hill and Wang, 1983).

16. Antiblackness manifested in the American School through the physical exclusion of black people from school structures as well as their exclusion from curricula. Black people were then confined to particular kinds of education (e.g. segregated, agricultural, and domestic training) when legally permitted into the American School and simultaneously confined by stereotypical representations when they were included in curricula.

17. Michael W. Apple, "The Politics of Official Knowledge: Does a National Curriculum Make Sense?," *Teachers College Record* 95, no. 2 (1993): 222–241; James C. Scott, *Domination and the Arts of Resistance: Hidden Transcripts* (New Haven, CT: Yale University Press, 1992), 4, 14; on "insurgent intellectual networks," see Aldon Morris, *The Scholar Denied: W. E. B. Du Bois and the Birth of Modern Sociology* (Oakland: University of California Press, 2015), 193.

18. Jones was an active board member and presidential candidate of the Louisiana Colored Teachers' Association. "Normal Founder Elected to Head Colored L.T.A.," *Rustin Daily Leader,* November 21, 1932; "'Of Importance' (Note about Including Negro History in Schools)," *Louisiana Colored Teachers' Journal,* January 1935, 36–38.

19. Paul Laurence Dunbar's 1895 poem "We Wear the Mask," in *The Complete Poems of Paul Laurence Dunbar* (Philadelphia: Hakim's Publishers, 1980).

20. "Representing power was essential to reproducing domination." Saidiya Hartman, *Scenes of Subjection: Terror, Slavery, and Self-Making in Nineteenth-Century America* (New York: Oxford University Press, 1997), 7. This intrusion on the sociality of black school life was such a familiar reality that dramatic accounts of white visitors and black schools appear widely across the archival record and black literature from the Jim Crow era. Angela Y. Davis, *Angela Davis: An Autobiography* (New York: Random House, 1974), 90–93; Zora Neale Hurston, *Dust Tracks on a Road: An Autobiography* (New York: Harper Collins, 2006), 34–35; Walker, *Lost Education,* 13; Du Bois, *Souls of Black Folk,* chap. "On the Coming of John"; Ralph Ellison, *Invisible Man,* 2nd ed. (New York: Vintage Books, 1995).

21. The metaphor of walking a tightrope is used by Albert Brooks, a Washington, DC, teacher, and similarly by the historian Glenda Gilmore to characterize the work of the educator Charlotte Hawkins Brown. Albert N. D. Brooks, "H. Councill

Trenholm," *Negro History Bulletin* 26, no. 8 (May 1, 1963): 231–233; Gilmore, *Gender and Jim Crow,* 185–186.

22. "Thompson 'Guarantees' School Board Harmony: Making No Mention of Resignation, Says 'Isms' All Banned; Offensive Text Referred to Lee," *Muskogee Daily Phoenix,* June 2, 1925, Oklahoma Historical Society (italics added).

23. Oliver R. Pope, *Chalk Dust* (New York: Pageant Press, 1967), 4; John Egerton, *Speak Now against the Day: The Generation before the Civil Rights Movement in the South* (Chapel Hill: University of North Carolina Press, 1995), 562.

24. Simone Browne, *Dark Matters: On the Surveillance of Blackness* (Durham, NC: Duke University Press Books, 2015), 6.

25. Houston A. Baker, "Meditation on Tuskegee: Black Studies Stories and Their Imbrication," *Journal of Blacks in Higher Education,* no. 9 (1995): 51–59; this autobiographical quote from Baker is a riff on James Weldon Johnson's "freemasonry of the race." See James Weldon Johnson, *The Autobiography of an Ex-Coloured Man* (New York: Vintage, 1989), 21–22, 74.

26. Al Sweeney, "Dr. Carter G. Woodson, 72, Has Written 19 Books, Published 64 Others; Hopes Day Will Come When There'll Be No Need for Negro History Week . . . ," *Afro Magazine,* 1948, 3, excerpt in box 370, folder 1, Claude Burnett Papers, Chicago History Museum.

27. Leo Strauss, *Persecution and the Art of Writing* (Chicago: University of Chicago Press, 1988), 24–25.

28. "If slavery persists as an issue in the political life of black America, it is not because of antiquarian obsession with bygone days or the burden of a too-long memory, but because black lives are still imperiled and devalued by a racial calculus and a political arithmetic that were entrenched centuries ago. This is the afterlife of slavery—skewed life chances, limited access to health and education, premature death, incarceration, and impoverishment." Saidiya Hartman, *Lose Your Mother: A Journey along the Atlantic Slave Route* (New York: Farrar, Straus and Giroux, 2008) 6; Carter G. Woodson, *Mis-education of the Negro* (Washington, DC: Association for the Study of African American Life and History), 47.

29. An extensive amount of scholarship has portrayed the character of black teachers as a professional group and the challenges they faced: Michael Fultz, "Teacher Training and African American Education in the South, 1900–1940," *Journal of Negro Education* 64, no. 2 (1995): 196–210; Michael Fultz, "African American Teachers in the South, 1890–1940: Powerlessness and the Ironies of Expectations and Protest," *History of Education Quarterly* 35, no. 4 (1995): 401–422; Ronald E. Butchart, *Schooling the Freed People: Teaching, Learning, and the Struggle for Black Freedom, 1861–1876* (Chapel Hill: University of North Carolina, 2010), esp. 17–52, "To Serve My Own People"; Katherine Mellen Charron, *Freedom's Teacher: The Life of Septima Clark* (Chapel Hill: University of North Carolina Press, 2012); Walker, *Lost Education;* V. P. Franklin, "'They Rose and Fell Together': Af-

rican American Educators and Community Leadership, 1795–1954," *Journal of Education* 172, no. 3 (1990): 39–64; Adam Fairclough, *A Class of Their Own: Black Teachers in the Segregated South* (Cambridge, MA: Belknap, 2007); Vanessa Siddle Walker, "Organized Resistance and Black Educators' Quest for School Equality, 1878–1938," *Teachers College Record* 107, no. 3 (2005): 355–388.

30. An important body of work has documented the intentional underdevelopment of black education and the ongoing precarious position of black teachers: Anderson, *Education of Blacks;* James D. Anderson, "Northern Foundations and the Shaping of Southern Black Rural Education, 1902–1935," *History of Education Quarterly* 18, no. 4 (1978): 371–396; William Watkins, *The White Architects of Black Education: Ideology and Power in America, 1865–1954* (New York: Teachers College Press, 2001); Fultz, "African American Teachers"; Michael Fultz, "Caught between a Rock and a Hard Place: The Dissolution of Black State Teachers Associations, 1954–1970," in *The SAGE Handbook of African American Education,* ed. Linda C. Tillman (Thousand Oaks, CA: SAGE, 2008), 67–82; Russell W. Irvine and Jacqueline Jordan Irvine, "The Impact of the Desegregation Process on the Education of Black Students: Key Variables," *Journal of Negro Education* 52, no. 4 (1983): 410–422; Woodson, *Mis-education;* W. E. B. Du Bois and Augustus Granville Dill, *The Common School and the Negro American: Report of a Social Study* (Atlanta, GA: Atlanta University Press, 1911).

31. See Gates's analyses of "the talking book" trope in early slave narratives. "The Trope of the Talking Book," in Henry Louis Gates, *The Signifying Monkey: A Theory of African-American Literary Criticism,* reprint ed. (New York: Oxford University Press, 1989), 139–154.

32. Butchart traces the major phases of scholarship on the history of black education in the following essay, beginning in the early twentieth century: Ronald E. Butchart, "'Outthinking and Outflanking the Owners of the World': A Historiography of the African American Struggle for Education," *History of Education Quarterly* 28, no. 3 (1988): 333–366.

33. Scholars have observed unbalanced critiques of black teachers in historical scholarship across time; see, for instance, Tondra L. Loder-Jackson, *Schoolhouse Activists: African American Educators and the Long Birmingham Civil Rights Movement* (Albany: SUNY Press, 2015), 2–3; and Vanessa Siddle Walker, "African American Teaching in the South: 1940–1960," *American Educational Research Journal* 38, no. 4 (December 2001): 752–753.

34. Earl Lewis, "Invoking Concepts, Problematizing Identities: The Life of Charles N. Hunter and the Implications for the Study of Gender and Labor," *Labor History* 34, no. 2–3 (June 1993): 293; Al-Tony Gilmore, *A More Perfect Union: The Merger of the South Carolina Education Association and the Palmetto Education Association* (self-pub., CreateSpace Independent Publishing Platform, 2017), 45.

35. Loder-Jackson, *Schoolhouse Activists,* 9–10, quote from 105.

36. Davis, *Angela Davis;* Ossie Davis and Ruby Dee, *With Ossie and Ruby: In This Life Together* (New York: It Books, 2000); Benjamin Mays and Orville Burton, *Born to Rebel: An Autobiography* (Athens: University of Georgia Press, 2003); Albert Murray, *South to a Very Old Place* (New York: Vintage, 1991).

37. The theory and concepts presented in this book draw from and clarify black people's traditions in education, hence "a grammar of"; but they also name distinct social relations of power and structural elements that shaped the context of these experiences, "a grammar for." This latter point is a riff on Hortense J. Spillers, "Mama's Baby, Papa's Maybe: An American Grammar Book," *Diacritics* 17, no. 2 (1987): 65–81.

38. Neil Roberts, *Freedom as Marronage* (Chicago: University of Chicago Press, 2015), 8–11.

39. Walter Johnson, *Soul by Soul: Life inside the Antebellum Slave Market* (Cambridge, MA: Harvard University Press, 1999), 19–22.

40. Orlando Patterson, *Slavery and Social Death: A Comparative Study,* 2nd ed. (Cambridge, MA: Harvard University Press, 2018), xiv, 13.

41. Birgit Brander Rasmussen, "'Attended with Great Inconveniences': Slave Literacy and the 1740 South Carolina Negro Act," *PMLA* 125, no. 1 (2010): 201–203; Williams, *Self-Taught,* 13; Carter G. Woodson, *The Education of the Negro Prior to 1861: A History of the Education of the Colored People of the United States from the Beginning of Slavery to the Civil War* (New York: Putnam and Son's, 1915), chap. 1, 8–9: "The prohibitive legislation extended over a period of more than a century, beginning with the act of South Carolina in 1740. But with the exception of the action of this State and that of Georgia the important measures which actually proscribed the teaching of Negroes were enacted during the first four decades of the nineteenth century."

42. George McDowell Stroud, *Sketch of the Laws Relating to Slavery in the Several States of the United States of America* (Philadelphia: Kimber and Sharpless, 1827), 88–90 (italics added).

43. Hilary J. Moss, *Schooling Citizens: The Struggle for African American Education in Antebellum America* (Chicago: University of Chicago Press, 2010), 18–19; "dangerous undertaking" quoted in Davison Douglas, *Jim Crow Moves North: The Battle over Northern School Segregation, 1865–1954* (New York: Cambridge University Press, 2005), 41 (see "Struggle for Black Education in the Antebellum North") (italics added). For a discussion of educator Octavius Catto's killing in Philadelphia for his political activism, see Jelani M. Favors, *Shelter in a Time of Storm: How Black Colleges Fostered Generations of Leadership and Activism* (Chapel Hill: The University of North Carolina Press, 2019), 18.

44. Frederick Douglass, *My Bondage and My Freedom* (New York: Miller, Orton & Mulligan, 1855), 146. "Most slaves who once were counted as valuable, on account of their ability to read and write the English language, were thereafter con-

sidered unfit for service in the South and branded as objects of suspicion." Woodson, *Education of the Negro,* 10.

45. Toni Morrison, "The Site of Memory," in *Inventing the Truth: The Art and Craft of Memoir,* ed. William Zinsser, 2nd ed. (Boston: Houghton Mifflin Harcourt, 1995), 89.

46. There are expansive references to fugitive slaves and literacy, largely recovered from newspaper ads for runaways, in John Hope Franklin, *Runaway Slaves: Rebels on the Plantation* (Oxford: Oxford University Press, 2000), 66, 109, 145, 172, 231.

47. See Du Bois's discussion of "the general strike" in W. E. B. Du Bois and David Levering Lewis, *Black Reconstruction in America, 1860–1880* (New York: Free Press, 1998), 55–61. Douglass explained, "In the old slave times, the colored people were expected to work without thinking. . . . *They were to be hands—only hands, not heads.* Thought was the prerogative of the master." Frederick Douglass, "Blessings of Liberty and Education," Teaching American History, September 3, 1894, https://teachingamericanhistory.org/library/document/blessings-of-liberty -and-education/.

48. Williams, *Self-Taught,* 98, 122.

49. Vincent Harding, *There Is a River: The Black Struggle for Freedom in America* (New York: Houghton Mifflin Harcourt, 1981), 265; Woodson, *Education of the Negro;* Anderson, *Education of Blacks;* Webber, *Deep like the Rivers;* Williams, *Self-Taught.*

50. David Walker, *David Walker's Appeal to the Coloured Citizens of the World* (Baltimore: Black Classic, 1830 / 1992), 52; Douglass, *My Bondage,* 146. "Among the blacks is misery enough, God knows, but no poetry. . . . Religion indeed has produced a Phyllis Whately [sic]; but it could not produce a poet. The compositions published under her name are below the dignity of criticism." Thomas Jefferson, *Notes on the State of Virginia* (Philadelphia: Prichard and Hall, 1787), 150.

51. See introduction of Zora Neale Hurston, *Mules and Men* (Philadelphia: J. B. Lippincott Co, 1935).

52. "Got one mind" quoted in Robert L. Harris Jr., "Review of Roderick A. Mc-Donald's *The Economy and Material Culture of Slaves: Goods and Chattels on the Sugar Plantations of Jamaica and Louisiana,*" *African American Review* 29, no. 3 (Fall 1995): 510.

53. Brooks, "H. Councill Trenholm."

54. Fred Moten, "Black Optimism / Black Operation" (Chicago, October 19, 2007); John Hope Franklin Humanities Institute, *The Black Outdoors: Fred Moten and Saidiya Hartman in Conversation with J. Kameron Carter and Sarah Jane Cervenak* (Goodson Chapel, Duke Divinity School, 2016).

55. Account of principal being fired for use of Woodson's textbook: "Thompson 'Guarantees' School Board Harmony: Making No Mention of Resignation, Says 'Isms' All Banned; Offensive Text Referred to Lee."

56. John W. Blassingame, ed., *Slave Testimony: Two Centuries of Letters, Speeches, Interviews, and Autobiographies* (Baton Rouge: LSU Press, 1977), 465; Williams, *Self-Taught,* 28.

57. Building from James Scott's "everyday resistance" and "infrapolitics," fugitive pedagogy interprets the common, everyday acts of subversion by black teachers as extending from a politics cultivated in black educational intuitions and a larger plot against the American School. These were not isolated, sporadic acts. They extended from a black politics of education that became formalized over time. On everyday resistance as it pertains to enslaved people, Scott writes, "The rare, heroic, and foredooms gestures of a Nat Turner or a John Brown are simply not the places to look for the struggle between slaves and their owners. One must look rather at the constant, grinding conflict over work, food, autonomy, ritual—at everyday forms of resistance." He continues, "Where everyday resistance most strikingly departs from other forms of resistance is in its implicit disavowal of public and symbolic goals. Where institutionalized politics is formal, overt, concerned with systematic, de jure change, everyday resistance is informal, often covert, and concerned largely with immediate, de facto gains." James C. Scott, *Weapons of the Weak: Everyday Forms of Peasant Resistance* (New Haven, CT: Yale University Press, 1987), xvi, 33; on "infrapolitics," see Scott, *Domination;* also, on black working-class infrapolitics, see Robin D. G. Kelley, *Race Rebels: Culture, Politics, and the Black Working Class* (New York: Free Press, 1996), 25–33.

58. White, *Tropics of Discourse,* 84, 109–111.

59. Pero Dagbovie, *The Early Black History Movement: Carter G. Woodson and Lorenzo Johnston Greene* (Urbana: University of Illinois Press, 2007).

60. Thomas L. Dabney, "The Study of the Negro," *Journal of Negro History* 19, no. 3 (1934): 266–307.

61. "Jamaica Branch in History Week," *New York Amsterdam News,* February 18, 1939, 11.

62. Woodson was professor and dean at Howard University from 1919 to 1920 and then at West Virginia State for one year, after being a schoolteacher since the 1890s. See Chapters 1 and 2.

63. Mabel Grant, *Del Sudoeste Yearbook,* 1939 (San Diego, CA: Associated Students of San Diego State College, 1939), 132; Mabel Grant, *Del Sudoeste Yearbook,* 1938 (San Diego, CA: Associated Students of San Diego State College, 1938), 151.

64. Tamah Richardson and Annie Rivers, "Progress of the Negro: A Unit of Work for the Third Grade," *Virginia Teachers Bulletin,* May 1936, 3–8.

65. "Schoolmaster to His Race Mourned," *Washington AfroAmerican,* April 8, 1950.

66. Carter G. Woodson, "The Miseducation of the Negro," *The Crisis,* August 1931; Woodson, *Mis-education,* 105, reference to schooling and lynching on p. 4.

67. "Teachers Urged by Dr. Woodson to Adopt More Realistic Approach: Delegates Pack Sisters Chapel," *Atlanta Daily World*, April 17, 1942, 1 and 6;

68. Du Bois, *Souls of Black Folk*, 23.

69. See critique of "disciplinary decadence" and discussion of Black Studies and methods in Lewis Gordon, "Africana Thought and African-Diasporic Studies," in *A Companion to African-American Studies*, ed. Jane Anna Gordon and Lewis Gordon (Malden, MA: Wiley-Blackwell, 2006), 591.

70. Michel-Rolph Trouillot, *Silencing the Past: Power and the Production of History* (Boston: Beacon, 1997), 26: "Silences enter the process of historical production at four crucial moments . . . the making of sources . . . the making of archives . . . the making of narratives . . . the making of history in the final instance"; Marisa J. Fuentes, *Dispossessed Lives: Enslaved Women, Violence, and the Archive* (Philadelphia: University of Pennsylvania Press, 2016), 4.

71. The scientific nomenclature of "quarantine" is an intentional nod toward pseudoscientific research that informed and justified racist educational practices. See the following: "Scientific Racism and Black Education," in Watkins, *White Architects*, 89; Thomas Fallace, *Race and the Origins of Progressive Education, 1880–1929* (New York: Teachers College Press, 2015). "The nether edge of campus" is taken from the writer David Bradley's discussion of a black student center at the University of Pennsylvania, which was positioned at the margins of campus. This location indexed deeper truths about the physical and symbolic relationship between blacks and the university. David Bradley, "Black and American, 1982," *Esquire*, May 1982, 69.

72. Rebecca Schneider, "Performance Remains," *Performance Research* 6, no. 2 (January 1, 2001): 102.

73. Toni Morrison, "Unspeakable Things Unspoken: The Afro-American Presence in American Literature (1988)," in *The Source of Self-Regard: Selected Essays, Speeches, and Meditations* (New York: Knopf, 2019), 173.

74. W. E. B. Du Bois, "My Evolving Program of Negro Freedom (1944)," *Clinical Sociological Review* 8, no. 1 (1990): 47.

75. Baker, "Meditation on Tuskegee."

76. In referring to this as a genre of theory, I intentionally leave room to consider, for instance, bodies of educational criticism by Native American educators and thinkers, Marxist educators, and feminist teachers and thinkers, among others who understand their political motivations for teaching to be in direct tension with the protocols and dominant ideology of the American School. This book, however, is concerned with what I am referring to as the tradition of "black educational criticism" or "African American educational criticism." While some have referred to this as black educational thought, I find the language of "criticism" to be a more apt description. See also Zeus Leonardo, "Educational Criticism as a New Specialization," *Research in Education* 96, no. 1 (November 1, 2016): 87–92.

77. William Henry Watkins, *Black Protest Thought and Education* (New York: Peter Lang, 2005); Carl Grant, Keffrelyn Brown, and Anthony L. Brown, *Black Intellectual Thought in Education: The Missing Traditions of Anna Julia Cooper, Carter G. Woodson, and Alain LeRoy Locke* (New York: Routledge, 2015).

78. Woodson, *Mis-education,* chap. 18.

1. Between Coffle and Classroom

1. Carter G. Woodson, "Coffle and Classroom Negro Against Bondage," *Negro History Bulletin,* February 1938, 3; Frances Ellen Watkins Harper, "Learning to Read by Frances Ellen Watkins Harper (1825–1911)," Poetry Foundation (Poetry Foundation, June 29, 2020), https://www.poetryfoundation.org; Frederick Douglass, *My Bondage and My Freedom* (New York, Miller, Orton & Mulligan, 1855), 146; Carter G. Woodson, *The Education of the Negro Prior to 1861: A History of the Education of the Colored People of the United States from the Beginning of Slavery to the Civil War* (New York: Putnam and Son's, 1915), 10.

2. Birgit Brander Rasmussen, "'Attended with Great Inconveniences': Slave Literacy and the 1740 South Carolina Negro Act," *PMLA* 125, no. 1 (2010): 201–203.

3. Hilary J. Moss, *Schooling Citizens: The Struggle for African American Education in Antebellum America* (Chicago: University of Chicago Press, 2010).

4. See Mill's analysis of the failures of social contract theory to account for race: Charles Mills, *The Racial Contract* (Ithaca, NY: Cornell University Press, 1999).

5. Janet D. Cornelius, *When I Can Read My Title Clear: Literacy, Slavery and Religion in the Antebellum South* (Columbia: University of South Carolina Press, 1992), 9.

6. "Intelligent Negroes" who "secretly communicated to their fellow men what they knew." Woodson, *Education of the Negro,* 13, 208.

7. Woodson, *Education of the Negro,* 13; Norman R. Yetman, "Elizabeth Sparks Interview," in *Life under the "Peculiar Institution": Selections from the Slave Narrative Collection* (New York: Holt, Rinehart and Winston, 1970), 296–299; Heather Williams, *Self-Taught: African American Education in Slavery and Freedom* (Chapel Hill: University of North Carolina Press, 2007), 7–8.

8. Appendix in Williams, *Self-Taught,* 209.

9. Frederick Douglass, "The Day of Jubilee Comes (1862)," in *The Portable Frederick Douglass,* ed. John Stauffer (New York: Penguin, 2016), 303–305.

10. Booker T. Washington, *Up from Slavery* (New York: Dover, 1995).

11. Charlotte Forten Grimke, "Life on the Sea Islands (1864)," in *The Portable Nineteenth-Century African American Women Writers,* ed. Hollis Robbins and Henry Louis Gates (New York: Penguin Classics, 2017), 130–163; J. W. Alvord, "First Semi-Annual Report on Schools and Finances of Freedmen, January 1, 1866"

(Washington, DC: Bureau Refugees, Freedman and Abandoned Lands, 1868); see pp. 1–9 of "Inspector's Report" from January 1866.

12. James Anderson, *The Education of Blacks in the South, 1860–1935* (Chapel Hill: University of North Carolina Press, 1988); Williams, *Self-Taught,* 7–8.

13. "Always bard and actor, sometimes con-man and wit-worker, the black preacher is doubtlessly the first spokesman in slave communities and after that time he *and the black educator* are the first leaders of freedmen." Hortense J. Spillers, "Fabrics of History: Essays on the Black Sermon" (PhD diss., Brandeis University, 1974), 3 (italics added).

14. Sylvia Wynter, "No Humans Involved: An Open Letter to My Colleagues," *Forum N. H. I. Knowledge for the 21st Century* 1, no. 1 (Fall 1994): 70.

15. In the post-Emancipation period, black Americans were aware that their education began in covert fashion during slavery. This was not just something of the past; it was also living history, family stories of those who achieved education against great odds or stories told by those who were alive to bear witness. Woodson's portrait of enslaved people "snatching learning in forbidden fields" or a black teacher in Chicago lecturing in the 1930s about slaves "steal[ing] away to learn" was, in effect, a retelling of the origin story of black American education. It is an origin story rooted in historical fact, a collection of isolated incidents that black people collectively understood as a more general story of their shared educational past.

I am suggesting here that even after slavery ended, black Americans inherited stories about those that came before them and how they struggled to become educated under violent persecution. Furthermore, it was through this knowledge that their own educational struggles, post-Emancipation, were put into perspective. Black people lived their educational lives through the frame of this origin story. It informed the purpose and meaning of their educational strivings. Lawrence W. Levine, *Black Culture and Black Consciousness: Afro-American Folk Thought from Slavery to Freedom* (New York: Oxford University Press, 1978), 386–387. Stories of Susie King Taylor and Frederick Douglass are prominent examples of these stories; see Susie King Taylor, *Reminiscences of My Life in Camp with the 33D United States Colored Troops Late 1st S. C. Volunteers* (Boston: the author, 1902); Douglass, *My Bondage and My Freedom.* McKissack discusses the story of her formerly enslaved grandmother's struggle to read as the motivation for her children's novel about an enslaved girl secretly learning to read. Patricia McKissack, *A Picture of Freedom* (New York: Scholastic, 1997). Carter G. Woodson, *The Negro in Our History* (Washington D.C.: Associated Publishers, 1922), 108.

16. Carter G. Woodson, "John Morton Riddle Obituary in 'Notes,'" *Journal of Negro History* 27, no. 2 (1942): 243–246.

17. Carter G. Woodson, "George Washington Was the Most Liberal Slaveholder," *New Journal and Guide,* February 29, 1936.

18. Woodson, "John Morton Riddle Obituary"; Carter G. Woodson, "My Recollections of Veterans of the Civil War," *Negro History Bulletin*, February 1944, 103–104.

19. William T. Alderson, "The Freedmen's Bureau and Negro Education in Virginia," *North Carolina Historical Review* 29, no. 1 (1952): 85–86; Anderson, *Education of Blacks;* Williams, *Self-Taught;* Woodson, "John Morton Riddle Obituary," 245.

20. Alderson, "Freedmen's Bureau," 70, 74, 77–78.

21. Rayford Whittingham Logan, *The Negro in American Life and Thought: The Nadir, 1877–1901* (New York: Dial, 1954).

22. Frank G. Ruffin, *The Cost and Outcome of Negro Education in Virginia: Respectfully Addressed to the White People of the State* (Richmond, VA: E. Waddey, 1889), 6–7, 12, 15, 16; William Watkins, *The White Architects of Black Education: Ideology and Power in America, 1865–1954* (New York: Teachers College Press, 2001), 43–47.

23. On "the chattel principle," see Walter Johnson, *Soul by Soul: Life inside the Antebellum Slave Market* (Cambridge, MA: Harvard University Press, 1999).

24. Carter G. Woodson, "Carter G. Woodson Autobiographical Narrative" (c. 1938), Daryl M. Scott's personal collections.

25. Mary McLeod Bethune, "True Leadership Is Timeless," *Negro History Bulletin*, May 1950, 173.

26. Reference to driving garbage wagon and scarcity of food and clothes: Carter G. Woodson and Jesse E. Moorland, "Letter from Carter G. Woodson to Jesse Moorland," May 22, 1920, box 126–134, folder 695, the Jesse E. Moorland Papers, Moorland Spingarn Research Center, Howard University (hereafter cited as Moorland Papers).

27. Ibid.; for a general history of Woodson's early life, education, and family genealogy, see the biography Jacqueline Goggin, *Carter G. Woodson: A Life in Black History* (Baton Rouge: LSU Press, 1997).

28. *McGuffey's Fourth Eclectic Reader,* rev. ed. (Cincinnati: Van Antwerp, Bragg, 1879), 110–115; Department of Public Instruction of Virginia, "Outline of Primary and Grammar School Curriculum in Virginia," in *Proceedings of the Conference of County and City Superintendents of Schools of Virginia Held in the City of Richmond* (Richmond, VA: James E. Goode, 1897), 53–56.

29. Woodson, "Autobiographical Narrative," 1.

30. This assertion is informed by scholarship that pushes for a more expansive understanding of American empire that includes, say, Manifest Destiny and westward expansion into territories previously labeled "Indian Country," even in the early nineteenth century. This is an understanding of American empire not predicated on expansion beyond the North American territory but one that sees those incidents of expansion as part of a much longer narrative of American imperialism.

See, for instance, Daniel Immerwahr, *How to Hide an Empire: A History of the Greater United States* (New York: Farrar, Straus and Giroux, 2019).

31. *McGuffey's Fourth Eclectic Reader,* 117, 163.

32. Woodson, "My Recollections of Veterans."

33. Ibid., 2; Goggin, *Carter G. Woodson,* 10–11.

34. Woodson, "My Recollections of Veterans," 116.

35. See, for instance, Scott's discussion of Denmark Vesey and the social function of literacy; Vesey read newspaper passages about the slave rebellion in Santo Domingo aloud to his coconspirators, in preparation for their planned slave uprising: Julius S. Scott, *The Common Wind: Afro-American Currents in the Age of the Haitian Revolution* (London: Verso, 2018), 210; Cornelius, *When I Can Read.*

36. Jacqueline Bacon, "Literacy, Rhetoric, and 19th Century Print Culture," ed. Phyllis M. Belt-Beyan and Shirley Wilson Logan, *Journal of African American History* 95, no. 3–4 (2010): 422.

37. Williams, *Self-Taught.*

38. Woodson, "My Recollections of Veterans," 116.

39. Burnis R. Morris, *Carter G. Woodson: History, the Black Press, and Public Relations* (Jackson: University Press of Mississippi, 2017), 37–38; Ancella R. Bickley, "Carter G. Woodson: The West Virginia Connection," *Appalachian Heritage* 36, no. 3 (2008): 59–69.

40. Carter G. Woodson, *Early Negro Education in West Virginia,* vol. 3, Studies in Social Science 6 (Charleston: West Virginia Collegiate Institute, 1921).

41. Morris, *Carter G. Woodson,* 37.

42. See Woodson, *Early Negro Education,* chap. 6; Barnett is also listed as a key speaker in the proceedings of the WVTA meeting in 1898; see J. R. Trotter, "'The W. VA. Teachers" Association," in *Biennial Report of the State Superintendent of Free Schools of West Virginia for the Two Years Ending June 30, 1898* (Charleston, West Virginia, 1899), 61–62.

43. See Woodson, *Early Negro Education,* chap. 3.

44. Cicero M. Fain III, *Black Huntington: An Appalachian Story* (Urbana: University of Illinois Press, 2019), 103–105.

45. W. E. B. Du Bois, *The Souls of Black Folk* (New York: Barnes & Noble Classics, 2005), chap. "Of the Meaning of Progress."

46. Woodson, "Autobiographical Narrative," 2; "The Commencement of Douglass High School," *Huntington Advertiser,* May 8, 1896, excerpts transcribed by Nelson Barnett, in the possession of Burnis Morris.

47. "Separate Coaches Constitutional," *Huntington Advertiser,* May 18, 1896, excerpts transcribed by Nelson Barnett, in the possession of Burnis Morris.

48. For more on Woodson's time at Berea, see Goggin, *Carter G. Woodson,* 12–14; Lincoln University, "Minutes of the Faculty of Arts," September 28, 1897, Lincoln University of Pennsylvania, Langston Hughes Memorial Library Special

Collections; Lincoln University, "Sophomore Class," in *Catalogue of Lincoln University, 1897–1898,* 1897, 22, Lincoln University of Pennsylvania, Langston Hughes Memorial Library Special Collections. A local newspaper in Kentucky also took note of Woodson's time at Berea in an announcement about local college news; see "College Items ('Carter G. Woodson')," *The Citizen,* April 23, 1903.

49. Lincoln University, "Sophomore Class Examination Ending Fall 1897," in *Lincoln University Grade Book,* 448, Lincoln University of Pennsylvania, Langston Hughes Memorial Library Special Collections.

50. Bickley, "Carter G. Woodson," 63.

51. Jacqueline G. Burnside, "Suspicion versus Faith: Negro Criticisms of Berea College in the Nineteenth Century," *Register of the Kentucky Historical Society* 83, no. 3 (1985): 254–256. Berea's practice of coeducation of the two races ultimately became illegal in 1904 with the passage of the Day Law in the state of Kentucky. Ibid., 261, 265–266.

52. "Assignment of Teachers," *Huntington Advertiser,* September 15, 1900, sec. 4, excerpts transcribed by Nelson Barnett, in the possession of Burnis Morris.

53. For more discussion on Barnett's role in Huntington and the political controversy surrounding his firing, see Morris, *Carter G. Woodson,* 37; and Bickley, "Carter G. Woodson," 63.

54. Woodson's "Teacher's High School Certificate," reprinted in *Negro History Bulletin,* May 1950, 180.

55. "The Douglas High School Graduating Exercises at Davis Opera House Last Evening," *Huntington Advertiser,* May 11, 1901, sec. 4, excerpts transcribed by Nelson Barnett, in the possession of Burnis Morris.

56. "Services at Douglass High School," *Huntington Advertiser,* September 23, 1901, sec. 3, excerpts transcribed by Nelson Barnett, in the possession of Burnis Morris.

57. Funds raised by the Douglass School under Woodson's principalship are listed in "The McKinley Memorial Fund," *West Virginia School Journal* 21, no. 12 (March 1902): 24.

58. "Douglass School Library," *Huntington Advertiser,* October 7, 1901, sec. 3, excerpts transcribed by Nelson Barnett, in the possession of Burnis Morris.

59. "Douglass High School Commencement: Closing Exercises of Colored School at Theatre Last Night," *Huntington Advertiser,* May 10, 1902, sec. 2, excerpts transcribed by Nelson Barnett, in the possession of Burnis Morris.

60. Kellie Carter Jackson, *Force and Freedom: Black Abolitionists and the Politics of Violence* (Philadelphia: University of Pennsylvania Press, 2019), 4–5.

61. University of Chicago Registrar's Office, "Carter Godwin Woodson University of Chicago Transcript," Summer 1902–Summer 1908, University of Chicago Registrar Archives.

62. See Woodson, *Early Negro Education,* chap. 6.

63. Carter G. Woodson, "Between Him and the Fire," *Chicago Defender,* January 6, 1934.

64. Booker T. Washington was scheduled to speak in Boston at the Zion Church, and local dissenters, including William Monroe Trotter, staged a demonstration. The police were called, and the conflict led to a police officer being stabbed and numerous protestors being arrested, Trotter included. The event was covered in a Kentucky newspaper: "A Miniature Riot," *Evening Bulletin,* July 31, 1903.

65. Du Bois, *Souls of Black Folk,* chap. "On Booker T. Washington and Others."

66. Watkins, *White Architects.*

67. Clif Stratton, *Education for Empire: American Schools, Race, and the Paths of Good Citizenship* (Oakland: University of California Press, 2016), 2.

68. Sarah Steinbock-Pratt, *Educating the Empire: American Teachers and Contested Colonization in the Philippines* (Cambridge, UK: Cambridge University Press, 2019), Atkinson quote cited on p. 17.

69. Quoted in Roland Sintos Coloma, "'Destiny Has Thrown the Negro and the Filipino under the Tutelage of America': Race and Curriculum in the Age of Empire," *Curriculum Inquiry* 39, no. 4 (2009): 504.

70. Woodson's official appointment is dated as December 19, 1903, in the following report: "Quarterly Report of Changes, Bureau of Education, Appointments" (Manila, Philippines, January 1, 1904), box 372, file 4096-16 (Education, Government Schools and Teachers), US National Archives, Bureau of Insular Affairs, RG 350 I-3 5-A General Classified Files, 1898–1945 (1898–1913 Segment); for additional discussion of Woodson's time in the Philippines, see Goggin, *Carter G. Woodson,* 16–18.

71. "List of Teachers Selected," *Huntington Advertiser,* May 27, 1902, sec. 2, excerpts transcribed by Nelson Barnett, in the possession of Burnis Morris.

72. "Quarterly Report of Changes, Bureau of Education, Appointments."

73. Ibid., 40, 96.

74. Glenn A. May, "Social Engineering in the Philippines: The Aims and Execution of American Educational Policy, 1900–1913," *Philippine Studies* 24, no. 2 (1976): 153.

75. Quote taken from 1903 Superintendent Report reprinted in May, "Social Engineering," 156.

76. Goggin, *Carter G. Woodson,* 18.

77. Sister Mary Anthony Scally, "The Philippine Challenge," *Negro History Bulletin,* January 1981, 17.

78. Francisco Benitez, "American Education in the Philippines," *The Filipino* 1, no. 3 (May 1906): 26.

79. Carter G. Woodson, *The Mis-Education of the Negro* (Washington D.C.: Association for the Study of African American Life and History, 2008).

80. Ibid., 84–85.

81. University of Chicago Registrar's Office, "Carter Godwin Woodson University of Chicago Transcript"; Woodson, "Autobiographical Narrative."

82. These were graduate-level courses offered through the Sorbonne's public education program, where scholars who were not formally enrolled students could learn free of charge. "L'Université De Paris Et Les Établissements Parisiens D'Enseignement Supérieur—Programmes Sommaires (Année Scolaire 1906–1907)," 1906, Student Booklets and Course Catalogues, The Sorbonne (University of Paris) Archives.

83. University of Chicago Registrar's Office, "Carter Godwin Woodson University of Chicago Transcript"; a list of courses completed at the University of Paris is included in the following: Carter G. Woodson, "Letter from Woodson to Dean of Harvard Graduate School of Arts and Science," August 19, 1908, Woodson student file in off-site storage, Harvard University Archives and Special Collections.

84. Carter G. Woodson, "Letter from Carter Godwin Woodson to W. E. B. Du Bois, February 18, 1908," W. E. B. Du Bois Papers (MS 312), Special Collections and University Archives, University of Massachusetts Amherst Libraries (hereafter cited as Du Bois Papers).

85. Woodson, "Letter from Woodson to Dean of Harvard Graduate School of Arts and Science."

86. University of Chicago Registrar's Office, "Carter Godwin Woodson University of Chicago Transcript."

87. George W. Robinson, "Carter G. Woodson's Letter of Acceptance to Harvard University Graduate School of Arts and Sciences," September 22, 1908, Woodson student file in off-site storage, Harvard University Archives and Special Collections.

88. Woodson, "Letter from Woodson to Dean of Harvard Graduate School of Arts and Science."

89. Carter G. Woodson, "Harvard University Application for Admission to the Candidacy for a Degree in Arts or Philosophy," September 12, 1908, Woodson student file in off-site storage, Harvard University Archives and Special Collections.

90. Woodson identifies a discussion in graduate school when his professor dismissed the idea that black people had any bearings on the development of the American Revolution. Carter G. Woodson, "The George Washington Bicentennial Eliminates March 5th, Crispus Attucks Day," *New York Age*, January 2, 1932, 9.

91. Goggin, *Carter G. Woodson*, 21–26; for extensive coverage of the racist ideas of Woodson's graduate school professors, see Jeffrey Aaron Snyder, *Making Black History: The Color Line, Culture, and Race in the Age of Jim Crow* (Athens: University of Georgia Press, 2018), quotes from Channing on pp. 23–24, 176n26.

92. August Meier and Elliott Rudwick, *Black History and the Historical Profession, 1915–1980* (Urbana: University of Illinois Press, 1986), 3–4.

93. Woodson passed his exams in January 1910.

94. Pero G. Dagbovie, *Carter G. Woodson in Washington, D.C.: Father of Black History* (Charleston, SC: Arcadia, 2014).

95. Carter G. Woodson, "Knockers Make Capital Graveyard of Ambition, Proclaims Woodson," *Atlanta Daily World,* April 7, 1932, 2.

96. Charles H. Wesley, *History of Sigma Pi Phi: First of the Negro-American Greek-Letter Fraternities,* 50th anniv. ed. (Washington DC: Association for the Study of Negro Life and History, 1954), 76–78.

97. William Nelson, "The Campaign for the Study of Negro Literature and History," *The Oracle: Semi-Annual Publication of the Grand Chapter of The Omega Psi Phi Fraternity,* August 1921, 31–33.

98. Michael Dawson, "A Black Counterpublic? Economic Earthquakes, Racial Agenda(s), and Black Politics," *Public Culture,* no. 7 (1994): 195–223.

99. Imani Perry, *May We Forever Stand: A History of the Black National Anthem* (Chapel Hill: University of North Carolina Press, 2018), 6.

100. For more discussion of Woodson's involvement in DC's political organizations, see Dagbovie, *Carter G. Woodson,* 68.

101. Wesley, *History of Sigma Pi Phi,* 75, 77.

102. Ibid., 29; "Biographical Sketch," *Negro History Bulletin,* May 1950, 171–173; Rayford W. Logan, "Carter G. Woodson: Mirror and Molder of His Time, 1875–1950," *Journal of Negro History* 58, no. 1 (January 1973): 6.

103. Mary Church Terrell, "History of the High School for Negroes in Washington," *Journal of Negro History* 2, no. 3 (July 1917): 252–266; Henry S. Robinson, "The M Street High School, 1891–1916," *Records of the Columbia Historical Society, Washington, D.C.,* no. 51 (1984): 119–143. The first principal was Emma J. Hutchins, a white woman from New Hampshire.

104. Mr. Francis L. Cardoza, who later served as principal, graduated from Glasgow University in Scotland and founded the Avery Institute in South Carolina in 1867, the first free secondary school for African Americans. The school also had a medical doctor and a judge as its principals during the years leading it into the twentieth century.

105. Robinson, "M Street High School," 122–123.

106. Mary Gibson Hundley, *The Dunbar Story, 1870–1955,* 1st ed. (New York: Vantage, 1965), 64; Thomas Sowell, "Black Excellence: The Case of Dunbar High School," *Public Interest,* April 1, 1974, 3–21.

107. Hundley, *Dunbar Story,* 164.

108. Jacqueline Goggin, "Carter G. Woodson and the Movement to Promote Black History" (ProQuest Dissertations Publishing, 1984), 5.

109. Burroughs was a respected leader in the National Baptist Convention. See Evelyn Brooks Higginbotham, *Righteous Discontent: The Women's Movement in the Black Baptist Church, 1880–1920* (Cambridge, MA: Harvard University Press, 1994).

110. Robinson, "M Street High School," 140.

111. Ibid., 131. The legacy of Dunbar loomed large in M Street's academic culture. His sonnet "Keep A-Pluggin' Away" was even adopted as the school creed. Hundley, *Dunbar Story, 1870–1955,* 59.

112. Edward C. Williams, "Report of Principal of M Street High School, 1909–1910," Annual Report of the Commissioners of the District of Columbia Year Ended June 30, 1910, Report of the Board of Education, 1910.

113. Roscoe Bruce, "Report of the Assistant Superintendent in Charge of Colored Schools," Annual Report of the Commissioners of the District of Columbia Year Ended June 30, 1915, Report of the Board of Education, July 1, 1915.

114. Edward C. Williams, "Report of Principal of M Street High School, 1909–1910," Annual Report of the Commissioners of the District of Columbia Year Ended June 30, 1910, Report of the Board of Education, 1910, p. 240.

115. Jessie H. Roy, "Some Personal Recollections of Dr. Woodson," *Negro History Bulletin,* May 1965, 185, 192.

116. Roy, "Some Personal Recollections,"185, 192

117. Logan, "Mirror and Molder," 8–9; William M. Cobb, "Carter G. Woodson: The Father of Negro History," *Journal of the National Medical Association* 62, no. 5 (September 1970): 389; Goggin, *Carter G. Woodson,* 29–30.

118. Roy, "Some Personal Recollections," 185, 192

119. Goggin, *Carter G. Woodson,* 23–25.

120. See Richard R. Wright's recollections of Harvard professor John Fiske; Richard R. Wright, "Negro Companions of the Spanish Explorers," *Phylon (1940–1956)* 2, no. 4 (1941): 325–322; "denaturalizing" knowledge is a term presented by Sylvia Wynter in a phone conversation regarding Woodson's philosophical contributions.

2. "The Association . . . Is Standing Like the Watchman on the Wall"

Epigraphs: Carter G. Woodson, "Association on Guard," Norfolk Journal and Guide, October 17, 1936; W. E. B. Du Bois, "As the Crow Flies," to be published in Chicago Globe (April 7, 1950), 6, Du Bois Papers (MS 312).

1. Khalil Gibran Muhammad, *The Condemnation of Blackness: Race, Crime, and the Making of Modern Urban America* (Cambridge, MA: Harvard University Press, 2011).

2. W. E. B. Du Bois, "Slanderous Film," *The Crisis,* December 1915, 76–77; Ed Guerrero, *Framing Blackness: The African American Image in Film* (Philadelphia: Temple University Press, 1993), 11–13.

3. "Lynching Statistics by Year, Provided by Tuskegee University Archives," UMKC Law School (website), accessed July 5, 2020, http://law2.umkc.edu/faculty /projects/ftrials/shipp/lynchingyear.html.

4. Michael Dawson, "A Black Counterpublic? Economic Earthquakes, Racial Agenda(s), and Black Politics," *Public Culture,* no. 7 (1994): 195–223; on "civic estrangement," see Salamishah Tillet, *Sites of Slavery: Citizenship and Racial Democracy in the Post–Civil Rights Imagination* (Durham, NC: Duke University Press, 2012), 3–10.

5. See Perry's treatment of "black institutional life" in relationship to her analysis of "Lift Every Voice and Sing," and other scholarship pertaining to the covert activities of black religious and educational institutions. Imani Perry, *May We Forever Stand: A History of the Black National Anthem* (Chapel Hill: University of North Carolina Press, 2018), 6–12, 145; Albert J. Raboteau, *Slave Religion: The "Invisible Institution" in the Antebellum South* (Oxford: Oxford University Press, 2004); Vanessa Siddle Walker, *The Lost Education of Horace Tate: Uncovering the Hidden Heroes Who Fought for Justice in Schools* (New York: New Press, 2018); Howard Holman Bell, *A Survey of the Negro Convention Movement 1830–1861* (New York: Arno Press and the New York Times, 1969).

6. Pero G. Dagbovie, *Carter G. Woodson in Washington, D.C.: Father of Black History* (Charleston, SC: Arcadia, 2014).

7. Elinor Des Verney Sinnette, *Arthur Alfonso Schomburg: Black Bibliophile and Collector* (Detroit: Wayne State University Press, 1989), 53; Alfred A. Moss, *The American Negro Academy: Voice of the Talented Tenth* (Baton Rouge: Louisiana State University Press, 1981).

8. Randall K. Burkett, Pellom McDaniels, and Tiffany Gleason, *The Mind of Carter G. Woodson as Reflected in the Books He Owned, Read, and Published* (Atlanta: Emory University, 2006).

9. Arthur Alfonso Schomburg, *Racial Integrity a Plea for the Establishment of a Chair of Negro History in Our Schools and Colleges, etc.* (New York: A. V. Bernier, 1913); Richard Robert Wright, "The Possibilities of the Negro Teacher," *AME Church Review* 10, no. 4 (April 1894): 459–470; Leila Amos Pendleton, *A Narrative of the Negro* (Washington, DC: Press of R. L. Pendleton, 1912).

10. Roscoe Bruce, "Report of the Assistant Superintendent in Charge of Colored Schools," Annual Report of the Commissioners of the District of Columbia Year Ended June 30, 1915, Report of the Board of Education, July 1, 1915, pp. 249–250.

11. E. Renee Ingram, "Bruce, Roscoe Conkling, Sr.," in *Harlem Renaissance Lives: from the African American National Biography*, ed. Henry Louis Gates Jr. and Evelyn Brooks Higginbotham (New York: Oxford University Press, 2009), 84–86.

12. Ida B. Wells-Barnett, "Negro Fellowship League," *Broad Ax*, August 7, 1915, 4.

13. Jacqueline Goldsby, *A Spectacular Secret: Lynching in American Life and Literature* (Chicago: University of Chicago Press, 2006), 58–59.

14. James E. Stamps, "The Beginning of the ASNLH," *Negro History Bulletin*, November 1965. It is also noted that Claude A. Barnett, who would later found the Associated Negro Press, had a booth at the exposition selling "high quality" prints of distinguished black figures and scenes from Negro life. It is unclear if Woodson sold pictures printed by Barnett's company. "Race Shows Wonderful Progress in 50 Years," *Chicago Defender*, September 4, 1915, 3.

15. "Pictures of Distinguished Negroes," box 1, folder 3, Carter Godwin Woodson Collection, Manuscript, Archives, and Rare Book Library, Emory University (hereafter cited as Woodson Collection); Woodson notes that the ASNLH supplied

printed photographs for classroom use as early as 1927; see Carter G. Woodson, "The Annual Report of the Director," *Journal of Negro History* 12, no. 4 (1927): 568.

16. Carter G. Woodson and Jesse E. Moorland, "Letter from Carter G. Woodson to Jesse Moorland," August 24, 1915, box 126–134, folder 695, Moorland Papers; Jesse E. Moorland to Carter G. Woodson, "Letter from Jesse Moorland to Carter G. Woodson," September 2, 1915, box 126–134, folder 695, Moorland Papers.

17. Jacqueline Goggin, *Carter G. Woodson: A Life in Black History* (Baton Rouge: LSU Press, 1997), 33–34.

18. Stamps, "Beginning of the ASNLH."

19. Alexander L. Jackson, "Reminiscences, Greetings, Challenges . . . ," *Negro History Bulletin,* Summer 1965.

20. "Y.M.C.A. Bldg Dedicated with Imposing Ceremonies," *Chicago Defender,* June 21, 1913, 1.

21. Stamps, "Beginning of the ASNLH."

22. Ibid.

23. Charles H. Wesley, "Our Fiftieth Year: The Golden Anniversary, 1965," *Negro History Bulletin,* Summer 1965, 195.

24. Patricia W. Romero, "Carter G. Woodson: A Biography" (PhD diss., Ohio State University, 1971), 92.

25. Stamps, "Beginning of the ASNLH."

26. ASNLH Articles of Incorporation, Papers of Carter G. Woodson and the Association for the Study of Negro Life and History, 1915–1950, University Publications of America, Microfilm, UC Berkeley, reel 1 (hereafter cited as Woodson Microfilm Collection).

27. Wesley, "Our Fiftieth Year."

28. Carter G. Woodson, *Journal of Negro History* 1, no. 1 (1916): Woodson, "Notes," 98; J. R. Fauset, review of *Review of the Haitian Revolution, 1791 to 1804,* by T. G. Steward, *Journal of Negro History* 1, no. 1 (1916): 93; W. B. Hartgrove, "The Story of Maria Louise Moore and Fannie M. Richards," *Journal of Negro History* 1, no. 1 (1916): 23–33.

29. Roscoe Bruce, "Report of the Assistant Superintendent in Charge of Colored Schools," *Report of the Commissioners of the District of Columbia,* June 30, 1916, 249–250.

30. Rayford W. Logan, *Howard University: The First Hundred Years 1867–1967* (New York: NYU Press, 1969), 171.

31. Roscoe Bruce, "Report of the Assistant Superintendent in Charge of Colored Schools (1919)," Annual Report of the Commissioners of the District of Columbia Year Ended June 30, 1919, Report of the Board of Education, June 30, 1919, 237–238.

32. "1918–19: Catalog of the Officers and Students of Howard University" (Howard University, January 1, 1918), Howard University Catalogs, no. 45, 106–108.

33. Carter G. Woodson, *The Negro in Our History* (Washington, DC: Associated Publishers, 1922), 326–328; David F. Krugler, *1919, the Year of Racial Violence: How African Americans Fought Back* (New York: Cambridge University Press, 2014), 72–73.

34. Woodson, *Negro in Our History*, 261.

35. Arnett G. Lindsay, "Dr. Woodson as a Teacher," *Negro History Bulletin*, May 1950, 183.

36. In addition to the US history courses he taught in the History Department, Woodson also taught a course on the history of political theory in the Political Science Department. "1919–20: Catalog of the Officers and Students of Howard University" (Howard University, January 1, 1919), Howard University Catalogs, no. 46, 157–161, Moorland Spingarn Research Center, Howard University.

37. Carter G. Woodson, "Twenty Years Wasted, Says D.C. Historian," *Negro World*, March 21, 1931, 1, 8.

38. Carter G. Woodson, "The George Washington Bicentennial Eliminates March 5th, Crispus Attucks Day," *New York Age*, January 2, 1932, 9.

39. Ibid.; Lindsay, "Dr. Woodson as a Teacher," 191; see also Woodson's treatment of Attucks in *Negro in Our History*, 58–59.

40. Arnett G. Lindsay, "Diplomatic Relations between the United States and Great Britain Bearing on the Return of Negro Slaves, 1783–1828," *Journal of Negro History* 5, no. 4 (October 1, 1920): 391–419; Woodson and Lindsay sustained their relationship over the years. It was Lindsay who found Woodson on the afternoon of April 3, 1950, after he had passed away unexpectedly in his sleep. He subsequently served as a pallbearer at Woodson's funeral and chaired the first executive meeting of the ASNLH after Woodson's passing to discuss the publication of the *Journal of Negro History* and the *Negro History Bulletin*. A number of Woodson's past students and mentees were present for this meeting; see "Minutes Held at the Y.W.C.A. May 3, 1950," box 4, folder 8, Woodson Collection.

41. Logan, *Howard University*, 167.

42. Ibid., 208; Goggin, *Carter G. Woodson*, 51–52.

43. "Letter from Carter G. Woodson to Jesse E. Moorland (May 22, 1920)," May 22, 1920, box 126–134, folder 695, Moorland Papers; "Letter from Carter G. Woodson to Jesse Moorland," May 20, 1920, box 126–134, folder 695, Moorland Papers.

44. Carter G. Woodson, *The Mis-education of the Negro* (Washington DC: Association for the Study of African American life and History, 2008), 14, chap. 3.

45. Romero, "Carter G. Woodson: A Biography," 80.

46. "ASNLH Brochure" (n.d.), box 1, folder 31, Woodson Collection; Geneva C. Turner, "A Look at the Association: Past, Present, Future," *Negro History Bulletin*, May 1965, 184; Dagbovie, *Carter G. Woodson*.

47. See Favors's discussion of the "second curriculum" of HBCUs: Jelani M. Favors, *Shelter in a Time of Storm: How Black Colleges Fostered Generations of*

Leadership and Activism (Chapel Hill: University of North Carolina Press, 2019), 7, 107.

48. W. Daykin, "Nationalism as Expressed in Negro History," *Social Forces,* no. 13 (1934): 257–263; Sister Anthony Scally, "Phelps-Stokes Confidential Memorandum for the Trustees of the Phelps-Stokes Fund Regarding Dr. Carter G. Woodson's Attacks on Dr. Thomas Jesse Jones," *Journal of Negro History* 76, no. 1/4 (1991): 48–60.

49. Carter G. Woodson, "Ten Years of Collecting and Publishing the Records of the Negro," *Journal of Negro History* 10, no. 4 (1925): 602; August Meier and Elliott Rudwick, *Black History and the Historical Profession, 1915–1980* (Urbana: University of Illinois Press, 1986), 20.

50. Woodson, "Ten Years of Collecting and Publishing," 602–603; Meier and Rudwick, *Black History,* 35.

51. Ibid., 27–35.

52. Jameson quoted in Darlene Clark Hine, "Carter G. Woodson, White Philanthropy and Negro Historiography," *History Teacher* 19, no. 3 (1986): 411.

53. Jones quoted in Hine, "Carter G. Woodson," 414.

54. Letter from Carter G. Woodson to Benjamin Brawley, January 7, 1932, Du Bois Papers (MS 312).

55. Zora Neale Hurston, "What White Publishers Won't Print (Negro Digest, April 1950)," in *Hurston: Folklore, Memoirs, and Other Writings* (New York: Literary Classics of the United States, 1995), 950–955.

56. W. E. B. Du Bois, "As the Crow Flies," to be published in *Chicago Globe* (April 7, 1950), 6, Du Bois Papers (MS 312).

57. James Anderson, *The Education of Blacks in the South, 1860–1935* (Chapel Hill: University of North Carolina Press, 1988), Woodson, *Mis-education.*

58. Meier and Rudwick, *Black History,* 60

59. Carter G. Woodson, "An Accounting for Twenty-Five Years," *Journal of Negro History* 25, no. 4 (1940): 426

60. Woodson, "Association on Guard."

61. Carter G. Woodson, *Carter G. Woodson's Appeal,* ed. Daryl Michael Scott, limited ed. copy (Washington, DC: Association for the Study of African American Life and History, 2008).

62. For a treatment of the ASNLH in comparison to mainstream academic organizations, see Romero, "Carter G. Woodson," 216.

63. Moss, *American Negro Academy.*

64. A similar observation is made in Jacqueline Goggin, "Carter G. Woodson and the Movement to Promote Black History" (ProQuest Dissertations Publishing, 1984), 12.

65. Pero Gaglo Dagbovie, "Black Women, Carter G. Woodson, and the Association for the Study of Negro Life and History, 1915–1950," *Journal of African American History* 88, no. 1 (January 1, 2003): 21; see "Teachers and Preachers," in

Evelyn Brooks Higginbotham, *Righteous Discontent: The Women's Movement in the Black Baptist Church, 1880–1920* (Cambridge, MA: Harvard University Press, 1994), 41.

66. "The Negro in Our History 4th Edition Advertisement" (n.d.), box 1, folder 1, Woodson Collection.

67. "The Annual Report of the Director for the Year 1922–1923," *Journal of Negro History* 8, no. 4 (October 1923): 467.

68. "An Appeal for Members," 1928, box 1, folder 31, Woodson Collection.

69. "25th Anniversary Meeting Program" (1940), box 1, folder 9, Woodson Collection.

70. Romero, "Carter G. Woodson," 215.

71. Ibid., 143.

72. Ibid., 120.

73. ASALH, *Reflections of Carter G. Woodson: With John Hope Franklin and Adelaide Cromwell*, DVD (ASALH 91st Annual Convention, Atlanta, GA, 2006).

74. Dagbovie, *Carter G. Woodson in Washington D.C.*, 57.

75. Wilhelmina M. Crosson, "Reminiscences, Greetings, Challenges . . . ," *Negro History Bulletin*, Summer 1965.

76. Letter from Clarke Leo Smith Jr. to Woodson (undated), Woodson Microfilm Collection, reel 2; biography of Smith found on "Happy Father's Day to My Dad, Clarke L. Smith, Jr. (1915–1984)," by Yvonne May (daughter), http://www.clarkesmithphotography.com/blog (accessed April 8, 2015).

77. Aldon Morris, *The Scholar Denied: W. E. B. Du Bois and the Birth of Modern Sociology* (Oakland: University of California Press, 2015), 141, 144.

78. Dorothy Height, testimonial, prerecorded for ASALH Founder's Day Event 2009 (Prince George County, 2009), in personal collection of Mrs. Barbara Spencer Dunn.

79. Letter reprinted in *Negro History Bulletin* (May 1950) under the title, "The Death of the Founder," 170, 176

80. Crosson, "Reminiscences, Greetings, Challenges."

81. "Schoolmaster to His Race Mourned," *Washington Afro-American*, April 8, 1950.

82. Jessie H. Roy, "Some Personal Recollections of Dr. Woodson," *Negro History Bulletin*, May 1965, 185, 192.

83. Jessie Roy and Geneva Turner, *Pioneers of Long Ago* (Washington DC: Associated Publishers, 1951), xi–xii.

84. Woodson's ATA "Life Member" certificate reproduced in Willie Miles' "Dr. Carter G. Woodson as I Recall Him, 1943–1950," *Journal of Negro History* 76, no. 4 (1991): 99; see also Thelma Perry, *History of the American Teachers' Association* (Washington, DC: National Education, 1975).

85. Meier and Rudwick, *Black History*, 75, 90; Lorenzo J. Greene, *Selling Black History for Carter G. Woodson: A Diary, 1930–1933*, ed. Arvarh E. Strickland

(Columbia: University of Missouri Press, 1996); Francille Rusan Wilson, *The Segregated Scholars: Black Social Scientists and the Creation of Black Labor Studies, 1890–1950* (Charlottesville: University of Virginia Press, 2006); Dagbovie, *Carter G. Woodson.*

86. "ASNLH Brochure" (n.d.), box 1, folder 31, Woodson Collection; "The Annual Report of the Director for the Year 1922–1923," *Journal of Negro History* 8, no. 4 (October 1923): 466–471.

87. Zora Neale Hurston, Deborah G. Plant, and Alice Walker, *Barracoon: The Story of the Last "Black Cargo"* (London: Amistad, 2018), 6, 118–119.

88. Alrutheus A. Taylor, "Dr. Carter G. Woodson: Inspirer and Benefactor of Young Scholars," *Negro History Bulletin,* May 1950, 186; "Dr. Woodson as I Knew Him," 1976, box 92, Lorenzo Johnston Green Papers, Manuscript Division, Library of Congress, Washington, DC; Meier and Rudwick, *Black History,* 94.

89. Morris, *Scholar Denied,* 144.

90. Malcolm X and Alex Haley, *The Autobiography of Malcolm X* (New York: Ballantine Books, 1965): 178.

91. Mary McLeod Bethune, "True Leadership Is Timeless," *Negro History Bulletin,* May 1950, 173.

92. W. E. B. Du Bois, *Dusk of Dawn: An Essay toward an Autobiography of a Race Concept* (New York: Harcourt, Brace, 1940), 203.

93. Du Bois, "As the Crow Flies," 7.

3. A Language We Can See a Future In

Epigraph: Sylvia Wynter, "Race and Our Biocentric Belief System: An Interview with Sylvia Wynter (June 2000)," in *Black Education: A Transformative Research and Action Agenda for the New Century,* ed. Joyce Elaine King (Washington, DC: American Educational Research Association, 2005), 365.

1. Lewis R. Gordon, "Africana Thought and African Diasporic Studies," *Black Scholar* 30, no. 3–4 (2000): 25.

2. Norman R. Yetman, "Elizabeth Sparks Interview," in *Life Under the "Peculiar Institution": Selections from the Slave Narrative Collection* (New York: Holt, Rinehart and Winston, 1970), 299: "Niggers used to go way off in quarters and slip and have meetins'. They called it stealin the meetin'. The children used to teach me to read."

3. Frederick Douglass, *My Bondage and My Freedom* (New York: Miller, Orton & Mulligan, 1855), 146.

4. For discussion on major themes in what I am calling black educational criticism, see William Henry Watkins, *Black Protest Thought and Education* (New York: Peter Lang, 2005); Carl Grant, Keffrelyn Brown, and Anthony L. Brown, *Black Intellectual Thought in Education: The Missing Traditions of Anna Julia Cooper, Carter G. Woodson, and Alain LeRoy Locke* (New York: Routledge, 2015); Wil-

liam H. Watkins, "Black Curriculum Orientations: A Preliminary Inquiry," *Harvard Educational Review* 63, no. 3 (1993): 321–338; Michael J. Dumas and kihana miraya ross, "'Be Real Black for Me': Imagining BlackCrit in Education," *Urban Education* 51, no. 4 (April 1, 2016): 415–442.

5. Lauryn Hill, *The Miseducation of Lauryn Hill,* audio CD (Sony Legacy, 1998).

6. Carter G. Woodson, *The Mis-education of the Negro* (Washington DC: The Association for the Study of African American Life and History), 3.

7. Ibid., 106.

8. Michael W. Apple, "The Politics of Official Knowledge: Does a National Curriculum Make Sense?," *Teachers College Record* 95, no. 2 (1993): 222–241.

9. C.f. Jeffrey Aaron Snyder, "Progressive Education in Black and White: Rereading Carter G. Woodson's *Miseducation of the Negro,*" *History of Education Quarterly* 55, no. 3 (August 1, 2015): 273–293.

10. Henry W. Elson, *Modern Times and the Living Past* (New York: American Book Company, 1935), 13.

11. Carter G. Woodson, "Twenty Years Wasted, Says D.C. Historian," *Negro World,* March 21, 1931, 1, 8.

12. Woodson, *Mis-education,* 33, 83.

13. Ibid., 5 (italics added).

14. Carter G. Woodson, "Some Thoughts of C.G. Woodson" (n.d.), p. 3, Papers of Carter G. Woodson and the Association for the Study of African American Life and History, 1915–1950, Microfilm Collection, University Publications of America.

15. Woodson, *Mis-education,* 19.

16. Ibid., 83 (italics added).

17. Carter G. Woodson, "Differentiation in Education with Respect to Races," *New York Age,* January 27, 1934, 5 (italics added).

18. Ibid., 75.

19. Ibid., 75.

20. Ibid., 107.

21. Ibid., 64.

22. Mary McLeod Bethune, "The Association for the Study of Negro Life and History: Its Contribution to Our Modern Life," *Journal of Negro History* 20, no. 4 (1935): 407–408.

23. Woodson, *Mis-education,* 47.

24. Achille Mbembe, *Critique of Black Reason* (Durham, NC: Duke University Press Books, 2017), 28.

25. Heather Williams, *Self-Taught: African American Education in Slavery and Freedom* (Chapel Hill: University of North Carolina Press, 2007), 136.

26. Saidiya Hartman, *Scenes of Subjection: Terror, Slavery, and Self-Making in Nineteenth-Century America* (New York: Oxford University Press, 1997), 129–130.

27. Woodson, *Mis-education,* 14.

28. Ibid.

29. See Chapter 5 for a discussion on Woodson's critiques of black teachers / teacher training.

30. William Watkins, *The White Architects of Black Education: Ideology and Power in America, 1865–1954* (New York: Teachers College Press, 2001).

31. Quote taken from correspondence from Woodson to William C. Graves (secretary of philanthropist Julius Rosenwald), May 4, 1922, Rosenwald Papers, cited in Jacqueline Goggin, "Carter G. Woodson and the Movement to Promote Black History" (University of Rochester, Proquest Dissertations Publishing, 1984), 265.

32. Letter from Carter G. Woodson to Benjamin Brawley, January 7, 1932, Du Bois Papers (MS 312).

33. W. E. B Du Bois to Carter G. Woodson, "Letter from W. E. B. Du Bois to Carter G. Woodson, January 29, 1932," January 29, 1932, Du Bois Papers (MS 312) (italics added).

34. Letter from Carter G. Woodson to Benjamin Brawley, January 7, 1932, Du Bois Papers (MS 312).

35. Darlene Clark Hine, "Carter G. Woodson, White Philanthropy and Negro Historiography," *History Teacher* 19, no. 3 (1986): 405–425; "Notes," *Journal of Negro History,* January 1932.

36. Carter G. Woodson, "Letter from Carter G. Woodson to W. E. B. Du Bois," January 7, 1932, Du Bois Papers (MS 312).

37. Letter from Carter G. Woodson to Benjamin Brawley, January 7, 1932, Du Bois Papers (MS 312).

38. Carter G. Woodson, "Letter from Carter G. Woodson to W. E. B. Du Bois," February 11, 1932, Du Bois Papers (MS 312).

39. Carter G. Woodson, "Letter from Carter G. Woodson to Edwin C. Embree," August 12, 1931, box 170, folder 6, Julius Rosenwald Fund Records, Fisk University Special Collections; Woodson expressed the following: "I am now fifty-five years old, and before I begin to decline I want to write the history of the Negro in five large volumes, it will require about four years. I have practically all of the data on hand, but my other duties are such that I do not have time to take up this important task. . . . As I grow older and see the income upon which I have to depend remaining about constant, I become more and more apprehensive of the loss which may be sustained in my carrying with me to my grave the vast amount of information which I have collected during the last generation. What I am asking for, therefore, is the opportunity to assemble these facts in scientific form to make a complete story of the rise and development of the Negro."

40. David Levering Lewis, *W. E. B. Du Bois: The Fight for Equality and the American Century 1919–1963,* 1st ed. (New York: Henry Holt, 2000), 447–448.

41. ASALH, "Henry Louis Gates Jr. on Carter G. Woodson: Open Letter to Dr. Henry Louis Gates, Jr., Harvard University, from the Executive Council—

Association for the Study of African American Life and History," *Journal of African American History* 88, no. 2 (March 25, 2003): 221–222.

42. Al Sweeny interview with Carter G. Woodson, "Dr. Carter G. Woodson, 72, Has Written 19 Books, Published 64 Others," *Afro Magazine*, 1948, box 370, folder 1, Claude A. Barnett Papers, Chicago History Museum.

43. Woodson, *Mis-education*, 108.

44. Jarvis Ray Givens, "'A Grammar for Black Education beyond Borders': Exploring Technologies of Schooling in the African Diaspora," *Race, Ethnicity and Education* 19, no. 6 (2016): 1288–1302.

45. Carter G. Woodson, "Thomas Jesse Jones," *Journal of Negro History*, January 1950, 107–109.

46. Woodson, *Mis-education*, 108.

47. At the ASNLH's annual meeting in 1938, Woodson hosted feature sessions where Yergan and Robeson presented, and in 1945 Woodson wrote a supportive review of Yergan and Robeson's *For a New Africa*. Sister Anthony Scally, "Phelps-Stokes Confidential Memorandum for the Trustees of the Phelps-Stokes Fund Regarding Dr. Carter G. Woodson's Attacks on Dr. Thomas Jesse Jones," *Journal of Negro History* 76, no. 1 / 4 (1991): 48–60; C. G. Woodson, review of *Review of For a New Africa*, by Max Yergan and Paul Robeson, *Journal of Negro History* 30, no. 3 (1945): 346–348; C. G. Woodson, "Proceedings of the Annual Meeting of the Association for the Study of Negro Life and History Held in New York City November 11, 12, and 13, 1938," *Journal of Negro History* 24, no. 1 (1939): 1–8.

48. Richard Robert Wright, "The Colored Farm Laborers and Farmers of Georgia (Augusta, Ga., November 23, 1883)," Report of the Committee of the Senate upon the Relations between Labor and Capital IV (1885), 811–820; Charlotte Forten Grimke, "Life on the Sea Islands (1864)," in *The Portable Nineteenth-Century African American Women Writers,* ed. Hollis Robbins and Henry Louis Gates (New York: Penguin Classics, 2017), 130–163; Edward A. Johnson, *A School History of the Negro Race in America from 1619 to 1890* (Raleigh: Edwards & Broughton, 1890).

49. Robert Allen, *Black Awakening in Capitalist America: An Analytic History,* 1st ed. (Trenton, NJ: Africa World, 1969); Robert L. Allen, "Reassessing The Internal (Neo) Colonialism Theory," *Black Scholar* 35, no. 1 (2005): 2–11; Stokley Carmichael and Charles V. Hamilton, *Black Power: The Politics of Liberation in America* (New York: Random House, 1967), esp. "White Power: The Colonial Situation," 15–16.

50. John Henrik Clarke, "Education for a New Reality in the African World" (Annual Meeting of the National Alliance of Black Educators, New York, NY, November 14, 1985); Bernard Coard, *How the West Indian Child Is Made Educationally Sub-Normal in the British School System: The Scandal of the Black Child in Schools in Britain.* (London: New Beacon for the Caribbean Education and Community Workers' Association, 1971); Joyce Elaine King, "Diaspora Literacy and

Consciousness in the Struggle against Miseducation in the Black Community," *Journal of Negro Education* 61, no. 3 (1992): 317–340; Kassie Freeman and Ethan Johnson, *Education in the Black Diaspora: Perspectives, Challenges, and Prospects* (New York: Routledge, 2011); Sam Mchombo, "Language, Learning, and Education for All in Africa1," in *Giving Space to African Voices*, ed. Zehlia Babaci-Wilhite (Rotterdam: Sense Publishers, 2014), 21–47.

51. Sylvia Wynter, "No Humans Involved: An Open Letter to My Colleagues," *Forum N. H. I. Knowledge for the 21st Century* 1, no. 1 (Fall 1994): 70; Sylvia Wynter, "The Ceremony Must Be Found: After Humanism," *Boundary* 2, no. 12 / 13 (1984): 19–70; Greg Thomas, "PROUD FLESH Inter / Views: Sylvia Wynter," *ProudFlesh: New Afrikan Journal of Culture, Politics and Consciousness*, no. 4 (2006), http://www.africaknowledgeproject.org/index.php/proudflesh/article/view/202.

52. Woodson, *Mis-education*, 21.

53. Wynter, "No Humans Involved," 58.

54. Ibid., 62, 58.

55. Woodson, *Mis-education*, 106–108.

56. Wynter, "No Humans Involved," 59, 70.

57. Ibid., 58.

58. Sylvia Wynter, "Textbooks and What They Do: The Conceptual Breakthrough of Carter G. Woodson," in *Do Not Call Us Negro: How "Multicultural" Textbooks Perpetuate Racism* (San Francisco: Aspire, 1990), 20, 23.

59. Woodson, *Mis-education*, 106.

60. Ngũgĩ wa Thiong'o, *Decolonising the Mind: The Politics of Language in African Literature* (Oxford, UK: James Currey Ltd., 1986), 3.

61. Ibid., 9.

62. Woodson, *Mis-education*, 267.

63. Thomas Fallace, *Race and the Origins of Progressive Education, 1880–1929* (New York: Teachers College Press, 2015).

64. Carter G. Woodson, review of *The Myth of the Negro Past* by Melville Herskovits, *Journal of Negro History*, January 1942, 115–118.

65. Edward Franklin Frazier, *The Negro Family in Chicago*, University of Chicago Sociological Series (Chicago, University of Chicago Press, 1932); Melville Herskovits, *The Myth of The Negro Past* (New York: Harper and Brothers, 1941).

66. Carter G. Woodson, Review of *Life in a Haitian Valley* by Melville Herskovits, *Journal of Negro History*, July 1937, 366–369; Woodson also endorsed the academic work of such scholars as Lorenzo Turner and Zora Neale Hurston, who studied cultural patterns (particularly linguistic and religious) in specific black communities in the United States. In 1927 Woodson reported that the ASNLH had been supporting Hurston to do research on Negro folklore in Florida and Alabama; see Carter G. Woodson, "The Annual Report of the Director," *Journal of Negro History* 12, no. 4 (October 1927): 570–571.

67. Chinua Achebe, "An Image of Africa: Racism in Conrad's *Heart of Darkness*," *Massachusetts Review* 57, no. 1 (Spring 2016): 14–27.

68. Mbembe, *Critique of Black Reason*, 38.

69. Raymond Williams, "Culture Is Ordinary," in *Resources of Hope: Culture, Democracy, Socialism* (London: Verso, 1989), 3–14.

70. Georg Wilhelm Friedrich Hegel, *The Philosophy of History (1837)*, trans. J. Sibree (Kitchener, Canada: Batoche Books, 2001), 111, 117; on p. 109 Hegel asserts, "Africa proper, as far as History goes back, has remained—for all purposes of connection with the rest of the World—shut up; it is the Gold-land compressed within itself—the land of childhood, which lying beyond the day of self-conscious history, is enveloped in the dark mantle of Night."

71. Olufemi Taiwo, "Exorcising Hegel's Ghost: Africa's Challenge to Philosophy," *African Studies Quarterly* 1, no. 4 (1998): 3–16.

72. More discussion on Hegel's exclusion of Africa in his *Philosophy of History* can be found in Stephanie Shaw's work on Du Bois. She demonstrates how Du Bois built on and offers a corrective to Hegel's thinking. Paul Gilroy offers a similar discussion of Hegel's influence on Du Bois from his time in Germany. Stephanie J. Shaw, *W. E. B. Du Bois and 'The Souls of Black Folk,'* reprint ed. (Chapel Hill: University of North Carolina Press, 2015), 6; Paul Gilroy, *The Black Atlantic: Modernity and Double-Consciousness*, reissue ed. (Cambridge, MA: Harvard University Press, 1993), 134.

73. C. L. R. James, "Fanon and the Caribbean," in *International Tribute to Frantz Fanon: Record of the Special Meeting of the United Nations Special Committee against Apartheid, 3 November 1978* (New York: United Nations Centre against Apartheid, 1979), 43–46.

74. Aime Césaire, *Discourse on Colonialism* (New York: Monthly Review Press, 2000), 41.

75. Ibid., 42 (italics added).

76. Woodson, *Mis-education*, xiii.

77. Thomas and Wynter, "PROUD FLESH Inter / Views," 7.

78. Adelaide Casley-Hayford, "A Girl's School in West Africa," *Southern Workman*, October 1926, 450; Rina Okonkwo, "Adelaide Casley Hayford Cultural Nationalist and Feminist," *Phylon* 42, no. 1 (1981): 41–51; Coard, *West Indian Child*, 13, 39; Kehinde Andrews, *Resisting Racism: Race, Inequality and the Black Supplementary School Movement* (London: Trentham Books, 2013).

79. Givens, "Grammar for Black Education"; Brent Hayes Edwards, *The Practice of Diaspora: Literature, Translation, and the Rise of Black Internationalism* (Cambridge, MA: Harvard University Press, 2003).

80. Carter G. Woodson, "Observations: The Trend of Current Thought and Discussion; Is the Educated Negro a Liability?," *Chicago Defender*, May 21, 1932, 2.

81. Woodson, *Mis-education*, xviii.

82. Ibid., 108.

83. Woodson, "Differentiation in Education" (italics added).

84. Ibid., xii.

85. Gloria Ladson-Billings, "From the Achievement Gap to the Education Debt: Understanding Achievement in U.S. Schools," *Educational Researcher* 35, no. 7 (October 1, 2006): 3–12.

86. Snyder, "Progressive Education," 273–293; Fallace, *Race and the Origins,* 108–122.

87. Williams, *Self-Taught.*

88. Carter G. Woodson, "Comments on Negro Education by Carter G. Woodson: Vocational Guidance," *New York Age,* May 7, 1932.

89. Woodson was enrolled in Educational Psychology, and John Dewey is listed as the instructor in Chicago's course catalogue. University of Chicago Registrar's Office, "Carter Godwin Woodson University of Chicago Transcript," Summer 1902-Summer 1908, University of Chicago Registrar Archives; "Circular of Information: Preliminary Announcements for the Summer Quarter 1902" (University of Chicago, February 1902).

90. Daniel Perlstein, "Minds Stayed on Freedom: Politics and Pedagogy in the African-American Freedom Struggle," *American Educational Research Journal* 39, no. 2 (2002): 257; Lisa D. Delpit, "The Silenced Dialogue: Power and Pedagogy in Educating Other People's Children," *Harvard Educational Review* 58, no. 3 (1988): 280–298.

91. Russell Rickford, *We Are an African People: Independent Education, Black Power, and the Radical Imagination* (Oxford: Oxford University Press, 2016).

92. Rayford Whittingham Logan, *The Negro in American Life and Thought: The Nadir, 1877–1901* (New York: Dial, 1954).

93. Gordon, "Africana Thought," 25.

94. Richard Robert Wright, "The Possibilities of the Negro Teacher," *AME Church Review* 10, no. 4 (April 1894): 459–470.

4. The Fugitive Slave as a Folk Hero in Black Curricular Imaginations

Epigraphs: Richard Robert Wright, "The Possibilities of the Negro Teacher," AME Church Review 10, no. 4 (April 1894): 468–469; W. E. B. Du Bois, "Does the Negro Need Separate Schools?," Journal of Negro Education 4, no. 3 (1935): 328–335.

1. Albert J. Raboteau, *Slave Religion: The "Invisible Institution" in the Antebellum South* (Oxford: Oxford University Press, 2004); Eddie S. Glaude Jr., *Exodus! Religion, Race, and Nation in Early Nineteenth-Century Black America* (Chicago: University of Chicago Press, 2000); Julius S. Scott, *The Common Wind: Afro-American Currents in the Age of the Haitian Revolution* (London: Verso, 2018).

2. Susan Paul, *Memoir of James Jackson, The Attentive and Obedient Scholar, Who Died in Boston, October 31, 1833, Aged Six Years and Eleven Months, By His Teacher (Originally Published 1835)*, ed. Lois Brown (Cambridge, MA: Harvard University Press, 2000), 11.

3. Vanessa Siddle Walker, *The Lost Education of Horace Tate: Uncovering the Hidden Heroes Who Fought for Justice in Schools* (New York.: New Press, 2018), 149.

4. Charlotte Forten Grimke, "Life on the Sea Islands (1864)," in *The Portable Nineteenth-Century African American Women Writers*, ed. Hollis Robbins and Henry Louis Gates (New York: Penguin Classics, 2017), 130–163.

5. James W. C. Pennington, *Text Book of the Origin and History of the Colored People* (Hartford, CT: L. Skinner, Printer, 1841); Webster quoted in Stephen G. Hall, *A Faithful Account of the Race: African American Historical Writing in Nineteenth-Century America* (Chapel Hill: University of North Carolina Press, 2009), 49.

6. Jacqueline Bacon, "The History of Freedom's Journal: A Study in Empowerment and Community," *Journal of African American History* 88, no. 1 (2003): 1–20; Jacqueline Bacon, "Literacy, Rhetoric, and 19th-Century Black Print Culture," ed. Phyllis M. Belt-Beyan and Shirley Wilson Logan, *Journal of African American History* 95, no. 3–4 (2010): 417–423.

7. Nathaniel Mackey, "Other: From Noun to Verb," *Representations*, no. 39 (1992): 55.

8. William Wells Brown, *The Black Man: His Antecedents, His Genius, and His Achievements* (New York: Thomas Hamilton; Boston: R. F. Wallcut, 1863).

9. This idea of the fugitive slave as a folk hero builds on the thinking of Margaret Walker in her critique of William Styron's novel *Confessions of Nat Turner*. "The racism in that book is the damage that he does to the hero for the black child. Nat Turner represents to black people, first of all, a preacher and that is one of our heroes—you see, folk heroes; and then he represents a leader—a slave leader and a man, an insurrectionist. He was fighting against all of the tyranny and hatred and dominance of the society and of a feudal system that was doomed. Styron maligned Nat Turner in every possible way. Styron attacks his personality. He attacks him as a folk hero." Margaret Walker, *Conversations with Margaret Walker*, ed. Maryemma Graham (Jackson: University of Mississippi Press, 2002), 24.

10. Orrin E. Klapp, "The Folk Hero," *Journal of American Folklore* 62, no. 243 (1949): 17, 20.

11. Charles H. Wesley, "Creating and Maintaining an Historical Tradition," *The Journal of Negro History* 49, no. 1 (1964): 13–33; Lawrence W. Levine, *Black Culture and Black Consciousness: Afro-American Folk Thought from Slavery to Freedom* (New York: Oxford University Press, 1978), 77, 97, 386. Hurston also plays with notions of time, distance, and relevance of African American folklore and stories of their heroes from slavery in the post-Emancipation period. Zora Neale Hurston, "High John de Conquer (The American Mercury, October 1943)," in *Hurston:*

Folklore, Memoirs, and Other Writings (New York: Literary Classics of the United States, 1995), 922–931.

12. George Washington Williams, *History of the Negro Race in America from 1619 to 1880* (New York: G. P. Putnam's Sons, 1885), 91 (italics added).

13. Grimke, "Life on the Sea Islands"; "Printed Record of the Board of President and Directors" (St. Louis, MO: St. Louis Public Schools, July 1889), St. Louis Public Schools Records, Missouri Historical Society Archives, St. Louis; "Named for Negroes: And the Great Anti-Slavery Leaders Left Unremembered," *St. Louis Post-Dispatch,* December 10, 1890.

14. Jarvis R. Givens, "'He Was, Undoubtedly, a Wonderful Character': Black Teachers' Representations of Nat Turner During Jim Crow," *Souls: A Critical Journal of Black Politics Culture and Society* 18, no. 2–4 (October 2016): 215–234; Lawrence D. Reddick, "Racial Attitudes in American History Textbooks of the South," *Journal of Negro History* 19, no. 3 (1934): 225–265.

15. Edward A. Johnson, *A School History of the Negro Race in America from 1619 to 1890: With a Short Introduction as to the Origin of the Race: Also a Short Sketch of Liberia* (Raleigh: Edwards & Broughton, Printers, 1890), 90–92; Leila Amos Pendleton, *A Narrative of the Negro* (Washington, DC: Press of R. L. Pendleton, 1912), 116; John W. (John Wesley) Cromwell, *The Negro in American History: Men and Women Eminent in the Evolution of the American of African Descent* (Washington, DC: American Negro Academy, 1914), 16.

16. Carter G. Woodson, *The Negro in Our History* (Washington, DC: Associated Publishers, 1922), 263, 83, 235, 210, 233.

17. Ira B. Bryant, "Study Guide Negro History, Public School, Houston, Texas," 1936, box 4, folder 3, Thelma S. Bryant and Ira B. Bryant Collection (MSS 0452), Houston Metropolitan Research Center, African American Library at the Gregory School; George Longe, "A Tentative Approach to Negro History for Use in Grades 1–4, New Orleans Colored Public Schools, Literature and Music," 1936, box 2, folder 7, George Longe Papers, Amistad Research Center, New Orleans, LA; Bessie King and Madeline Stratton, "Supplementary Units for the Course of Study in Social Studies, Grades 7–8" (Chicago: Bureau of Curriculum, Board of Education, City of Chicago, 1942), box 2, folder 2, Madeline Stratton Morris Papers, Vivian G. Harsh Research Collection of Afro-American History and Literature, Chicago Public Library.

18. E. Belfield Spriggins, "Dr. Du Bois Holds Audience Spellbound on 'Negro and Reconstruction,'" *Louisiana Weekly,* February 24, 1934, Louisiana Weekly Microfilm Collection, Amistad Research Center, New Orleans, LA; marginal note on p. 5 of Madeline Morgan, "Negro Achievement in Chicago Public Schools" (June 22, 1942), box 2, folder 3, Madeline Stratton Morris Papers, Vivian G. Harsh Research Collection of Afro-American History and Literature, Chicago Public Library.

19. Tamah Richardson and Annie Rivers, "Progress of the Negro: A Unit of Work for the Third Grade," *Virginia Teachers Bulletin,* May 1936, 3–8; Angela Y. Davis,

Angela Davis: An Autobiography (New York: Random House, 1974), 100; on "innocence amusements," see Saidiya Hartman, *Scenes of Subjection: Terror, Slavery, and Self-Making in Nineteenth-Century America* (New York: Oxford University Press, 1997), 8, 43.

20. Effie Lee Morris (The HistoryMakers A2005.242), interviewed by Loretta Henry, October 13, 2005, session 2, tape 4, story 4, Effie Lee Morris describes her work at the Cleveland Public Library, HistoryMakers Digital Archive.

21. These approved textbooks are listed in the state's curriculum manual: State Department of Education of Louisiana, "Louisiana High School Standards Manual of Organization and Administration (Section on Social Science Curriculum)," bulletin no. 161 (Baton Rouge, LA: State Department of Education of Louisiana, July 1, 1929), 69, Harvard Graduate School of Education, Gutman Library Special Collections.

22. Henry W. Elson, *Modern Times and the Living Past* (New York: American Book Company, 1935), iii–iv.

23. Ibid., 13 (italics added).

24. Ibid., 14 (italics added).

25. Sylvia Wynter, "No Humans Involved: An Open Letter to My Colleagues," *Forum N. H. I. Knowledge for the 21st Century* 1, no. 1 (Fall 1994): 70; Michael W. Apple, "The Politics of Official Knowledge: Does a National Curriculum Make Sense?," *Teachers College Record* 95, no. 2 (1993): 222–241.

26. Nathaniel Wright Stephenson, *An American History* (Boston: Ginn, 1919), 118.

27. Ibid., 386.

28. Reference to black Civil War soldiers, see ibid., 440.

29. Ibid., 399–400 (italics added).

30. Ibid., 482.

31. Carter G. Woodson, "Woodson Renews Attack on History Propogandist: Assails Enemies Who Undermine History Ass'n," *New Journal and Guide,* February 7, 1931.

32. Reddick, "Racial Attitudes."

33. This chapter focuses on textbooks published by black teachers who created their texts intentionally for classroom instruction and school age children. I begin with Edward A. Johnson's (1891) textbook because it was intentionally written for classroom instruction, whereas those before it were written for a more general audience. Also, these three texts are not the only textbooks published by black schoolteachers. For instance, Woodson's American Negro Academy colleague John Cromwell and Silas X. Floyd, who was a school principal and leader in the National Association of Teachers in Colored Schools, both published books for school children, the first a history book and the latter a series of short stories. The three textbooks were popularly received and representative of the range of this tradition. For more on black textbooks, see Hall, *Faithful Account of the Race.*

34. Johnson, *School History*.

35. Pendleton, *Narrative of the Negro*.

36. For additional discussion on Woodson's textbooks in relationship to others published by his contemporaries, see Jeffrey Aaron Snyder, *Making Black History: The Color Line, Culture, and Race in the Age of Jim Crow* (Athens: University of Georgia Press, 2018), 55–61.

37. The frame of "race vindication" was widely used by nineteenth-century black intellectuals and encompasses a broad intellectual practice that can be traced throughout African American history; see Edward Blyden's *A Vindication of the African Race* published in 1857; William Wells Brown's *The Black Man: His Antecedents, His Genius, and His Achievements* (1863), which sought to "aid in vindicating the Negro's character, and show that he is endowed with those intellectual and amiable qualities which adorn and dignify human nature." Similarly, the American Negro Academy was founded in 1897 by leading black scholars of the era; their constitution outlined that "the Academy shall endeavor with care and diligence . . . to aid, by publications, the dissemination of the truth and the vindication of the Negro race from vicious assaults."

38. Givens, "'Wonderful character,'" 218.

39. This idea of race vindication as descriptive, corrective, and prescriptive is my reading of the term through Manning Marable's conceptualization of the intellectual demands of Black Studies: Manning Marable, "Black Studies and the Racial Mountain," *Souls* 2, no. 3 (2000): 17–36; Givens, "'Wonderful Character.'"

40. Carter G. Woodson, "Edward Austin Johnson," *Journal of Negro History* 29, no. 4 (1944): 506.

41. Johnson, *School History*, iii–v.

42. See Brittney Cooper's definition of race women and their "attention to 'proving the intellectual character' of the race." Brittney C. Cooper, *Beyond Respectability: The Intellectual Thought of Race Women* (Urbana: University of Illinois Press, 2017), 11–12.

43. Frank Lincoln Mather, *Who's Who of the Colored Race: A General Biographical Dictionary of Men and Women of African Descent* (publisher not identified, 1915); Laurie Maffly-Kipp and Kathryn Lofton, *Women's Work: An Anthology of African-American Women's Historical Writings from Antebellum America to the Harlem Renaissance* (Oxford: Oxford University Press, 2010); Pero Dagbovie, "Black Women Historians from the Later 19th Century to the Dawning of the Civil Rights Movement," *Journal of African American History* 89, no. 3 (2004): 249.

44. Pendleton's letter is reprinted in "How the Public Received the Journal of Negro History," *Journal of Negro History* 1, no. 2 (1916): 225–226.

45. Jessie Fauset's review of Pendleton's book in "What to Read" section of *The Crisis*, August 1912; "A Selected List of Books," *The Crisis*, August 1914; "A Selected List of Books," *The Crisis*, April 1922. Further discussion of Pendleton's textbooks can be found in Dagbovie, "Black Women Historians," 249.

46. Leila Amos Pendleton, "Aunt Calline's Sheaves," *The Crisis,* June 1917; Leila Amos Pendleton, "'The Foolish and the Wise: Sallie Runner Is Introduced to Socrates' and 'The Black Swan,'" *The Crisis,* March 1921; Leila Amos Pendleton, "An Apostrophe to the Lynched," *The Crisis,* June 1916.

47. Pendleton, *Narrative of the Negro,* 6.

48. Francille Rusan Wilson, *The Segregated Scholars: Black Social Scientists and the Creation of Black Labor Studies, 1890–1950* (Charlottesville: University of Virginia Press, 2006), 2; see also, Pero Gaglo Dagbovie, "'Among the Vitalizing Tools of the Radical Intelligentsia, of Course the Most Crucial Was Words': Carter G. Woodson's 'The Case of the Negro' (1921)," *Journal for the Study of Radicalism* 3, no. 2 (2009): 88.

49. "Dr. Woodson As I Knew Him," 1976, box 92, Lorenzo Johnston Green Papers, Manuscript Division, Library of Congress, Washington, DC.

50. Alain Locke, review of *The Negro in Our History,* by Carter G. Woodson, *Journal of Negro History* 12, no. 1 (1927): 100.

51. LaGarrett J. King, Ryan M. Crowley, and Anthony L. Brown, "The Forgotten Legacy of Carter G. Woodson: Contributions to Multicultural Social Studies and African American History," *Social Studies* 101, no. 5 (August 23, 2010): 211–215 Carl Grant, Keffrelyn Brown, and Anthony L. Brown, *Black Intellectual Thought in Education: The Missing Traditions of Anna Julia Cooper, Carter G. Woodson, and Alain LeRoy Locke* (New York: Routledge, 2015); William Henry Watkins, *Black Protest Thought and Education* (New York: Peter Lang, 2005); Alana D. Murray, "Countering the Master Narrative: The Development of the Alternative Black Curriculum in Social Studies, 1890–1940" (PhD diss., University of Maryland, 2012).

52. Pendleton, *Narrative of the Negro,* 19.

53. Ibid.

54. Chinua Achebe, "An Image of Africa: Racism in Conrad's *Heart of Darkness,*" *Massachusetts Review* 57, no. 1 (Spring 2016): 14–27.

55. D. W. Griffith, *The Birth of a Nation* (Epoch Producing Corporation, 1915); W. E. B. Du Bois and David Levering Lewis, *Black Reconstruction in America, 1860–1880* (New York: Free Press, 1998).

56. LaGarrett J. King, Christopher Davis, and Anthony L. Brown, "African American History, Race and Textbooks: An Examination of the Works of Harold O. Rugg and Carter G. Woodson," *Journal of Social Studies Research* 36, no. 4 (2012): 359–386.

57. Harold Ordway Rugg, *A History of American Government and Culture: America's March toward Democracy* (Boston: Ginn and Company, 1931), 367–368 (italics added).

58. Woodson, *Negro in Our History,* 251–254 (italics added).

59. Ibid., 124.

60. Ibid., 127.

61. V. P. Franklin and Mary Frances Berry, *Black Self-Determination: A Cultural History of African-American Resistance* (Brooklyn, NY: Lawrence Hill Books, 1992), 6.

62. Johnson, *School History,* 48.

63. Ibid.

64. Woodson, *Negro in Our History,* 31.

65. Pendleton, *Narrative of the Negro,* 181 (italics added).

66. Adalaine Holton, "Decolonizing History: Arthur Schomburg's Afrodiasporic Archive," *The Journal of African American History* 92, no. 2 (2007): 222.

67. Jarvis Ray Givens, "'A Grammar for Black Education beyond Borders': Exploring Technologies of Schooling in the African Diaspora," *Race, Ethnicity and Education* 19, no. 6 (2016): 1288–1302.

68. Carter G. Woodson, "Back Matter—Two Valuable School Books Now Available," *Journal of Negro History* 16, no. 1 (1931).

69. Carter G. Woodson, "The Annual Report of the Director," *Journal of Negro History* 12, no. 4 (1927): 570–571. The ASNLH supported "Miss Zora Neale Hurston collecting Negro folklore in Florida . . . and a similar study of Plateau or the negro settlement just outside of Mobile which sprang from landing there in 1859 the last cargo of slaves brought from Africa to the United States." More discussion of Woodson's support of research on African retentions provided in Chapter 3.

70. Carter G. Woodson, *Negro Makers of History* (Washington, DC: Associated Publishers, 1928), 346–347 (italics added).

71. Woodson also shared these ideas publicly through the black press; see, for instance, Woodson, "Woodson Renews Attack."

72. Johnson, *School History,* 142, 196, 145.

73. Pendleton, *Narrative of the Negro,* 54.

74. Jessie Fauset, "What to Read," *The Crisis,* August 1912, 183.

75. Woodson, *Negro in Our History,* 108.

76. Givens, "Grammar for Black Education"; Achille Mbembe, *Critique of Black Reason* (Durham, NC: Duke University Press Books, 2017).

77. William Watkins, *The White Architects of Black Education: Ideology and Power in America, 1865–1954* (New York: Teachers College Press, 2001); King, Davis, and Brown, "African American History"; Fallace, *Race and the Origins.*

78. Pendleton, *Narrative of the Negro,* 98.

79. Johnson, *School History,* 84.

80. Ibid., 82–83 (italics added).

81. Woodson, *Negro in Our History,* 12–14 (italics added).

82. Reddick, "Racial Attitudes"; King, Davis, and Brown, "African American History."

83. Reddick, "Racial Attitudes," 237.

84. Stephenson, *American History,* 118, 386.

85. Johnson, *School History*, 24.

86. Ibid., 90–92.

87. Reddick, "Racial Attitudes," 237.

88. Givens, "'Wonderful Character'," 228.

89. Ibid., 95.

90. Pendleton, *Narrative of the Negro*, 63.

91. Ibid., 65.

92. Woodson, *Negro in Our History*, 92.

93. Wesley, "Creating and Maintaining," 21.

94. Rayford Whittingham Logan, *The Negro in American Life and Thought: The Nadir, 1877–1901* (New York: Dial, 1954).

95. Johnson, *School History*, 47.

96. Ibid., 144.

97. Ibid., 63 (italics added).

98. Pendleton, *Narrative of the Negro*, 98.

99. Reddick, "Racial Attitudes," 261.

100. Pendleton, *Narrative of the Negro*, 165.

101. Woodson, *Negro in Our History*, 161.

102. Johnson, *School History*, 102–103.

103. Evelyn Brooks Higginbotham, *Righteous Discontent: The Women's Movement in the Black Baptist Church, 1880–1920* (Cambridge, MA: Harvard University Press, 1994), 186–187.

104. Paisley Jane Harris, "Gatekeeping and Remaking: The Politics of Respectability in African American Women's History and Black Feminism," *Journal of Women's History* 15, no. 1 (2003): 212–220.

5. Fugitive Pedagogy as a Professional Standard

1. Heather Williams, "How Slavery Affected African American Families," accessed March 20, 2016, http://nationalhumanitiescenter.org/tserve/freedom/1609 -1865/essays/aafamilies.htm; Diane Burke, "'Mah Pappy Belong to a Neighbor': The Effects of Abroad Marriages on Missouri Slave Families," in *Searching for Their Places: Women in the South across Four Centuries*, ed. Thomas Appleton and Angela Bosewell (Columbia: University of Missouri Press, 2003), 57–78; Thomas L. Webber, *Deep like the Rivers: Education in the Slave Quarter Community, 1831–1865* (New York: Norton, 1978), 28–29.

2. Correspondence, Clark Leo Smith to Woodson (n.d.), Papers of Carter G. Woodson and the Association for the Study of Negro Life and History, 1915–1950, Microfilm Collection, University Publication of America.

3. Michele Mitchell, *Righteous Propagation: African Americans and the Politics of Racial Destiny after Reconstruction* (Chapel Hill: University of North Carolina Press, 2004), 9.

4. Andrew Billingsley, for example, discussed the role of nonnuclear family models among enslaved black communities. He offered that fictive kinship and extended family played critical roles in raising children and supporting community members during slavery and even thereafter. Andrew Billingsley, *Climbing Jacob's Ladder: The Enduring Legacies of African-American Families* (New York: Touchstone, 1994).

5. Ibid., 7.

6. Vanessa Siddle Walker and Ulysses Byas, *Hello Professor: A Black Principal and Professional Leadership in the Segregated South* (Chapel Hill: University of North Carolina Press, 2009), 8.

7. Ohio Colored Teachers' Association, *Transactions of the First Annual Meeting of the Colored Teachers Association Held at Springfield, Ohio, December 25, 26 & 27, 1861,* 1861, 8.

8. Ronald E. Butchart, *Schooling the Freed People: Teaching, Learning, and the Struggle for Black Freedom, 1861–1876* (Chapel Hill: University of North Carolina, 2010), 27.

9. Mitchell, *Righteous Propagation,* 8.

10. William Watkins, *The White Architects of Black Education: Ideology and Power in America, 1865–1954* (New York: Teachers College Press, 2001), 20.

11. Watkins, *White Architects;* quote by Samuel Armstrong cited in James Anderson, *The Education of Blacks in the South, 1860–1935* (Chapel Hill: University of North Carolina Press, 1988), 45, 291.

12. Michael Fultz, "Teacher Training and African American Education in the South, 1900–1940," *Journal of Negro Education* 64, no. 2 (1995): 207.

13. Anderson, *Education of Blacks,* 110–147.

14. The Slater Fund was established in 1881 and from its inception emphasized industrial/practical education. Ibid., 66, 138; see also the discussion of training schools versus high schools in Fultz, "Teacher Training," 203.

15. Anderson, *Education of Blacks,* 110–111.

16. W. E. B Du Bois, Augustus Granville Dill, and Conference for the Study of the Negro Problems, eds., *The Common School and the Negro American* (Atlanta: Atlanta University Press, 1911), 7.

17. Anderson, *Education of Blacks,* 188, 145.

18. Thelma D. Perry, *History of the American Teachers Association* (Washington: National Education Association, 1975); Fultz, "Teacher Training."

19. Jacqueline Goggin, *Carter G. Woodson: A Life in Black History* (Baton Rouge: LSU Press, 1997), 31.

20. Julia Davis to Woodson, February 17, 1927, Papers of Carter G. Woodson and the Association for the Study of Negro Life and History, 1915–1950, Microfilm Collection, University Publication of America, (italics added).

21. Letter reprinted in Perry, *American Teachers Association,* 197 (italics added).

22. List of schools using textbook in "The Negro in Our History 4th Edition Advertisement," n.d., box 1, folder 1, Woodson Collection.

23. He also encouraged Sadie Daniel to feature Burroughs in her book, *Women Builders*. See Carter G. Woodson to Nannie Burroughs, August 15, 1930, box 32, Nannie Helen Burroughs Papers, Manuscript Division, Library of Congress, Washington, DC; Sadie Iola Daniel, *Women Builders* (Washington, DC: Associated Publishers, 1931).

24. "Dr. Woodson As I Knew Him," 1976, box 92, Lorenzo Johnston Greene Papers, Manuscript Division, Library of Congress, Washington, DC (hereafter cited as Greene Papers).

25. This event was covered both locally in Muskogee and nationally in the black press: "Thompson 'Guarantees' School Board Harmony: Making No Mention of Resignation, Says 'Isms" All Banned; Offensive Text Referred to Lee,'" *Muskogee Daily Phoenix*, June 2, 1925, Oklahoma Historical Society; "Dr. Woodson's Negro History Confiscated in Oklahoma," *Afro-American*, August 1, 1925.

26. "Dr. Woodson's Negro History Confiscated."

27. Vanessa Siddle Walker, *The Lost Education of Horace Tate: Uncovering the Hidden Heroes Who Fought for Justice in Schools* (s.l.: New Press, 2018), 214–220; Heather Williams, *Self-Taught: African American Education in Slavery and Freedom* (Chapel Hill: University of North Carolina Press, 2007), 121–123; Campbell Scribner, "The Destruction of African-American Schoolhouses in the South, 1864–1876," unpublished manuscript (University of Maryland, November 2018).

28. Jarvis R. Givens, "'There Would Be No Lynching If It Did Not Start in the Schoolroom': Carter G. Woodson and the Occasion of Negro History Week, 1926–1950," *American Educational Research Journal* 56, no. 4 (2019): 1457–1494.

29. "Negro History Week 1934 Brochure," p. 3, 1934, box 1, folder 36, Woodson Collection.

30. "Negro History Week," *Journal of Negro History* 11, no. 2 (April 1926): 238.

31. Ibid., 240.

32. Ibid.

33. Julia Davis to Woodson, February 17, 1927, Papers of Carter G. Woodson and the Association for the Study of Negro Life and History, 1915–1950, Microfilm Collection, University Publication of America.

34. Carter G. Woodson, "Negro History Week—the Fourth Year," *Journal of Negro History* 14, no. 2 (April 1929): 114.

35. "Prominent Educators to Address Teachers at National Meeting," *The Bulletin: Official Organ of the National Association of Teachers in Colored Schools* 9, no. 7 (June–July 1929): 10, in National Education Association: Special Collections records, series 1: American Teachers Association 1911–1986, box 3044, folder 10, Special Collections Research Center, George Washington University.

36. Speech excerpt reprinted in Perry, *American Teachers Association*, 197.

37. Alice Harris to Woodson (February 28, 1930), including the following newspaper clipping, "Negro History Pageant Marked by Good Acting," *St. Luke Herald,* February 22, 1930, Papers of Carter G. Woodson and the Association for the Study of Negro Life and History, 1915–1950, Microfilm Collection, University Publication of America.

38. Carter G. Woodson, "Negro History Week—the Fifth Year," *Journal of Negro History* 16, no. 2 (1931): 125.

39. Ibid., 126, 128–129.

40. Perry, *American Teachers Association,* 195.

41. Ibid.

42. Ibid., 192–193.

43. Ambrose Caliver, *National Survey of the Education of Teachers, Bulletin, 1933, No. 10; Volume IV: Education of Negro Teachers* (Washington, DC: Office of Education, US Department of the Interior, 1933), 68.

44. Carter G. Woodson, *The Mis-Education of the Negro* (Washington, DC: Association for the Study of African American Life and History, 2008), 35 (italics added).

45. David Howard-Pitney, "The Enduring Black Jeremiad: The American Jeremiad and Black Protest Rhetoric, from Frederick Douglass to W. E. B. Du Bois, 1841–1919," *American Quarterly* 38, no. 3 (1986): 481–492.

46. Suzanne Dovi, "Political Representation," in *The Stanford Encyclopedia of Philosophy,* ed. Edward N. Zalta, Fall 2018 (Metaphysics Research Lab, Stanford University, 2018), https://plato.stanford.edu/archives/fall2018/entries/political-representation/.

47. Woodson, *Mis-education,* preface.

48. Carter G. Woodson, "Twenty Years Wasted, Says D.C. Historian," *Negro World,* March 21, 1931, 1, 8.

49. Woodson, "Negro History Week—the Fourth Year," 109–115.

50. Carter G. Woodson, "Progressive Work of Negro Teachers Association Is Praised," *Pittsburg Courier,* July 23, 1932, A8.

51. Ibid.

52. Woodson, *Mis-Education,* 83.

53. James C. Scott, *Domination and the Arts of Resistance: Hidden Transcripts* (New Haven, CT: Yale University Press, 1992), 4.

54. Glenda Gilmore, *Gender and Jim Crow: Women and the Politics of White Supremacy in North Carolina, 1896–1920* (Chapel Hill: University of North Carolina Press, 1996), 148.

55. "Normal Founder Elected to Head Colored L.T.A.," *Rustin Daily Leader,* November 21, 1932.

56. Gilmore, *Gender and Jim Crow,* 186.

57. John Henrik Clarke, "The Influence of Arthur A. Schomburg on My Concept of Africana Studies," *Phylon* 49, no. 1 / 2 (1992): 7; Ralph L. Crowder, "Willis Na-

thaniel Huggins (1886–1941): Historian, Activist, and Community Mentor," *Afro-Americans in New York Life and History* 30, no. 2 (July 1, 2006): 127.

58. Clarke, "Influence."

59. Letter from Willis N. Huggins to *The Crisis,* April 18, 1933, and Program for Association for the Study of Negro Life and History, Inc., New York Branch, "First Annual Dinner of the Negro History Club," April 20, 1933, Du Bois Papers (MS 312); Carter G. Woodson, "Negro History Week—the Twelfth Year," *Journal of Negro History* 22, no. 2 (1937): 141–147.

60. Ancella R. Bickley, *History of the West Virginia State Teachers Association* (Washington, DC: National Education Association, 1979), 64.

61. J. Rupert Picott, *History of the Virginia Teachers Association* (Washington, DC: National Education Association, 1975), 207.

62. W. Fitzhugh Brundage, *The Southern Past: A Clash of Race and Memory* (Cambridge, MA: Belknap, 2008), 159.

63. "Annual Report of the Director," *Journal of Negro History* 20, no. 4 (October 1935): 369.

64. L. D. Reddick, "Twenty-Five Negro History Weeks," *Negro History Bulletin,* May 1, 1950, 178–180.

65. "Annual Report of the Director," *Journal of Negro History* 20, no. 4 (October 1935): 369.

66. "Negro History Week Brochure 1934," p. 5, box 1, folder 36, Woodson Collection.

67. August Meier and Elliott Rudwick, *Black History and the Historical Profession, 1915–1980* (Urbana: University of Illinois Press, 1986), 61.

68. Jerome A. Gray, Joe L. Reed, and Norman W. Walton, *History of the Alabama State Teachers Association* (Washington, DC: National Education Association, 1987), 91.

69. Ibid.

70. Table of contents of *The Handbook* are reprinted in Gray, Reed, and Walton, *Alabama State Teachers Association,* 92–94.

71. Franklin: ASALH, *Reflections of Carter G. Woodson: With John Hope Franklin and Adelaide Cromwell,* DVD (ASALH 91st Annual Convention, Atlanta, GA, 2006).

72. Ira B. Bryant, "Study Guide Negro History, Public School, Houston, Texas," 1936, box 4, folder 3, Thelma S. Bryant and Ira B. Bryant Collection (MSS 0452), Houston Metropolitan Research Center, African American Library at the Gregory School (italics added).

73. Ira B. Bryant, "Class Project, Social Problems, A Report on Negro Housing Conditions, High School Senior Class in Civics, Phillis Wheatley High School," 1936, box 4, folder 8, Thelma S. Bryant and Ira B. Bryant Collection (MSS 0452), Houston Metropolitan Research Center, African American Library at the Gregory School.

74. George Longe, "A Tentative Approach to Negro History for Use in Grades 1–4, New Orleans Colored Public Schools, Literature and Music," 1936, box 2, folder 7, George Longe Papers, Amistad Research Center, New Orleans, LA; Bessie King and Madeline Stratton, "Supplementary Units for the Course of Study in Social Studies, Grades 7–8" (Chicago: Bureau of Curriculum, Board of Education, City of Chicago, 1942), box 2, folder 2, Madeline Stratton Morris Papers, Vivian G. Harsh Research Collection of Afro-American History and Literature, Chicago Public Library.

75. "Proceedings of the Annual Meeting of the ASNLH, Held at Virginia State College, Petersburg, Virginia, October 25–28, 1936," *Journal of Negro History* 22, no. 1 (January 1937): 11.

76. Pero Gaglo Dagbovie, "Black Women, Carter G. Woodson, and the Association for the Study of Negro Life and History, 1915–1950," *Journal of African American History* 88, no. 1 (January 1, 2003): 21–41.

77. Mary McLeod Bethune, "The Association for the Study of Negro Life and History: Its Contributions to Our Modern Life," *Journal of Negro History* 20, no. 4 (October 1935): 408.

78. Her presidency (1936–1951) fortified the connection between black teachers and the work of the Association.

79. Daryl Michael Scott, "Seventy-Five Years of Educational Reform," *Black History Bulletin* 74, no. 2 (2010): 32; while I have never seen any recorded evidence that the *Negro History Bulletin* was Bethune's idea, there seems to be long-standing institutional knowledge that this is the case. In addition to this article by Scott, John Bracey and Darlene Clarke Hine emphasized this point in a conversation at the 2014 ASALH meeting in Memphis, Tennessee.

80. John Hope Franklin, "The Place of Carter G. Woodson in American Historiography," *Negro History Bulletin*, May 1950, 176.

81. Letter, Woodson to Lorenzo Greene, June 8, 1937, box 74, Greene Papers.

82. Letter, Woodson to Lorenzo Greene, June 25, 1937, box 74, Greene Papers.

83. Daryl Michael Scott, "Seventy-Five Years of Educational Reform," *Black History Bulletin* 74, no. 2 (2010): 32.

84. Carter G. Woodson, "What's Behind 'the Negro History Bulletin,'" *Negro History Bulletin*, October 1, 1943, 19.

85. Albert Brooks, "Dr. Woodson the Inspiration," *Negro History Bulletin*, December 1, 1956.

86. Albert Brooks, "On Alabama Racial Tightrope," *Negro History Bulletin*, May 1963, 231.

87. Albert Brooks, "Organizing Negro Leadership," *Negro History Bulletin*, May 1945, 180.

88. Woodson to Pearl Schwartz, November 10, 1937, box 75, Greene Papers; Greene to Woodson, November 13, 1937, box 74, Greene Papers.

89. Greene to Woodson, June 22, 1938, and Woodson to Greene, July 2, 1938, box 74, Greene Papers.

90. "Starting Right" *Negro History Bulletin*, February 1938, 12.

91. Ibid.

92. "Results Sought," *Negro History Bulletin*, February 1938, 13.

93. *Negro History Bulletin*, May 1938, 7.

94. Letter, Woodson to Greene, June 8, 1937, box 74, Greene Papers.

95. "The Negro Teacher at Work," *Negro History Bulletin*, October 1938, 5.

96. L. A. Duckett, "A Method for Studying Negro Contributions to Progress," *Negro History Bulletin*, October 1938, 3.

97. Ibid.

98. "The Struggle of the Negro Against Bondage," *Negro History Bulletin*, February 1938, 3.

99. Carter G. Woodson, "Educating the Negro before the General Emancipation," *Negro History Bulletin*, November 1939): 17.

100. "An Accounting for 25 Years," *Journal of Negro History* 25, no. 4 (October 1940): 43.

101. Michael Fultz, "African American Teachers in the South, 1890–1940: Powerlessness and the Ironies of Expectations and Protest," *History of Education Quarterly* 35, no. 4 (1995): 402; Fultz, "Teacher Training," 198.

102. Correspondence from Julia Davis to Woodson, February 17, 1927, Woodson Microfilm Collection, UC Berkeley; "Julia Davis," *Negro History Bulletin* 12, no. 2 (April 1, 1962): 168; a library branch would be named after Julia Davis in St. Louis because of her efforts.

103. Akiki K. Nyabongo, *Africa Answers Back* (London: Routledge, 1936); Prince Nyabongo, "African Life and Ideals," *Journal of Negro History* 26, no. 3 (1941): 279–298; Oscar Handlin and Lilian Handlin, *From the Outer World* (Cambridge: Harvard University Press, 1997), 128.

104. Correspondence from Akiki Nyabango to Woodson regarding Negro History Week Celebration in Montgomery, March 7, 1941, Papers of Carter G. Woodson and the Association for the Study of Negro Life and History, 1915–1950, Microfilm Collection, University Publication of America.

105. E. Horace Fitchett to Carter G. Woodson, May 30, 1941, Papers of Carter G. Woodson and the Association for the Study of Negro Life and History, 1915–1950, Microfilm Collection, University Publication of America.

106. Carter G. Woodson, "Notes," *Journal of Negro History*, April 1942, 242–243.

107. Carter G. Woodson, "What's Behind the Negro History Bulletin," *Negro History Bulletin*, October 1943, 16.

108. Ibid.

109. Carter G. Woodson, "Teachers Urged by Dr. Woodson to Adopt More Realistic Approach: Delegates Pack Sisters Chapel," *Atlanta Daily World*, April 17, 1942, 1, 6.

110. "Carter G. Woodson Addresses Teachers at Annual Meeting," *Chicago Defender*, April 7, 1934, 24.

111. Wilhelmina M. Crosson to W. E. B. Du Bois, January 28, 1933, Du Bois Papers (MS 312).

112. Brother David L. Carl, "The Origins of Black History Month in Boston," Omega Psi Phi Fraternity, Inc., Gamma Chapter (website), February 5, 2016, http://gamma1916.com/2016/02/658/.

113. C. G. Woodson, "What's behind 'the Negro History Bulletin,'" *Negro History Bulletin* 7, no. 1 (October 1, 1943): 19.

114. Carter G. Woodson, "The Annual Meeting," *Negro History Bulletin* 8, no. 3 (December 1, 1944): 60.

115. Ernest J. Middleton, *History of Louisiana Education Association* (Washington, DC: National Education Association, 1984) 65.

116. Ernest Becker, "Correspondence from Ernest O. Becker (Assistant Superintendent) to Miss Sue Hafley (Supervisor of School Libraries) and CC: Mr. George Longe," December 19, 1947, box 1, folder 1, George Longe Papers, Amistad Research Center, New Orleans, LA.

117. Carter G. Woodson, "'Race Leaders' Barred from History Conference—Ablest Scholars Have Been Poor Thinkers—Seventy-Five Per Cent of Colleges Should Be Closed," July 22, 1935, box 370, folder 1, Claude A. Barnett Papers, Chicago History Museum.

6. "Doomed to Be Both a Witness and a Participant"

Epigraph: W. E. B. Du Bois, *Darkwater: Voices from within the Veil* (New York: Washington Square, 2004), 63.

1. Nancy Faust Sizer and Theodore Sizer, *The Students Are Watching: Schools and the Moral Contract* (Boston: Beacon, 2000).

2. Reverend Jerry A. Moore Jr. (The HistoryMakers A2007.171), interviewed by Janet Sims-Wood, April 27, 2007, The HistoryMakers Digital Archive, session 1, tape 1, story 6, "Reverend Jerry A. Moore, Jr. recalls his father's position as a school supervisor."

3. bell hooks, "The Oppositional Gaze: Black Female Spectators," in *Black American Cinema*, ed. Manthia Diawara (New York: Routledge, 1993), 288–289.

4. Zeus Leonardo, "The Story of Schooling: Critical Race Theory and the Educational Racial Contract," *Discourse: Studies in the Cultural Politics of Education* 34, no. 4 (October 1, 2013): 606–608.

5. Hilary J. Moss, *Schooling Citizens: The Struggle for African American Education in Antebellum America* (Chicago: University of Chicago Press, 2010).

6. Tunde Adeleke, "Martin R. Delany's Philosophy of Education: A Neglected Aspect of African American Liberation Thought," *Journal of Negro Education* 63, no. 2 (1994): 221–223.

7. Jenny Proctor and Federal Writers Project, Narrative of Jenny Proctor, 1937, National Humanities Center, The Making of African American Identity: Vol. I, 1500–1865, http://nationalhumanitiescenter.org/pds/maai/enslavement/text1/jennyproctor.pdf (italics added).

8. Elizabeth Alexander, "'Can You Be Black and Look at This?': Reading the Rodney King Video(s)," in *The Black Interior* (Saint Paul, MN: Graywolf, 2004), 177.

9. "The Challenge to the Negro," 1926–1927, box 1, folder 33, Woodson Collection.

10. Mary McLeod Bethune, "The Association for the Study of Negro Life and History: Its Contributions to Our Modern Life," *Journal of Negro History* 20, no. 4 (October 1935): 407–408.

11. Rayvon Fouché, "Say It Loud, I'm Black and I'm Proud: African Americans, American Artifactual Culture, and Black Vernacular Technological Creativity," *American Quarterly* 58, no. 3 (2006): 658.

12. John Hope Franklin, Gerald Horne, Harold Cruse, Allen Ballard, and Reavis Mitchell, "Black History Month: Serious Truth Telling or a Triumph in Tokenism?," *Journal of Blacks in Higher Education,* no. 18 (1997): 91.

13. Jasmine Nichole Cobb, *Picture Freedom: Remaking Black Visuality in the Early Nineteenth Century* (New York: NYU Press, 2015), 19–21.

14. Na'ilah Nasir, *Racialized Identities: Race and Achievement among African American Youth* (Stanford, CA: Stanford University Press, 2011),131; Erving Goffman, *The Presentation of Self in Everyday Life* (New York: Anchor, 1959); Urie Bronfenbrenner, *The Ecology of Human Development: Experiments by Nature and Design* (Cambridge, MA: Harvard University Press, 1981).

15. "How We Have Been Helped by the Study of Negro History" and "January," Student Yearbook, 1929, box 312, Nannie Helen Burroughs Papers, Manuscript Division, Library of Congress, Washington, DC.

16. Carter G. Woodson, *The Negro in Our History* (Washington, DC: Associated Publishers, 1922), 179, 226.

17. Carlotta Walls Lanier, interviewed by Larry Crowe, July 8, 2002, The HistoryMakers Digital Archive.

18. The Honorable John Lewis, interviewed by Julieanna L. Richardson, April 25, 2001, The HistoryMakers Digital Archive; Congressman John Lewis, "Rep. John Lewis' Remarks at the Dedication of the National Museum of African American History and Culture," September 24, 2016, https://johnlewis.house.gov/media-center/press-releases/rep-john-lewis-remarks-dedication-national-museum-african-american.

19. Thelma D. Perry, *History of the American Teachers Association* (Washington: National Education Association, 1975), 195.

20. "Pictures of Distinguished Negroes," box 1, folder 3, Woodson Collection.

21. Dr. D.O.W. Holmes, "Spent Life Bringing About Respect for Race, Heritage," *Afro-American,* May 12, 1950 (italics added).

22. Franklin et al., "Black History Month," 91.

23. John Bracey, interview by Jarvis R. Givens, University of Massachusetts Amherst, audio, November 21, 2016, personal collection.

24. Imani Perry, *May We Forever Stand: A History of the Black National Anthem* (Chapel Hill: University of North Carolina Press, 2018), 12, 8.

25. Ibid., 80; Carter G. Woodson, "Proceedings of the Annual Meeting of the Association for the Study of Negro Life and History Held in St. Louis, Missouri, October 21 to 25, 1928," *Journal of Negro History* 14, no. 1 (1929): 4; J. O. Lucas, "In the Elementary School," *Negro History Bulletin*, February 1939, 40; Ruth White Willis, "Let Our Rejoicings Rise," *Negro History Bulletin* 4, no. 8 (May 1, 1941): 187; Muriel L. Wellington, "The Negro Anthem," *Negro History Bulletin*, November 1948, 40–41.

26. John Bracey, interview by Jarvis R. Givens, University of Massachusetts Amherst, audio, November 21, 2016, personal collection.

27. On "civic estrangement," see Salamishah Tillet, *Sites of Slavery: Citizenship and Racial Democracy in the Post–Civil Rights Imagination* (Durham, NC: Duke University Press, 2012), 3–10.

28. Laverne Spurlock, Teachers in the Movement Interview with Dr. Laverne Beard Spurlock, interview by Carmen Foster, video, December 5, 2016, "Teachers in the Movement" Video Collection, University of Virginia, Curry School of Education.

29. James E. Allen, "Surveys of Negro History Week Circulated by James E. Allen in New York Public Schools (1950)," 1950, box 29, folder 9, James E. Allen Papers, Amistad Research Center, New Orleans, LA.

30. James Weldon Johnson, *Along This Way: The Autobiography of James Weldon Johnson* (New York: Penguin Classics, 2008), 155.

31. Angela Davis, *Angela Davis on Black History Month* (Speech at Eastern Kentucky University, 2011), YouTube, posted by AfroMarxist, May 11, 2018, https://www.youtube.com/watch?v=u8_aJwvae4k.

32. Johnson, *Along This Way*, 119.

33. Frederick Douglass, *Narrative of the Life of Frederick Douglass, an American Slave* (Boston: Anti-Slavery Office, 1845), 5.

34. Heather Williams, *Self-Taught: African American Education in Slavery and Freedom* (Chapel Hill: University of North Carolina Press, 2007), 122–125.

35. Alexander, "'Can You Be Black,'" 194.

36. Goran Olsson, *The Black Power Mixtape 1967–1975* (MPI Home Video, 2011).

37. Frederick Douglass, *My Bondage and My Freedom* (New York: Miller, Orton & Mulligan, 1855), 155.

38. Proctor and Federal Writers Project, Narrative of Jenny Proctor.

39. William H. Holtzclaw, *The Black Man's Burden* (New York: Neale Publishing, 1915), 30.

40. Leila Amos Pendleton, *A Narrative of the Negro* (Washington, DC: Press of R. L. Pendleton, 1912), 6.

41. "History Quiz Stumps Many in Competition," *New York Amsterdam News*, February 15, 1933, 11.

42. Tamah Richardson and Annie Rivers, "Progress of the Negro: A Unit of Work for the Third Grade," *Virginia Teachers Bulletin,* May 1936, 3–7.

43. Ibid. (italics added).

44. Ibid.

45. Ibid.

46. Ibid.

47. Carter G. Woodson, *The Mis-education of the Negro* (Washington, DC: Association for the Study of African American Life and History, 2008), 107.

48. More on Junior Branches of ASNLH in "Notes," *Journal of Negro History* 14, no. 1 (January 1929): 106–107.

49. Carter G. Woodson to Martha Wilson, "Woodson to Martha M. Wilson," January 27, 1942, box 35, folder 984, Luther Porter Jackson Papers, Johnston Memorial Library, Special Collections and Archives, Virginia State University.

50. Luther Porter Jackson to Carter G. Woodson, March 1, 1942, box 35, folder 984, Luther Porter Jackson Papers, Johnston Memorial Library, Special Collections and Archives, Virginia State University.

51. John Bracey, interview by Jarvis R. Givens, University of Massachusetts Amherst, audio, November 21, 2016, personal collection.

52. Ibid.

53. Houston A. Baker, "Meditation on Tuskegee: Black Studies Stories and Their Imbrication," *Journal of Blacks in Higher Education,* no. 9 (1995): 51–59 (italics added).

54. "Negro History Week 1935," circular, box 41, Luther Porter Jackson Papers, Johnston Memorial Library, Special Collections and Archives, Virginia State University.

55. Carter G. Woodson, "Negro History Week—the Twelfth Year," *Journal of Negro History* 22, no. 2 (1937): 146–147 (italics added).

56. For "embodied learning," see Jarvis R. Givens, "'There Would Be No Lynching If It Did Not Start in the Schoolroom': Carter G. Woodson and the Occasion of Negro History Week, 1926–1950," *American Educational Research Journal* 56, no. 4 (2019): 1457–1494.

57. For discussion on black commemorative practices, rituals, and racial identity, see Eddie S. Glaude Jr., *Exodus!: Religion, Race, and Nation in Early Nineteenth-Century Black America* (Chicago: University of Chicago Press, 2000), 84–87.

58. Alice W. Magee, "Boston Children Celebrating," *Negro History Bulletin* 19, no. 6 (March 1948): 133, 139–140.

59. Angela Davis, *Angela Davis: An Autobiography* (New York: Random House, 1974), 90.

60. Angela Davis, *Angela Davis on Black History Month* (Speech at Eastern Kentucky University, 2011), YouTube, posted by AfroMarxist, May 11, 2018, https://www.youtube.com/watch?v=u8_aJwvae4k.

61. Michael Cole described prolepsis as the "cultural mechanism that brings the end into the beginning," whereby that which is aspired to is spoken / named / projected onto the identity of someone in the present. Michael Cole, *Cultural Psychology: A Once and Future Discipline* (Cambridge: Harvard University Press, 1996), 183–184.

62. Angela Davis, *Angela Davis on Black History Month*.

63. John Bracey, interview by Jarvis R. Givens, University of Massachusetts Amherst, audio, November 21, 2016, personal collection.

64. Jarvis Ray Givens, "'A Grammar for Black Education beyond Borders': Exploring Technologies of Schooling in the African Diaspora," *Race, Ethnicity and Education* 19, no. 6 (2016): 1288–1302.

65. Ossie Davis's references to Negro History Week: Charles Burnett, dir., *Nat Turner: A Troublesome Property*, documentary, produced by Frank Christopher, 2003; Ossie Davis, interview by Julieanna Richardson, March 9, 2001, History-Makers Digital Archive; Ossie Davis and Ruby Dee, *With Ossie and Ruby: In This Life Together* (New York: It Books, 2000), 25, 45.

66. Nathan Hare, interview by Loretta Henry, April 5, 2004, session 1, tape 2, story 2, HistoryMakers Digital Archive.

67. Vernon Jarrett, interview by Julieanna Richardson, video, June 27, 2000, HistoryMakers Digital Archive.

68. Daphne A. Brooks, *Bodies in Dissent: Spectacular Performances of Race and Freedom, 1850–1910* (Durham, NC: Duke University Press Books, 2006), 5–6.

69. Baker, "Meditation on Tuskegee," 54.

70. Robert L. Harris Jr. (Emeritus Professor, Cornell University) comment on Jarvis R. Givens, "Black Rebellion and the Political Imaginations of African American Teachers," *AAIHS* (blog), November 5, 2018, https://www.aaihs.org/black-rebellion-and-the-political-imaginations-of-african-american-teachers/.

Conclusion

Epigraph: W. E. B. Du Bois, "The Tragedy of 'Jim Crow,'" *The Crisis*, August 1923.

1. D. P. Simpson, "Paedagogus," *Cassell's Latin Dictionary* (New York: Macmillan, 1968), 419.

2. Lisa Maurice, *The Teacher in Ancient Rome: The Magister and His World* (Lanham, MD: Lexington Books, 2013), 112–113. While the paedagogus was a slave of "high status," they were property, nonetheless. The differential levels of status in ancient slavery had modern analogs as well; one might think of "house negroes"—in some cases, slaves of relatively "high status"—who were tasked with the informal teaching of children at times: this is key to "the Mammy" and "Uncle Remus," for instance. Deborah Gray White, *Ar'n't I a Woman? Female Slaves in the Plantation South* (New York: W. W. Norton, 1999), 46–48; William L. Andrews,

Slavery and Class in the American South: A Generation of Slave Narrative Testimony, 1840–1865 (New York: Oxford University Press, 2019).

3. See, also, Booker T. Washington's following recollection: "I had no schooling whatsoever while I was a slave, though I remember on several occasions I went as far as the schoolhouse door with one of my young mistresses to carry her books. The picture of several dozen boys and girls in a schoolroom engaged in study made a deep impression upon me, and I had the feeling that to get into a schoolhouse and study in this way would be about the same as getting into paradise." Booker T. Washington, *Up from Slavery* (New York: Dover, 1995).

4. D. P. Simpson, "Fugitivus," *Cassell's Latin Dictionary* (New York: Macmillan Publishing Company, 1968), 258.

5. Toni Morrison, "The Slavebody and the Blackbody," in *The Source of Self-Regard: Selected Essays, Speeches, and Meditations* (New York: Knopf, 2019), 74–78; Sylvia Wynter, "The Ceremony Must Be Found: After Humanism," *Boundary* 2, no. 12 / 13 (1984): 19–70.

6. Eric Robert Taylor, *If We Must Die: Shipboard Insurrections in the Era of the Atlantic Slave Trade* (Baton Rouge: LSU Press, 2009).

7. Carter G. Woodson, *The Negro in Our History* (Washington, DC: Associated Publishers, 1922), 108.

8. Carter G. Woodson, *The Mis-Education of the Negro* (Washington, DC: Association for the Study of African American Life and History, 2008), 47.

9. Robin D. G. Kelley, "Black Study, Black Struggle," *Boston Review*, March 7, 2016, http://bostonreview.net/forum/robin-d-g-kelley-black-study-black-struggle.

10. Du Bois, "The Tragedy of 'Jim Crow'" (italics added).

11. Sylvia Wynter, "Novel and History, Plot and Plantation," *Savacou*, no. 5 (1971): 99.

12. Sylvia Wynter, Afro-American Culture and Social Order ("Soundings" interview sponsored by the National Humanities Center), interview by Wayne J. Pond, audio, November 22, 1981.

13. Martha Biondi, *The Black Revolution on Campus* (Berkeley: University of California Press, 2014).

14. Hortense J. Spillers, "Brandeis Alumni Achievement Award and Talk Commemorating 50th Anniversary of Black Studies" (African American Studies 50th Anniversary Conference, Brandeis University, February 9, 2019), YouTube, posted by BrandeisUniversity, February 11, 2019, https://www.youtube.com/watch?v=gcFeVjb0VlY.

15. "Many Brave Storm to Hear Lecture of Carter G. Woodson, Historian: Much of History Read Today on Negro Is Mere Propaganda to Perpetuate 'White Supremacy,'" *New York Amsterdam News*, December 8, 1926.

16. Julie A. Reuben, *The Making of the Modern University: Intellectual Transformation and the Marginalization of Morality* (Chicago: University of Chicago Press,

1996), 211, 224–227; Andrew Jewett, *Science, Democracy, and the American University: From the Civil War to the Cold War* (Cambridge: Cambridge University Press, 2014), 13.

17. Pero Dagbovie, "Making Black History Practical and Popular: Carter G. Woodson, the Proto Black Studies Movement and the Struggle for Black Liberation," *Western Journal of Black Studies* 27, no. 4 (2003): 272.

18. "Black Studies has been around for a very long time. We called it something else. We called it Negro History, and perhaps Negro History is almost as old as the twentieth century. I guess you can say that Carter G. Woodson formalized it." Keith D. Leonard, "First Questions: The Mission of Africana Studies: An Interview with Hortense Spillers," *Callaloo* 30, no. 4 (2007): 1054.

19. Houston A. Baker, "Meditation on Tuskegee: Black Studies Stories and Their Imbrication," *Journal of Blacks in Higher Education,* no. 9 (1995): 51–59.

20. Biondi, *Black Revolution on Campus,* 47.

21. The ideals and political values informing the pedagogy of black schoolteachers were often cultivated by what Jelani Favors calls the "second curriculum" of HBCUs, the primary training grounds for black educators. Jelani M. Favors, *Shelter in a Time of Storm: How Black Colleges Fostered Generations of Leadership and Activism,* 1st ed. (Chapel Hill: University of North Carolina Press, 2019), 5.

22. Stefano Harney and Fred Moten, *The Undercommons: Fugitive Planning and Black Study* (Wivenhoe, UK: Autonomedia, 2013), 26.

23. Dorothy B. Porter, "The Organized Educational Activities of Negro Literary Societies, 1828–1846," *Journal of Negro Education* 5, no. 4 (1936): 555–576; Elizabeth McHenry, *Forgotten Readers: Recovering the Lost History of African American Literary Societies* (Durham: Duke University Press, 2002).

24. Daniel Perlstein, "Schooling the New Negro: Progressive Education, Black Modernity, and the Long Harlem Renaissance," in *Educating Harlem: A Century of Schooling and Resistance in a Black Community, Eds. Ansley Erickson and Ernest Morrell* (New York: Columbia University Press, 2019), 41.

25. Madeline Morgan, "Negro Achievement in Chicago Public Schools" (June 22, 1942), box 2, folder 3, Madeline Stratton Morris Papers, Vivian G. Harsh Research Collection of Afro-American History and Literature, Chicago Public Library.

26. Perlstein, "Schooling the New Negro," 42.

27. James Weldon Johnson, *Along This Way: The Autobiography of James Weldon Johnson* (New York: Penguin Classics, 2008), 155.

28. David Bradley, "Black and American, 1982," *Esquire,* May 1982, 69; Biondi, *Black Revolution on Campus,* 1; Ibram X. Kendi, *The Black Campus Movement: Black Students and the Racial Reconstitution of Higher Education, 1965–1972* (New York: Palgrave Macmillan, 2012), 2.

29. Huey P. Newton, *Revolutionary Suicide* (New York: Penguin Classics, 2009), 17–20.

30. Oral histories with many of these scholars can be found in the HistoryMakers Digital Archive, where they discuss their early education and their involvement in Black Studies.

31. Russell W. Irvine and Jacqueline Jordan Irvine, "The Impact of the Desegregation Process on the Education of Black Students: Key Variables," *Journal of Negro Education* 52, no. 4 (1983): 410–422; Vanessa Siddle Walker, *The Lost Education of Horace Tate: Uncovering the Hidden Heroes Who Fought for Justice in Schools* (New York: New Press, 2018).

32. On "first leaders of freedmen," see Hortense J. Spillers, "Fabrics of History: Essays on the Black Sermon" (PhD diss., Brandeis University, 1974), 3. "The land that never has been yet—And yet must be—the land where *every* man is free." Langston Hughes, "Let America Be America Again," in *The Collected Poems of Langston Hughes* (New York: Vintage Classics, 1995), 189–191.

Acknowledgments

The journey to writing this book began much earlier than I realized. It is marked by the Black History Month programs of my youth, which I participated in under the tutelage of black teachers. These annual events complemented the daily devotions at the small parochial school I attended in Compton, California, from the age of three until my adolescent years. Every morning included the ritual of singing "Lift Every Voice and Sing" and reciting "Dreams" by Langston Hughes in the school yard before heading to class. These practices situated me in an intellectual tradition I had no capacity to comprehend or appreciate as a child—but I remember the feelings, and I suspect I always will. This site of exposure is essential to my work. Relatedly, as a rising sophomore at UC Berkeley, I was required to read Woodson's *The Mis-education of the Negro* in my pursuit to become a member of Alpha Phi Alpha Fraternity, Inc. I had no idea—as I went to one bookstore after another searching for five copies of this text—that it would be at the center of my vocation in the years to come. I am indebted to the teachers of my youth and the brothers I gained in college for planting these early seeds. They exposed me to the heritage that is the subject and mode of study in this book.

Studying under the faculty in UC Berkeley's Department of African American Studies as an undergraduate and doctoral student for ten consecutive years was an extraordinary gift. Their multidisciplinary and interdisciplinary expertise pushed me to think against the grain and imagine new ways to tell stories about black education. I am especially grateful to my dissertation committee members—Professors Ula Taylor, Na'ilah Nasir, and Daniel Perlstein. They gave generously of their time and were stellar mentors and teachers. I was lucky to have them in my corner. I am equally thankful for my colleagues at Berkeley, in African American studies and the Graduate School of Education, especially Christina Bush, Ameer Loggins, Charisse Burden-Stelly, Zachary Manditch-Prottas, Mariko Pegs, Kim McNair, Jasmine Johnson, Michael Myers II, kihana ross, and Maxine McKinney de Royston, as well as Mahasan Chaney and the other members of Dr. Perlstein's research group on race and power in education. They supported me in various ways as I completed my dissertation and helped cultivate the early ideas for this book.

Many organizations and institutions have supported me with financial and professional support along the way. Cally Waite, from the Social Science Research Council (SSRC), and the Mellon Mays Undergraduate Fellowship (MMUF) community have been a tremendous blessing. The MMUF and SSRC professional development and writing seminars have been invaluable and, for me, a space of refuge. I am also appreciative of the Berkeley MMUF community and Josephine Moreno in particular, for being my bridge to such an important community of scholars. I feel similarly about the Ford Foundation fellowship network and the support I received at the predoctoral and dissertation stage of my research.

Over the course of writing this book, I benefited tremendously from the community of scholars I found in the Association for the Study of African American Life and History and the field of black education studies. Robert L. Harris Jr., Theresa Perry, Derrick Alridge, Lindsey Jones, Alex Hyres, Janaka Lewis, Elizabeth Todd-Breland, Jermaine Thibodeaux, Crystal Sanders, Julius Fleming, and Jarvis McInnis have all helped push my thinking about this project at key moments. Shameka Powell, Derron Wallace, and Bianca Baldridge have been a wonderful circle of writers and friends. Pero Dagbovie and Burnis Morris, both Woodson scholars, pointed me in the direction of scattered historical sources over the years and thoughtfully engaged my work. Barbara Spencer Dunn changed the trajectory of my thinking without even knowing it, when she invited me to listen to her collection of old ASALH videos in the storage room of her church in Maryland. The story of Tessie McGee became a cornerstone of this book. Finding McGee would not have been possible without the video of her former student bearing witness to her pedagogy. I am extremely appreciative of Vanessa Siddle Walker and Imani Perry, whose scholarship and commentary pushed me to think in more expansive ways about the stakes of my work and the critical role of teachers in the black freedom struggle.

Librarians and archivists are magicians. I was reminded of this every step of the way. I am grateful for Randall Burkett and the late Pellom McDaniels III, who sat me down and offered pointed advice during my first research trip to work with the Carter G. Woodson papers at Emory University in the summer of 2013. Many other archivists and librarians have helped along the way, such as DeLisa Harris of Fisk University and teams at the Amistad Research Center, Virginia State University's Special Collections, Howard University's Moorland-Spingarn Research Center, Alabama State University Archives, the Vivian G. Harsh Research Collection in the Chicago Public Library, the HistoryMakers Digital Archive, and so many others. The team at the Harvard Graduate School of Education's Gutman Library, especially Carla Lillvik, have been particularly supportive in helping me find my way through the records and identifying sources I would not have otherwise sought out.

The Harvard Graduate School of Education provided me with space, time, and resources to write the book I understood to be important, and my colleagues have offered feedback on the manuscript at various stages. Julie Reuben, Meira Levinson, and Jal Mehta's genuine collegiality and careful commentary on my writing have meant a great deal. I am also grateful for my colleagues in Harvard's Department of African and African American Studies, especially Evelyn Brooks Higginbotham and Brandon Terry. Evelyn made time to provide verbal and written feedback from book proposal stage to the final manuscript, and Brandon's theoretical insights helped clarify key aspects of my thinking, in my mind and on the page.

Andrew Kinney, my editor at Harvard University Press, understood the aims of the book after our first meeting. He supported me in thinking around and outside of rigid conventions of historical scholarship when they did not serve the interests of the work. I am thankful that he saw value in my ideas and stayed committed to shepherding this project through the publication process.

This book, in its final form, is the result of my excavating archives over the course of seven years and then piecing together the stories as well as concepts to interpret them; but equally important has been the long, ongoing conversations with my closest thought partners: Rhaisa Williams, Joshua Bennett, and Ernest Mitchell. They have truly been friends to my mind. I've learned a tremendous amount from them individually and collectively. This book is so much better because of them.

A big thank you and "I love you!" to my family, for always cheering me on from afar and supporting me in ways that only they can—especially my mother and grandmothers.

Lastly, I am grateful for the intellectual shoulders on which I stand, generations of black men and women who struggled to know themselves and the world on terms that defied the master's ideology, enslaved people and their descendants who created *their own tools* for thinking and building. Writing and studying history is my way of attending to them, my way of ensuring that our futures might encounter them. This book is possible because they chose to think otherwise.

Index

Page numbers in italics refer to illustrations.